Warman's
COMPANION
COLLECTIBLE
DOLLS

Dawn Herlocher

©2008 by Krause Publications

Published by

kp krause publications
An Imprint of F+W Publications

700 East State Street • Iola, WI 54990-0001
715-445-2214 • 888-457-2873
www.krausebooks.com

Our toll-free number to place an order or obtain
a free catalog is (800) 258-0929.

Library of Congress Control Number: 2008925075

ISBN-13: 978-0-89689-701-4
ISBN-10: 0-89689-701-X

Designed by Rachael Knier
Edited by Mary Sieber

Printed in China

Table of Contents

Introduction

There is probably no rational explanation for the feelings collectors have for their dolls. Perhaps it's because they awaken memories and dreams, stirring our feelings of nostalgia, or the simple pleasure gained in admiring the beauty of these present-day reminders of a long vanished era.

The attraction to dolls seems to be immediate and universal, made obvious by the thousands of new enthusiasts who have excitedly embraced the world of doll collecting in recent years.

It is our hope that this book will help both the beginning and the more advanced collector enjoy doll collecting as a rewarding experience by providing information to identify and evaluate a wide variety of dolls.

Warman's Companion: Collectible Dolls also emphasizes the importance of condition. Please take the time to thoroughly inspect a doll. An antique bisque doll head should be checked not only on the outside, but also from the inside, for at times a repair or hairline crack is only visible from the inside. Remember not to confuse maintenance with repairs. Reset eyes, restrung bodies, and patched leather are examples of necessary maintenance and are not repairs to a doll. Modern dolls should always be in perfect, complete condition. Inspect the markings of a doll. You may find them on the back of the head, the torso, the bottom of a foot, or even on the derriere. Of course, many fine dolls will have absolutely no markings. Learn from every doll you see or handle, for there is almost as much fun in learning about a doll as there is in owning it. Visit doll shows and museums.

I encourage you to read and study as much as you can about dolls. The two volumes of Dorothy S., Elizabeth A., and Evelyn J. Coleman's *The Collector's Encyclopedia of Dolls* (Crown Publishing 1972 and 1986) cover doll manufacturing prior to 1930. *Antique Trader's Doll Makers & Marks* (Krause Publications, 1999) is a concise directory for doll identification. *200 Years of Dolls Third Edition* (Krause Publications, 2005) is an expanded companion to *Warman's Companion: Collectible Dolls*. If you don't own a copy, visit a library that does.

Talk to other collectors. I have never met a doll collector who doesn't enjoy talking about his or her dolls. Consider joining a doll club. Clubs that are members of the United Federation of Doll Clubs (U.F.D.C.) "represent the highest standards of excellence for collectors to create, stimulate and maintain interest in all matters pertaining to doll collecting." Write the U.F.D.C. at P.O. Box 14146, Parkville, MO 64152 to obtain the address of a club near you.

The format of this book is really quite simple. Dolls are arranged alphabetically by manufacturer or type. Within each section, there are generalized subheadings presented by material or style. These are further described by particular doll model, either by name, mold number, or a visual clue that identifies a particular doll.

Warman's Companion: Collectible Doll focuses on 100 doll manufacturers. In narrowing to that number, we choose the dolls that you are most likely to discover on your journey of doll collecting.

The astute collector or interim caregiver can use this book for comparative purposes when assessing and evaluating their dolls, whether building a new collection or researching an existing one of a thousand dolls.

Collecting Tips

The following procedures are provided to inform and educate. Neither the author nor publisher accept liability or responsibility in respect to any type of loss or damage caused, or alleged to be caused, directly or indirectly, by the information or products contained in this book. We simply intend to share some old tricks and methods that have been used over the years.

Dolls require tender loving care. They need to be repaired, restored, handled, displayed, and stored properly. The following tips will help you develop skills to ensure that your dolls receive the loving treatment they deserve.

When restoring a doll, the best approach is to be a minimalist. Do only the bare minimum to bring a doll to display level—retain, rather than destroy. Period features count heavily in a doll's value. Plan any repairs in a step-by-step process, evaluating as you go along.

Always approach the cleaning or maintenance of dolls with the greatest of care and respect. If you're not sure how to perform a certain procedure, ask an expert. We have an obligation to future doll collectors to preserve the dolls in our care and to maintain them in as good or better condition than they were when we received them.

20" Simon & Halbig, marked "S 15 H 949," open mouth with teeth, blue eyes, fully jointed composition body, wearing a purple silk dress.

Price Adjustment Factors

No two dolls are exactly alike. A study of their various features indicates the factors that influence the value of a doll, including rarity, condition, quality of material, artistry, availability, originality, history of providence, and the ever-important visual appeal. All of these factors contribute to a doll's charisma.

An antique doll may need attention to bring her to display condition.

For example, the 20" Simon & Halbig, mold number 949 (above), is a rather rare doll to find, but she nevertheless needs some tender loving care that will undoubtedly be costly. The obvious costume replacement may easily cost several hundred dollars, as will the shoes and vintage human hair or mohair wig. So, although the "book value" is $3,200, when all the modifications and improvements are considered, a more realistic value would be closer to $2,000-$2,200.

Other examples highlighting the importance of condition are the two American Character Sweet Sue dolls below. An 18" Sweet Sue doll in good condition has a value of $500. (However, when the all-original Alice version is found with her wrist tag and bright facial coloring, she could have a value of $1,200.) Conversely, the inappropriately redressed Sweet Sue with pale, faded coloring, messed hair, and new shoes has a value of $50-$75.

The most frequently asked question is how I determine the prices in this guide. It is really quite simple; I keep in constant contact with many doll dealers, auctioneers, show promoters, and brokers. The influences within the doll world have changed drastically over the years. We are an international-global community. Dealers think nothing of flying to England for an opportunity to purchase dolls for an increasingly discriminating collecting pool.

Only a few years ago prices fluctuated greatly from one coast to the other. The globetrotting, migrating collector aided by the Internet has made the doll market a more level purchasing field. It is amazing how consistent doll trends are; no matter if it is a large international auction house or a small independent doll dealer, prices and demands are all relevant.

Prices in this book are based on dolls in good condition, appropriately dressed with no damage. Unfortunately, dolls frequently have a number of faults.

What follows is a method by which you can take the prices listed in this book and adjust them to fit the doll you are examining. Admittedly, some of these adjustments do require you to make a judgment call. When analyzing a doll, it's always best to use your head, not your heart. Hopefully, the suggestions offered here will make you a wise and savvy buyer and/or seller.

18" American Character Sweet Sue, hard plastic, sleep eyes, jointed body, strawberry blonde hair, redressed in cotton print rickrack dress.

American Character 18" Sweet Sue in authentic Alice costume in mint condition with wrist tag, **$1,200.**
Courtesy of Julia Burke, www.juliaburke.com

Bisque

Hairline crack or repair in back or under wig **−50%**
Hairline crack or repair to face **−70%**
Very poor body (beyond normal wear) **−35%**
Replaced body **−45%**
Tinted or untinted ornamentation damage **−25%**
Original super-pristine condition and/or with original box **up to +200%**

China

Head cracked or repaired **−75%**
Cracked or repaired shoulder **−50%**
Worn or replaced body **−40%**
Exceptional, original doll **+75% or more**

Cloth

Face stained or faded **−50%**
Tears or large holes in face **−80%**
Mint original or excellent condition **up to 200%**

Metal

Lightly dented or lightly chipped head **−50%**
Badly dented or badly chipped head **−80%**
Bucherer dolls are forgiven for some chips and damage. So desirable are these dolls that the adjustment would be only **−20% to −30%**, depending on severity and location.
Mint, original, or excellent condition **+25%**

Composition and Papier-Mâché

Very light crazing **Acceptable**
Heavy crazing or cracking **−50%**
Small splits at corners of eye and/or mouth **−10%**
Heavy chipping to face **−75%**
Face repainted **−80%**
Major cracks, splits, and peeling **−30%**
Redressed or undressed **−25%**
Mint and/or boxed **+200% or more**

Wax

Minor cracks or minor warp to head **−20%**
Major cracks or major warp to head **−50%**
Softening of features **−20%**
Rewaxed **−70%**
All original with sharp features and good color **+200% or more**

Celluloid

Cracks **−80%**
Discolored **−70%**
Mint **+50%**

Wood

Light crazing or minute paint touch-up **Acceptable**
Repainted head or heavy splits (depending on severity and location) **−50% to −80%**
Mint original or excellent condition **+100%**

Plastic

Cracks or discoloration **−75%**
Hair combed **−40%**
Shelf dirt **−10%**
Redressed or missing accessories **−50%**
1950s, mint, boxed **up to 200%***
1960s, mint, boxed **up to 150%***
1970s, mint, boxed **up to 50%***
1980s, mint, boxed **List Value**
1990s, mint, boxed **List Value**
Or more, depending on the desirability of the doll

Vinyl

Damaged, discoloration **−100%**
Hair combed, redressed, shelf dust **−95%**
Pre-1990, mint, boxed **+10%**

Alexander
Doll Company

The Alexander Doll Company was founded in 1923 by Beatrice Alexander Behman and her sisters, Rose Alexander Schrecking, Florence Alexander Rapport, and Jean Alexander Disick. It was through the ambition and creativity of Beatrice that the company grew to become a giant doll manufacturer.

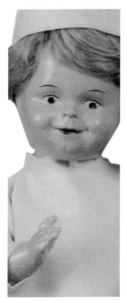

Alexander Doll Company's reputation for high quality has earned the respect of doll lovers of all ages. The dolls are outfitted in exquisitely trimmed silks, velvets, satins, and other fine fabrics, with beautiful accessories completing the costume.

In 1988 Beatrice Alexander sold the company to Chodorow and Smith, attorneys and businessmen. The Alexander Doll Company changed ownership again in 1995 when acquired by The Kalzen Breakthrough Partnership, a private capital fund managed by Gefinor Acquisition Partners.

Cloth

Prices listed are for appropriately costumed dolls with good color.

Early Cloth: 7", 9", 10", 12", 13", 14", 16", 18", 20", 22", 24", and 30"; flat or molded face socket head; pink cloth body; log-type legs; slightly bent arms; mohair wig; painted eyes; single stroke brows; closed heart-shaped mouth; typically unmarked; clothing tag with character name/"MADAME ALEXANDER/NEW YORK USA," gold octagon wrist tag with "character name/ALEXANDER DOLL COMPANY."

Child:

7"-12"	$700-$750
14"-18"	$800-$1,000
20"-30"	$1,050-$2,000

Baby and Infant:

12"	$450
16"	$600
24"	$800

Modern Cloth: 10", 12", 14", and 16"; stitched facial features; typically marked with cloth label "MADAME ALEXANDER/N.Y.N.Y."; clothing tag "MADAME ALEXANDER"; booklet-type wrist tag.

Child/Character/Baby:

10"-12"	$75
14"-16"	$85

Dionne Quintuplets: 17" and 24"; molded and painted facial features; yarn hair sewn to resemble curls tight to head; typically unmarked; clothing tag with character name/"MADAME ALEXANDER/NEW YORK USA."

17"	$1,100
4"	$1,500

Add $300 to any cloth doll with insert eyes.

15" Madame Alexander cloth Susie Q, **$900.**
Courtesy of McMasters-Harris Auction

Composition

Prices listed are for appropriately costumed dolls in good condition.

Tiny Betty Face Doll: 7" and 8" one-piece body and head; mohair wig; painted, side-glancing eyes; closed, heart-shaped mouth; painted-on black shoes and white socks. Typically marked "MmE. ALEXANDER" or "WENDY ANN"; clothing tag with character name "MADAME ALEXANDER/NEW YORK USA"; gold octagon wrist tag with character name "ALEXANDER DOLL CO."

7"	$375
8"	$500

Little Betty Face Doll: 9" and 11"; all jointed composition; molded hair or wig; painted side-glancing eyes; closed mouth; typically marked "MmE. ALEXANDER NEW YORK"; clothing tag with character name "MADAME ALEXANDER/NEW YORK USA"; gold octagon wrist tag with character name "ALEXANDER DOLL CO. N.Y./USA."

9"	$450
11"	$500

Betty Face Doll*: 13", 17", 19", and 22"; all jointed composition; mohair wig; tin or glassine sleep eyes; painted upper and lower or only lower lashes; tiny dimples on each side of closed mouth; typically unmarked; clothing tag with character name/ "Madame Alexander/New York"; rectangle or octagon wrist tag with character name/"Created by Madame Alexander/New York New York."

13"	$600
17"-19"	$700-$900
22"	$1,100

Add $600 for Nurse Leroux.

Wendy Ann Face Doll*: 9", 11", 13", 18", and 21"; all jointed composition; may have swivel waist; molded hair or wig; painted or sleep eyes; closed mouth; typically marked "WENDY ANN" or "WENDY ANN/MmE. ALEXANDER"; clothing tag with character name "MADAME ALEXANDER/NEW YORK USA" or a green foil, clover-shaped wrist tag with "WENDY ANN/ALEXANDER DOLL CO." and occasionally the character name.

9"-11"	$450-$500
13"-18"	$675-$750
21"	$1,200

Add $300 for Scarlett O'Hara (also spelled Scarlet) and Sonja Henie dolls; the 21" portraits can easily command two to three times the values given, depending on rarity and costume.

Princess Elizabeth Face Doll*: 13", 14", 15", 16", 17", 21", 24", and 27"; all jointed composition; mohair or human hair wig; tin or glassine sleep eyes; open mouth; typically marked "PRINCESS ELIZABETH/ALEXANDER DOLL CO."; clothing tag with character name "MADAME ALEXANDER NY/USA RIGHT RESERVE"; gold octagon wrist tag with character name/"ALEXANDER DOLL CO. NY."

13"	$600
14"	$800
15"-17"	$650-$750
21"	$900
24"	$1,100
27"	$1,500

Add $100 for Flora McFlimsy with red hair and freckles.

Margaret Face Doll*: 14", 18", and 21"; all jointed composition; mohair or human hair wig; single-stroke brows; sleep eyes; real upper and painted lower lashes; smiling mouth; typically marked "ALEXANDER"; clothing tag with character name "Madame Alexander NY/USA"; green foil, clover-shaped wrist tag with "ALEXANDER DOLL CO. N.Y. U.S.A." and occasionally character name.

14"	$1,500
18"	$1,900
21"	$2,000

Add $500 for Hulda doll.

Character Baby Face Doll*: 11", 12", 15", 19", 21", 23", and 24"; all composition; five-piece bent limb baby body or cloth body with composition head and limbs; molded and painted hair or mohair wig; sleep or painted eyes; open or closed mouth; clothing tag with baby's name/"MADAME ALEXANDER NEW YORK U.S.A."; gold octagon wrist tag with baby's name/"ALEXANDER DOLL CO. NEW YORK USA" or green foil, clover-shaped wrist tag with "ALEXANDER DOLL CO. NEW YORK USA."

11"-15"	$400-$475
19"-21"	$550-$575
23"-24"	$600-$650

Add $50 for Pinky Baby doll.
The more famous characters and elaborately costumed dolls will command higher prices.

Dionne Quintuplets: 7-1/2", 10-1/2", 14", 17", 19", and 23-1/2"; all composition; toddler body or cloth body with composition head and limbs; molded and painted hair or wig; typically marked "Dionne" and/or the individual name, "Dionne Alex," "Alexander," and possibly others.

7-1/2"-10"	$425-$550
14"	$800
17"	$650
19"	$1,100
23"	$900

Jane Withers: 13", 15", 17", and 20"; all jointed composition or cloth body with composition head and limbs; mohair wig; sleep eyes; long, painted upper and lower lashes; closed or open mouth; typically marked "JANE WITHERS/ALEX DOLL CO."; clothing tag "JANE WITHERS/ALL RIGHTS RESERVED MADAME ALEXANDER"; gold script name pin.

13"-15"	$1,500-$1,700
17"-20"	$2,000-$2,300

Jeannie Walker: 14" and 18"; all jointed composition; wooden walking mechanism; human hair wig; sleep eyes; closed mouth; typically marked "ALEXANDER DOLL CO./PAT NO. 2171271"; clothing tag "JEANNIE WALKER/MADAME ALEXANDER NY USA."

14"-18"	$1,200-$1,500

Sonja Henie: 15", 18", and 21"; all jointed composition body, may have swivel waist; blond mohair wig; sleep eyes; real eyelashes with dark eye shadow; dimples; open mouth; typically marked "SONJA HENIE/MADAME ALEXANDER"; clothing tag "SONIA HENIE MmM ALEXANDER/ALL RIGHTS RESERVED N.Y. U.S.A."; wrist tag with picture of Sonja Henie.

15"-18"	$1,100-$1,300
21"	$1,700

Note: The registration for Sonja Henie dolls reads, "to be dressed in elaborate skating costumes in assorted styles, skates attached to high skate shoes." Some smaller, closed-mouth Sonja Henie dolls used the Wendy Ann face.

Marionettes: 8", 10", and 12"; composition character face, torso, and lower limbs connected by cloth joints; typically marked "Tony Sarg/Alexander" on back and "Tony Sarg" on head; clothing tag "Madame Alexander" or may include character name. Tony Sarg designed and endorsed the marionettes including a special series commissioned for Walt Disney's Silly Symphonies and Snow White.

8"-10"	$325-$350
12"	$400

Note: Marionettes marked "Walt Disney's Marionettes" can easily demand two to three times the values given.

Individual Personalities

Occasionally, a personality was so popular that it merited its own face. Dolls that fall into this category include:

Dr. Dafoe: 14", Dionne Quintuplets doctor; cloth, chubby body; composition limbs; swivel composition head and shoulder plate; gray mohair wig; painted blue eyes with upper lashes only; smiling mouth; chin dimple; typically unmarked; white jumpsuit and doctor's coat; tagged "DR. DAFOE/MmE. ALEXANDER"; gold octagon Dr. Dafoe wrist tag..**$1,900**
Minister: Dr. Dafoe body and face; identified by clothing and/or wrist tag......**$1,400**
Priest: Dr. Dafoe body and face; identified by clothing and/or wrist tag..........**$1,500**
Baby Jane: 16", named for child star Juanita Quigley; all jointed composition; brown human-hair wig; brown sleep eyes; long, painted upper and lower lashes; open mouth; typically marked "BABY JANE/ALEXANDER"; clothing tag "BABY JANE/MmE. ALEXANDER." **$1,400**

14" Madame Alexander Dr. Dafoe, 13" Nurse Leroux, 7-1/2" Dionne Quintuplets with original boxes. It is so unusual to find the entire set in mint condition with original lithograph boxes that expect the value to exceed **$9,500.**
Courtesy of George and Kathleen Basset, gbasset1@tampabay.rr.com

Hard Plastic

Prices listed are for dolls in near-mint, original condition.

Wendy-Ann/Wendy/Wendy-Kins/Alexander-Kins and Billy (the boy)*: 7" to 8"; made continuously for the past 50 years; in 1955, "Ann" was dropped from the doll's name. All have chubby round faces; sleep eyes with molded upper and painted lower lashes; closed mouth; synthetic wigs; typically unmarked or marked "ALEX," after 1976 "ALEXANDER"; clothing tag "ALEXANDER-KINS," character name/"BY MADAME ALEXANDER REG U. S. PAT. OFF NY NY," or character name/"MADAME ALEXANDER/ALL RIGHTS RESERVED NEW YORK USA."

1953	Straight legs, non-walker	**$750**
1954-1955	Straight legs, walker	**$700**
1955-1964	Slightly bent legs, walker body	**$600**
1956	Jointed knees, walker with turning head	**$500**
1965-1972	Slightly bent or jointed knees, non-walker	**$550**
1973-1976*	Straight legs, jointed above the knees	**$275**
1982-1987	Straight leg	**$100**

*In 1974, a new series called "United States" was introduced. Tags may have a misspelled "Untied States," adding an additional $100.

Note: Also Baby Clown, Little Minister, Parlor Maid, Indian Girl, Agatha, Aunt Pitty Pat, Cousin Grace, Easter Wendy, Little Madeline, Little Victoria, My Shadow, Prince Charles, Princess Ann, Wendy in Easter Egg, and Bible characters can easily command two to three times the values given.

Margaret (O'Brien) Face Doll*, **: 14", 18", and 22"; all jointed hard plastic; mohair, floss, human hair, saran, or nylon wig; sleep eyes with real upper and painted lower lashes; slightly smiling mouth; typically marked "ALEXANDER"; clothing tag with character name.

14"-18"	$1,250-$1,500
22"	$1,900

*Godey, Renoir, Victoria, Fashion of Century, Queen Elizabeth, and Me and My Shadow Series can easily command twice the values given. Add $200 for black version Cynthia.
**The more famous characters and elaborately costumed dolls will command higher prices.

Maggie Face Doll*, **: 15", 18", and 23"; all jointed hard plastic; mohair, floss, human hair, saran, or nylon wig; closed mouth; typically marked "ALEXANDER"; clothing tag character name/"ALEXANDER N.Y., N.Y."

15"-18"	$900-$1,000
23"	$1,250

*Me and My Shadow Series, Century of Fashion, and Glamour Girls can easily command twice the values given.
**The more famous characters and elaborately costumed dolls will command higher prices.

Mary Ellen: 31"; all jointed hard plastic walker body; rooted nylon hair; wider smiling mouth; typically marked "MME ALEXANDER." **$900**

Madeline**: 14", 18"; hard plastic jointed body; vinyl head; rooted nylon or saran hair; sleep eyes; light dimples; open/closed, smiling mouth; typically marked "ALEXANDER."

14"-18"	$400-$600

**The more famous characters and elaborately costumed dolls will command higher prices.

Penny/Barbara Jane**: 29", 34", and 42"; soft cloth body; vinyl stuffed head, legs and arms; synthetic "Newtar" saran wig; sleep or painted eyes; wide smiling mouth; typically marked "ALEXANDER."

29"-31"	$550-$650
34"	$800

**The more famous characters and elaborately costumed dolls will command higher prices.

Cissy Face Dolls includes Winnie and Binnie Walker*, **: 15", 18", 20"/21", and 23"/25"; introduced in 1953 as Winnie Walker with walker child body, and in 1954 as Binnie Walker. Cissy was introduced in 1955 using the Winnie and Binnie face with an adult figure; high heel feet; jointed elbows, vinyl-over-hard-plastic arms on a walker body. The flat-footed Winnie and Binnie walkers are identified by their hairstyle. Winnie had a glued-on wig with a feather cut, combed in all directions. Binnie's hair is rooted to a vinyl skullcap with bangs; sleep eyes with real upper and painted lower lashes; closed, unsmiling mouth; typically marked "ALEXANDER"; clothing tag "CISSY, WINNIE, BINNIE," or character name.

15"-18"	$650-$700
20"/21"	$850
23"/25"	$950

*Lady in Red, Godey Portrait, Victoria, Lady Hamilton, Renoir, Gainsborough, Ice Capades Series, or elaborately accessorized costumes can easily command three to four times the values given.
**The more famous characters and elaborately costumed dolls will command higher prices.

Two 21" dolls (Shari Lewis and Sleeping Beauty) were released using the Cissy body, but with different faces. They also came in smaller sizes on different bodies.

Shari Lewis: 21"; hard plastic and vinyl jointed body; high heel feet; synthetic, dark blond pony tail; feathered brows; blue sleep eyes; real upper, painted lower lashes; very turned-up nose; pierced ears; closed, unsmiling mouth; typically marked "MmE 19©58 ALEXANDER." **$1,200**

Sleeping Beauty: 21"; hard plastic and vinyl jointed body; high heel feet; synthetic, blond wig; lightly feathered brows; sleep eyes; real upper, painted lower lashes; typically marked "ALEXANDER"; clothing tag "MADAME ALEXANDER PRESENTS WALT DISNEY'S AUTHENTIC SLEEPING BEAUTY." **$1,700**

Lissy Face Doll*, **: 11"; hard plastic jointed body; medium high heeled feet; small bosom; sleep eyes; real upper and painted lower lashes; closed mouth; typically unmarked; clothing tag with Lissy or character name; booklet-type wrist tags..**$600**

> *Katie, Tommy, Southern Belle, McGuffey Ana, or the trousseau sets can easily command twice the values given.
>
> **The more famous characters and elaborately costumed dolls will command higher prices.

11" Madame Alexander Lissy as *Little Women*. This is a rather common set, however, the condition of the dolls and original boxes increase the value to **$3,000**.

Courtesy of McMasters-Harris Auction

Elise Face Doll:** 16"; hard plastic body with vinyl arms; jointed elbows, knees, and ankles; oval eyes with real upper, painted lower lashes; pierced ears; closed mouth; typically marked "ALEXANDER" and "MmE ALEXANDER"; clothing tag with "ELISE/MeM ALEXANDER" or character name/"MeM ALEXANDER"; booklet-type wrist tag..**$550**

> **The more famous characters and elaborately costumed dolls will command higher prices.

Another doll introduced using the Elise body, but with its own face, was Sleeping Beauty. (The 21" Sleeping Beauty used the Cissy body.)

Sleeping Beauty: 16"; hard plastic, fully jointed body; blond synthetic wig; feathered brows; sleep eyes with real upper, painted lower lashes; smiling mouth; typically marked "ALEXANDER"; clothing tag "MADAME ALEXANDER PRESENTS WALT DISNEY'S AUTHENTIC SLEEPING BEAUTY." **$1,300**

Cissette Face Doll*, **: 10" to 11"; all jointed hard plastic; high heel feet; sleep eyes with real upper, painted lower lashes; most with pierced ears; closed mouth; typically marked "MmM ALEXANDER" or unmarked; clothing tag with character name or "CISSETTE" in turquoise, except blue in 1963; booklet-type wrist tag. **$600**

> **Gold Rush, Lady Hamilton, and Klondike Kate can easily command four to five times the values given.*
>
> ***The more famous characters and elaborately costumed dolls will command higher prices.*

Maggie Mix-Up: 8" and 17"; 8" all hard plastic, jointed body; straight orangish-red hair; freckles; sleep eyes; typically marked "ALEX"; clothing tag "Maggie"; booklet-type wrist tags.

10" Madame Alexander Cissette, **$600**.
Courtesy of McMasters-Harris Auction

    8" **$700**
    16" **$650**

Vinyl

Prices listed are for dolls in near-mint, original condition.

Kelly Face Doll: 12", 15", 17", and 22"; rigid, fully jointed vinyl bodies and limbs; rooted, synthetic hair; sleep eyes with molded lashes; open/closed mouth; typically marked "MME ALEXANDER" 1958 (same date used in 1958 and 1965); booklet-type wrist tag.

    12"-15" ....**$350-$400**
    17"-22" ....**$600-$625**

> *Note: Add $200 for "Marybel the Doll That Gets Well" in suitcase with sick child accessories.*

Jacqueline Face Doll: 21"; new face with jointed Cissy body. In 1962, White House Press Secretary Pierre Salinger requested that the Alexander Doll Company not make reference to First Lady Jacqueline Kennedy in advertising this doll. That year the Jacqueline doll was dropped, but was reintroduced as the Portrait Series in 1965 and continues to be used. Brown, short-rooted hair combed to the side; brown sleep eyes with thick lashes; eyeliner; closed mouth; typically marked "ALEXANDER 1961" (1961 remains in marking); booklet-type wrist tag. **$900**

    Portrait... **$1,300**

> *Note: The more famous characters and elaborately costumed dolls will command higher prices.*

Caroline Baby Face Doll: 15"; jointed hard plastic body; vinyl-head character baby; rooted blond hair, parted on side; big blue sleep eyes with lashes; dimpled, open, smiling mouth; typically marked "ALEXANDER/1961" and "ALEX. 1959/13"; booklet-type wrist tag..........**$500**

Joanie Face Doll: 36"; hard plastic jointed body; vinyl head; rooted saran hair; flirty eyes with long curly lashes; closed smiling mouth; typically marked "ALEXANDER/1959"; booklet-type wrist tag..**$700**

Mimi Face Doll: 30"; rigid, hard plastic jointed body; soft vinyl head and hands; rooted hair in various styles, from long curls to short bob cut; sleep eyes; molded lashes; single-stroke sweeping brows; closed mouth; typically marked "ALEXANDER/1961"; booklet-type wrist tag..**$650**

Smarty Face Doll*: 12"; jointed hard plastic toddler body; vinyl head; short, rooted hair; sleep eyes; molded lashes; open/closed smiling mouth; typically marked "ALEXANDER/1962"; booklet-type wrist tag...**$300**

> **Add $200 for Katie (black version) and $100 for Brother (dressed as a boy).*

Janie Face Doll*: 12"; Smarty body with chubby, character, occasionally freckled face; round eyes; closed, smiling mouth; typically marked "ALEXANDER/1964"; booklet-type wrist tag...**$375**

> **Add $100 for Lucinda, Rosy, or Suzy (identified by clothing label).*

Melinda Face Doll: 16" and 22"; hard plastic or vinyl body; swivel waist; almost white, rooted hair with full bangs; sleep eyes; open/closed smiling mouth with two teeth; typically marked "ALEXANDER/1962"; booklet-type wrist tag.

16"	**$350**
22"	**$450**

Brenda Starr (Yolanda): 12"; hard plastic; jointed adult body; Alexander's response to Barbie®; blond hair with one long lock on top; sleep eyes; long, molded lashes; closed, unsmiling mouth; typically marked "ALEXANDER/1964" and "ALEXANDER." **$400**

Polly Face Doll*: 17"; all jointed vinyl; rooted, long nylon hair; sleep eyes; closed, smiling mouth; typically marked "ALEXANDER DOLL CO. INC./1965"; clothing tag "Mary Ellen Playmate (Polly)"; booklet-type wrist tag. **$375**

> **Add $200 for Leslie (black version) and $100 if wearing a ring on the right hand (this accessory was included only in 1965, the year Polly was introduced).*

Mary Ann Face Doll: 14"; vinyl head; hard plastic jointed body; rooted nylon hair; sleep eyes with molded upper and painted side and lower lashes; closed mouth; typically marked "ALEXANDER/1965"; booklet-type wrist tag..............................**$275**

Coco*: (fashioned after Paris designer Coco, patented in 1966, and never used again); 21"; vinyl head and limbs; plastic body; jointed at waist, one-piece lower torso with bent right leg; rooted, blond shoulder length hair; sleep eyes; blue shadow; black eyeliner; feathered brows; typically marked "ALEXANDER/1966." ...... **$2,500-$2,800**

> **Add $500 for Coco Faced Portrait or Scarlett #2061.*

First Lady Complete Series: 14"

	$700
First Series	**$400**
Second Series	**$350**
Third, Fourth, Fifth, and Sixth Series	

Peter Pan Series:

	$450
Tinker Bell 10"	**$400**
Michael 12"	**$350**
Peter Pan or Wendy 14"	

Sound of Music Series: (all but the Kurt doll are available in two sizes)

Brigitta 10"& 14", Frederick 8"& 11", Gretl 8"& 11", Lisel 10" & 14", Martha 8" or 11"	**$200**
Louisa 10" & 14", Maria 12"	**$250**
Maria 17"	**$300**
Kurt 11"	**$400**

All Bisque

Bisque, china, parian, and porcelain are all forms of ceramics derived from a clay-based material to which feldspar and flint have been added. This mixture is molded, fired, painted, and fired again. Quality can range from the finest porcelain with beautifully detailed decoration to coarse and crudely painted "stone bisque." Factors determining a doll's quality include: the texture of the porcelain, the artistry applied in decorating the piece, the subject model, and the presence or absence of a glaze.

Prices listed are for appropriately costumed dolls in perfect condition.

French

Known as Mignonette; excellent quality bisque; unique "French Loop" or "Bell Top" (a molded loop found at the base of the neck, enabling the head to be strung to the body); kid-lined joints at neck, shoulder, and hip, occasionally elbows and/or knees; slender limbs connected by wooden pegs, wire, or elastic; nicely molded feet or painted shoes and socks; outstanding facial decorations; feathered brows; long eyelashes; solid dome or cork pate; good wig; closed mouth.

6" French Mignonette all bisque, **$3,400.**
From the collection of Trina and Bill Miller

Molded shoes/glass eyes:
5"-7"	**$2,000-$3,000**
9"-10"	**$5,200-$5,500**

Elbow joints/glass eyes:
5"-7"	**$3,000-$4,000**
9"	**$5,700**

Multi joints/glass eyes:
6"-8"	**$5,700-$6,500**
10"	**$6,800**

Wrestler-type/glass eyes:
5"-7"	**$2,000-$2,400**
8"-9"	**$3,000-$3,300**

SFBJ/Unis/later doll:
6"-9"	**$600-$800**
12"	**$1,000**

Painted eye:
4"-6"	**$500-$700**
9"-11"	**$800-$1,000**

Add $500 to any doll with molded bare feet.

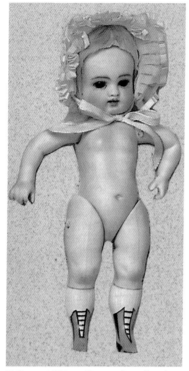

8" German all bisque Kestner often referred to as a Wrestler type, **$3,000.**
Courtesy of David Cobb Auction

German

German bisque can range from outstanding to quite poor; swivel neck may be attached to the body with wooden neck plug, or neck molded with holes on either side and strung with elastic; molded and painted hair or mohair wig; painted or glass eyes; open or closed mouth; typically marked "Germany," mold or size number or paper label on chest.

Prices given are for perfect dolls with nicely applied facial features; if crudely applied, expect to adjust the value accordingly.

Painted eyes/molded clothes
  2"-3" ....$75-$150
  4"-8" ....$200-$400
  9"-10" ....$425-$550
Painted eyes/various joints:
  2"-3" ....$125-$175
  4"-8" ....$225-$450
  9"-12" ....$500-$700
Glass eyes/arm and hip joints:
  4"-8" ....$350-$600
  10"-12" .... $1,200-$1,600
Glass eyes/fully jointed:
  4"-7" ....$450-$850
  8"-11" .... $1,200-$1,800
  12" $1,900
Glass eyes/molded bare feet:
  5" $2,700
  8" $4,200
  10" $4,600
Extraordinary/waist or knee joints:
  5"-7" .... $3,000-$4,000
  8"-10" .... $5,000-$6,000
Painted eyes/bent limb baby:
  4" $200
  8" $400
  12" $1,200
Glass eyes/bent limb baby:
  4" $350
  8" $700
  12" $1,500
Glass eyes/Wrestler-type:
  5" $2,000
  7"-8" .... $2,400-$3,000
  9" $3,300
  Add $100-$200 to any doll for swivel neck.

Babies and Characters

A few character dolls stand out as being very desirable, usually because of the character portrayed rather than superior quality. While purist collectors assign value to quality of artistry, the popularity of these dolls cannot be disputed.

Baby Bo-Kaye: swivel neck; glass eyes; typically marked with paper label.

5"-6"	$1,800-$2,200
8"	$3,500

Bonnie Baby: swivel neck; glass eyes; character face; molded teeth; typically marked with paper label.

5"	$1,300
7"-8"	$1,700-$1,900

Bye-Lo: typical Bye-Lo face; glass or painted eyes; typically marked with paper label or "Germany."

Painted eyes:

4"-6"	$450-$550
8"	$800

Glass eyes:

4"-6"	$650-$900
8"	$1,400

Orsini Girls: (Didi, Mimi, Vivi, Fefe) open/closed mouth; molded teeth; glass or painted eyes; typically marked with paper label.

Painted eyes:

5"-6"	$1,200-$1,400
8"	$1,800

Glass eyes:

5"-6"	$2,000-$2,500
8"	$4,000

Hebee and Shebee: cute, oversized face; molded clothes and shoes with holes for ribbons.

4"-6"	$700-$850
7"	$1,000
9"	$2,000

Max (123) and Moritz (124): 5"; character smiling face; typically marked "K ★ R."

5"	$2,400

Mildred the Prize Baby: happy round-faced baby with glass eyes; slightly parted, smiling lips, jointed at shoulder and hips; typically marked "208" (later dolls with deeply molded hair 880 are valued less); round paper label.

5"	$4,000

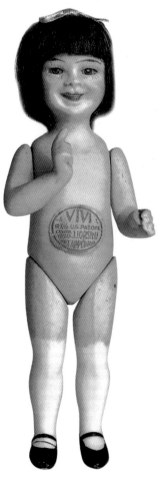

5" Vivi by Jeanne Orrsini, **$1,200.**
Courtesy of David Cobb Auction

Happifats: rotund boy and girl with down-glancing eyes; two tiny teeth; molded forehead hair lock and clothes.

4"	$300
6"	$500

Rag – Tag: cat and dog with swivel neck; glass eyes; molded booties; typically marked "Rag Trade Mark Corp by Georgene Averill 890 Germany"/ "Tag 891."

5"	$3,000

Other Animals (Rabbit or Bear):

2"-3"	$550-$600

Frog, Monkey, and Others:

4"-5"	$800-$900

Mibs, Baby Peggy, L. Amberg: character face; typically marked "1921" or with paper label.

4"-5"	$450-$500
6"	$625

Our Fairy #222: swivel neck; glass, side-glancing eyes; open/closed mouth with painted upper teeth; paper label.

4"	$750
7"	$1,200
9"	$2,000

Sonny: swivel neck; glass or painted eyes; round open/closed mouth; bare feet; typically marked with paper label.

Painted eyes:

6"	$925
7"	$1,250

Glass eyes:

6"	$3,100
7"	$3,500

Scootles: jointed shoulder and hip; molded wavy hair; painted, side-glancing eyes; closed, smiling mouth; typically marked "Germany."

4"	$750
7"	$1,200
9"	$2,000

Little Annie Rooney: jointed shoulders or no joints; yarn-braided wig; molded and painted dress and jacket; big eyes; wide, smiling, closed mouth; typically marked "Germany."

4"-5"	$400-$500

Googly Eyed: jointed shoulder and perhaps hip and neck; molded and painted hair or mohair wig; painted or glass eyes; closed mouth; typically marked "Germany" or a mold number.

Crawling Baby, Painted Eyes:

5"	$600

Glass Eyes, Elaborate Regional Costume:

5"	$900
6"	$1,300
7"	$1,400

Glass Eyes, Jointed Neck:

4"	$900
5"	$1,400
7"	$2,400

Round Face, Painted Eyes, Top Knot:
  7" $3,500
Painted Eyes:
  7" $800
Glass Eyes, mold #320:
  5" $1,200
Sad Mouth:
  4" $700
Glass Eyes, mold #65:
  4" $500
Glass Eyes, Fully Jointed, Including Elbows and Knees:
  5" $3,500
  7" $4,000

Frozen Charlotte

"Nacktfrosch" or "Naked Baby."

Frozen Charlotte and Frozen Charlie*: glazed or unglazed; solid, one-piece body, distinctive, bent arms; straight legs separated to knees; molded and painted hair; delicate facial features; undressed or rare molded clothing, hats, and/or boots; typically marked "Germany," mold number, or unmarked.

Charlotte or Charlie:
  3"-5" .... $100-$200
  8"-10" .... $300-$400
  12"-15" .... $600-$750
Pink tinted:
  3"-5" .... $300-$450
  8"-10" .... $600-$800
  12"-15" .... $900-$1,000
Black tinted:
  3"-5" .... $185-$235
  8"-10" .... $325-$425
  12"-15" .... $565-$775
Mold clothes or boots:
  3"-5" .... $285-$385
  7"-9" .... $450-$500
  10"-11" .... $525-$575
Unusual hair style:
  3"-5" .... $375-$425
  7"-9" .... $475-$525
  10"-11" .... $575-$600
  *Add $100 for unusual hats or footwear.

Later All Bisque

Pink Bisque: the bisque is not painted but tinted pink; jointed shoulder and hip; molded and painted bobbed hair or mohair wig; nicely painted facial features; textured stockings and single strap black shoes; typically marked "Germany."

12" Frozen Charlie, unmarked, pink tinted bisque, **$900.**
Courtesy of McMasters-Harris Auction

Glass eyes:

3" $165
4"-5" ....$200-$250
6"-7" ....$300-$400

Painted eyes:

3" $115
4"-5" ....$135-$165
6"-7" ....$220-$275

Unusual character or jointed waist:

3"-5" ....$350-$450
6" $500
7" $700

Painted Bisque: thin layer of flesh-colored paint applied over the entire doll but not fired or baked to a permanent application. Please note the difference between "cold painted," which has only particular parts painted, and "painted bisque," which is an all-over coating or wash. Jointed shoulder and hip; molded and painted hair or mohair wig; painted facial features; socks and single strap black shoes; typically marked "Germany."

2"-3" ....$60-$100
5" $150

Immobiles and Nodders

Prices listed are for average quality dolls. Extremely inferior or superior doll values fluctuate accordingly.

Immobiles*: no joints; molded and cold-painted features and clothing. Do not confuse immobiles with German bisque figurines or Frozen Charlottes. Immobiles used an inferior-quality bisque. The brightly colored, poorly applied, cold painted decoration may result in a worn appearance to facial features and clothing. Typically marked "Germany," a mold number, or unmarked. Adult or child*

2"-3" ....$60-$85
5"-7" ....$130-$185

*Add $100 for comic or personality characters.

Nodders: also known as knotters; solid, one-piece body, joined at the neck by elastic knotted through hole at top of head; molded and painted features; nodders representing people have molded

and painted clothes; most animal nodders have molded and painted fur; animal nodders with molded clothes are rare; typically unmarked.

Adult/child:

3"-4" ....$75-$85
5"-6" ....$100-$150

Comic character:

3"-4" ....$135-$150
5"-6" ....$175-$225

Personalities:

3"-4" ....$250-$285
5"-6" ....$300-$350

Animals*:

3"-4" ....$300-$400
5"-6" ....$500-$600

*Add $150 to any animal with molded clothes.

4" all bisque German character nodder, **$150.**
Courtesy of McMasters-Harris Auction

Japanese

Molded and painted hair and facial features; unjointed or jointed shoulder; rare examples have glass eyes, wigs, and/or additional joints; may have molded and painted clothes or no clothing; typically marked "Japan," "Nippon," or paper label.

Immobile adult/child:

3"-4"	$5-$10
5"-6"	$25-$35

Immobile characters:

3"-4"	$60-$65
5"-6"	$70-$75

Jointed adult/child:

5"-6"	$65-$75

Jointed characters/personalities*:

3"-5"	$100-$135
6"-7"	$150-$175

*Add $100 for Shirley Temple or known Disney characters.

Betty Boop: type with bobbed, wavy, molded hair; big, round, side-glancing eyes; spiked lashes; one-piece solid body; shoulder joints; often found wearing a crepe paper dress.

3-1/2"	$30
5"	$35
7"	$45

Box Set: such as bridal party, circus troupe, Snow White and dwarfs, Three Little Pigs and wolf, and others.

4"	$250
5"	$350
6"	$400

4"-6" all bisque Japan "Dolly Nippon" characters, nicely decorated and very appealing, **$125-$150.**
Courtesy of McMasters-Harris Auction

Alma Italian Felts

Alma, of Turin, Italy, manufactured beautiful felt dolls resembling the popular Lenci dolls. The dolls were exceptionally well made and exquisitely costumed.

Identifying characteristics include a hollow torso covered in light flesh-colored felt; ladder-like stitched seams; and attached ears made from folded and gathered material. The most unique construction aspect is the method used to attach the limbs. Unlike other cloth dolls that have limbs sewn onto the body, Alma dolls are jointed by elastic stringing.

12" and 13" Alma Boy, **$500**, and Girl, **$550**, marked "Alma Made in Italy."
Courtesy of McMasters-Harris Auction

Prices listed are for original costumed dolls with good color. Loose or wobbly joints do not greatly affect the price.

Child/Character Dolls*: all felt; socket head; covered hollow torso; limbs with no top stitching, attached with elastic; mohair sewn onto head in strips; painted side-glancing eyes; white dot highlights; painted outside-corner lashes; attached ears; closed or open mouth with teeth; beautifully costumed; typically unmarked or with wrist tag only.

Child:

9"-13"	$240-$550
16"-20"	$750-$950
22"	$1,100
26"	$1,400

Character:

6"	$950
20"	$1,500
28"	$2,200
30"	$2,700

*Exceptional or elaborately costumed characters, such as Russian Cossack Dancer, can easily be worth double the amounts listed.

Alt, Beck & Gottschalck

Alt, Beck & Gottschalck was located in Nauendorf, near Ohrdruf, Thuringia, Germany, from 1854 until 1930. A.B.G. (as it is commonly known) is credited by most doll historians with producing traditional bisque child and character babies as well as a series of beautifully detailed glazed and unglazed shoulder heads. More than 50 mold numbers, all between 639 and 1288, have been identified. Old bisque will have a slightly rough feel.

Prices listed are for appropriately costumed dolls in good condition.

Bisque Shoulder Head: bisque shoulder head or socket head and separate shoulder plate; kid or cloth body; cloth, kid, or bisque limbs; short neck; molded and painted hair or wig; may have bonnet, hat, scarf, or other molded ornamentation; painted or glass eyes; pierced or unpierced ears; open or closed mouth ("1/2" after the mold number indicates open mouth); typically marked "693," "698," "772," "882," "890," "889," "894," "926," "974," "978," "980," "990," "996," "998," "1000," "1002," "1008," "1022," "1024," "1028," "1044," "1054," "1056," "1062," "1064," "1123," "1127," "1142," "1154," "1214," "1218," "1222," "1226," "1234," "1235," "1254," "1288," "1304" and possibly others, followed by "XX" (double X's misaligned), "#," "No.," "1/2," size number, and/or "Germany."

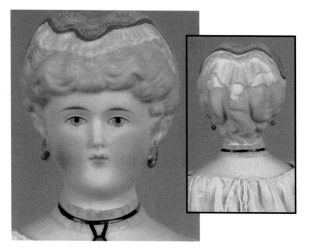

Alt, Beck & Gottschalck 20" closed mouth, molded hat and neck scarf with pierced ears and painted eyes, **$2,200.**

Courtesy of McMasters-Harris Auction

Closed mouth/painted eyes/molded
hair:
 12"-16" ....$450-$550
 18"-24" ....$600-$800
 27"-29" .... $1,100-$1,300
Closed mouth/glass eyes/molded
hair:
 12"-16" ....$700-$875
 18"-24" .... $1,000-$1,500
 27"-29" .... $1,750-$2,000
Closed mouth/elaborately molded
hair*, **:
 12"-16" .... $1,200-$1,500
 18"-24" .... $1,750-$2,200
 27"-29" .... $2,500-$3,000
 Closed mouth/molded hat or scarf:
 12"-16" .... 1,500-$1,800
 18"-24" .... $2,000-$2,500
 27"-29" .... $2,700-$3,200
Closed mouth/glass eye/with wig:
 12"-16" .... $1,000-$1,400
 18"-24" .... $1,700-$2,200
 27"-29" .... $2,700-$3,100
Open mouth:
 12"-16" ....$700-$750
 18"-22" ....$850-$950
 24"-27" .... $1,200-$1,450
 29" $1,800

China Shoulder Head*, **: china shoulder head extends over tops of arms; kid or cloth body; cloth, kid, or china limbs; short neck; molded and painted hair; many with molded bonnet, scarf, or other headwear; painted eyes, but at least one china head (mold 1008) has been found with glass eyes; many with pierced ears; closed mouth; typically marked "784," "880," "882," "1000," "1008," "1028," "1030," "1046," "1056," "1112," "1142," "1210," or "1214," followed by "XX" (double X's misaligned), "#," "No.," and size number.

 China head:
 12" $350
 14"-18" ....$450-$550
 22" $675
 24"-27" ....$750-$825
 29" $900

 Add $100 for pierced ears.

 **Add $300 for glass eyes.*

19" closed mouth Alt, Beck & Gottschalck,
$1,800.
Courtesy of Susan Miller

Closed Mouth Child: bisque socket head; composition-and-wood ball-joint body or kid body with kid lined bisque shoulder plate; good wig; glass eyes; typically marked "630," "911," "916," "938," "989," and possibly others.

 911/916/630/1322:
 12"-18" .... $2,200-$3,000
 22"-26" .... $3,000-$4,500
 938/989:
 12"-18" .... $3,500-$4,300
 22"-26" .... $4,300-$6,000
 1450/smiling character:
 12" $15,000
 16" $19,000
 20" $22,000

Open mouth: bisque socket head; composition-and-wood ball-joint body; good wig; glass eyes; typically marked "630," "1321," "1326," "1329," "1357," "1358," "1359," "1361," "1362," or "1367."

 Dolly face:
 14" $550
 20"-24" .... $800-$1,000
 30" $1,700

Molds 630/1321/1329/1357/1358/1359:

14" $1,500
16"-18" .... $2,000-$2,400
20" $2,700

Character Baby*: bisque socket head; composition bent-limb baby body; good wig; glass eyes; may have pierced nostrils; open mouth with teeth and tongue; typically marked "1322," "1352," or "1361."

10" $550
12"-16" .... $600-$800
20"-24" .... $900-$1,550
30" $2,400

*Add $150 for flirty eyes and $500 for jointed toddler body to any character baby.

Alt, Beck & Gottschalck 27" #1367 character breather baby, **$1,500,** and Bähr & Pröschild 18" #585 character baby, **$1,400.**
Courtesy of David Cobb Auction

Louis Amberg
& Son

Louis Amberg & Son was located in Cincinnati, Ohio, in 1878, and in New York City from 1893 until 1930. Amberg imported and manufactured both bisque and composition dolls. In 1907, Amberg's son, Joshua, joined the firm, and it became Louis Amberg & Son. In 1909, Louis Amberg was listed as the artist and owner of "Lucky Bill," the first known American copyrighted composition doll head. By 1928, Louis Amberg advertised over 600 style numbers available (including some imported from Germany and France). Louis Amberg & Son was sold to E. I. Horsman in 1930.

Bisque

Prices listed are for appropriately costumed dolls in good condition.

Baby Peggy: bisque shoulder or socket head; jointed composition-and-wood or kid body; happy or sad expression; mohair wig with bobbed style; glass eyes; closed mouth with smiling or serious expression; typically marked "19 c 24/LA & S/Germany/-50-/" followed by style number "972," "973," "983," or "982."

Shoulder head:
18"-20" .... $2,500-$2,700
22"-24" .... $2,850-$3,250
Socket head:
18"-20" .... $2,850-$3,100
22"-24" .... $3,250-$3,550

Fulper: bisque socket head; jointed composition-and-wood body; good wig; glass sleep eyes; thick upper and lower lashes; open mouth; two upper teeth; typically marked "Amberg Dolls the World Standard Fulper Made in USA."

Better quality:
14" $600
20" $850
24" $1,050
Standay quality:
14" $475
20" $625
24" $700

Newborn Baby (a.k.a. "Bottle Baby" or "My Playmate"): designed to represent a two-day-old infant; bisque flange neck; cloth body; solid dome; lightly spray-painted hair; flat, broad nose; sunken chin; full cheeks; small, flat ears; closed mouth; typically marked "L. A. & S. 1914/No.G45520," "L.A.S. 371 DRGM Germany," or "Newborn Baby 45520," "LAS 886."

8"-10"	$425-$475
12"	$575
14"	$725
17"	$950

Vanta Baby: bisque flange neck; cloth body; bent, composition limbs; lightly spray-painted hair; glass sleep eyes; real lashes; open mouth; two teeth; original Vanta Baby undergarments; with rattle, Baby's Record Book, and gift card; marked "Vanta Baby/LA & S 3/0 D.R.G.M Germany."

18"	$1,300
20"-22"	$1,500-$1,700
24"	$1,900

Louis Amberg & Son 25" bisque Vanta Baby, marked "Vanta Baby L.A. & S. Made in Germany," **$1,900.**

Courtesy of David Cobb Auction

Composition

Prices listed are for appropriately costumed dolls in good condition.

Babies: all composition; bent-limb baby body; molded and painted hair; painted eyes; closed mouth; typically marked "L.A.S. c/414/1911."

12"-14"	$300-$350
20"-22"	$500-$700

Baby Peggy: composition shoulder head and limbs; (more closely resembles a child) cloth body; molded and painted brown hair in bobbed style or mohair wig; painted eyes; open/closed mouth with teeth showing:

20"	$1,100

Charlie Chaplin: composition portrait head and hands; cloth body; dark molded and painted hair; painted, side-glancing eyes; closed mouth below molded and painted moustache; typically marked with cloth label "Charlie Chaplin Doll/Worlds Greatest Comedian/Made Exclusively by Louis Amberg & Son N.Y./By Special Arrangement with Essanay Film Co."

14"	$800
20"	$1,000

Lucky Bill: composition boy's character face; teddy-bear-type body. This rare doll's desirability is due more to its historical significance than artistic value.

14" $600

Mibs: composition shoulder head and limbs cloth body; slightly bowed legs; molded and painted strawberry blond hair with wave falling down the center of the forehead; perplexed expression; detailed, painted blue eyes looking down; thick lashes; slightly feathered brows; closed mouth; typically marked "L. A. & S. 1921/Germany" or unmarked; clothing tag "Amber Dolls/Please Love Me/I'm Mibs"; wrist tags "Amberg Dolls/Please Love Me/I'm Mibs" or "Please Love Me/I'm Mibs."

10" $1,100
16" $1,400

Sis Hopkins: composition shoulder or socket head on shoulder plate; cloth body; composition or sateen arms; character face of laughing child; molded hair with pigtails or wig with two braids; painted, side-glancing eyes; open/closed mouth, grinning with top and bottom teeth, or molded tongue sticking out; marked "SIS HOPKINS."

14" $750
16" $900
20" $1,300

Sunny Orange Blossom: composition shoulder head; cloth body and limbs; molded and painted bonnet, resembling an orange with holes for ribbon to tie; painted eyes; closed mouth; original orange organdy dress with "Sunny Orange Blossom" ribbons; painted socks and shoes; typically marked "L.A. & S./1924."

14" $1,500

Vanta Baby: composition shoulder head and bent limbs; cloth body with crier; molded and painted hair; tin sleep or painted eyes; open mouth with two teeth; original Vanta baby undergarments; celluloid baby rattle, gift card, and Dolly Record Book; typically marked "Vanta Baby" or "Vanta Baby/Trade Mark Reg./An Amberg Doll."

14" $450
18"-20" .... $500-$550
24"-25" .... $700-$900

Victory Doll: composition socket head, jointed wood-and-composition body; good wig; glass, sleep eyes; open mouth; typically marked "Amberg Victory Doll."

16" $350
20" $450
24" $600

Edwine/IT/Peter Pan/Sue/Tiny Tots: all composition; one-piece upper body and head, separate lower body; straight arms and legs; body-twist joint at waist; constructed with a rounded ball in the lower half of the body and a socket in the upper waist; typically marked "Amberg/Pat. Pend/L.A.S. R.C.P. 1928."

8" $400
14" $650

Felt

Louis Amberg responded to the public's desire for Lenci-style dolls: jointed at the neck, shoulder, and hip; washable faces; nicely dressed with bonnets or hats and single-strap shoes.

Prices listed are for appropriately costumed dolls with good color.

16"-18" .... $800-$900
24" $1,000

American Character

The American Character Doll Company was located in New York City from 1919 until 1968. Early in the company's history, composition dolls were made with the trade name Aceedeecee.

Composition

Prices listed are for appropriately costumed dolls in good condition.

Puggy: all composition; character face; male companion to the Campbell Kids; frowning expression; molded and painted hair; small, painted eyes; appropriately costumed; typically marked "A/Petite/Doll."

 12" $750

Character Babies: petite Babies and Mama Dolls; composition head; cloth body; bent limbs; molded and painted hair or good wig; sleep eyes; open or closed mouth; typically marked "Petite American Character," "Amer. Char. Doll Co.," "AC," or "Wonder Baby."

 12" $285
 14"-22" ....$300-$400
 24"-28" ....$450-$600

Tots: composition shoulder or socket head on shoulder plate; cloth or composition body; good wig; tin or glassine sleep eyes; real lashes; open or open/closed mouth with teeth; typically marked "Petite Am. Char."

 12"-16" ....$275-$350
 20"-22" ....$375-$400
 24" $425

Child: composition socket head on shoulder plate; composition limbs; cloth body; molded and painted hair or good wig; painted or glassine sleep eyes; typically marked "Amer. Char.," "Petite Sally," or "Sally" below a horseshoe with an embossed doll standing in the center.

 14"-16" ....$375-$425
 22"-24" ....$500-$600

Older Child/Teen (Sally, Carol Ann Berry)*: all composition; jointed at neck, shoulder, and hip; molded and painted hair and eyes or good mohair wig and glassine sleep eyes; typically marked "AmCharacter."

 12"-14" ....$300-$400
 16" $450
 24" $750

 *Add $200-$300 for original Carol Ann Berry (the Two-some Doll) with special crown braided hair.

American Character 12" composition Puggy, marked "Puggy A Petite Doll" hangtag, **$750.**
Courtesy of McMasters-Harris Auction

American Character 18"
Sweet Sue in authentic Alice
costume in mint condition
with wrist tag, **$1,200.**

*Courtesy of Julia Burke,
www.juliaburke.com*

Vinyl and Hard Plastics

Prices listed are for dolls in near-mint, original condition.

Ben Cartwright: solid jointed vinyl; molded hair;
painted features; molded clothes; typically marked "C/
American Character."

7-1/2" $120

Betsy McCall: hard plastic, vinyl, or combination of
both; socket head; rooted hair; sleep eyes with lashes;
closed mouth; typically marked "McCall Corp" in a circle, "McCall 1958," or unmarked.

7-1/2"-14" .... $400-$450
20"-22" .... $600-$650
30" $750
36"-39" .... $900-$1,100

Cricket/Teessy: plastic and vinyl teenage body; hair
grows when stomach button is pushed, shortens when
key is inserted and turned in back; painted eyes; closed
mouth; typically marked "American Character."

10" $150
13"-14" .... $200-$225

Eloise: all cloth; yellow yarn hair; painted eyes; character molded face; tiny nose; closed mouth; typically
marked with hangtag only "Amer. Char. Doll/Corp."

16" $600
22" $750

Freckles: small, two-faced girl changes expression
when left arm is moved up (happy) and down (sad);
rooted hair; painted eyes; mouth either open/closed
smiling, or closed sad expression; freckles; typically
marked "Amer. Char. Inc./1966."

14" $75
20"-22" .... $100-$125

Hedda Get Bedda: all vinyl; hard plastic bonnet; three-
sided vinyl head; knob on top of bonnet rotates molded
faces (awake and smiling, asleep and grinning, or sick
child); typically marked "American Doll and Toy Corp.
1961" and "Whimsie/Amer. Doll and Toy Corp. 1960";
(issued with two dates).

22" $275

Little Miss Echo: hard plastic; battery-operated recorder housed within the torso allows the doll to repeat
whatever is said to her.

30" $350

Little Ricky Jr.: vinyl socket head; one-piece body; molded and painted hair; sleep eyes; open nurser mouth; typically marked "Amer. Char. Doll."

14"-16"	$150-$225
21"-21"	$275-$300

Sandy: vinyl head; hard plastic, jointed body; advertised as "Sandy McCall, Betsy McCall's big brother"; molded and painted hair; sleep eyes; open/closed mouth; typically marked "Amer-Char," "McCall Corp.," or "American Character."

36"	$900

Sweet Sue and Toni*: hard plastic socket head; plastic and vinyl or all hard plastic body (walker or non-walker); arms slightly bent; well manicured hands; jointed shoulder and hip; various combinations of joints; wig or rooted hair; sleep eyes with real lashes; closed mouth; (Toni had high heel feet and pierced ears); typically marked "Amer. Char. Doll," "American Character Doll," "Amer Char," "A.C.," or unmarked.

Close-up of Sweet Sue showing outstanding quality and beautiful coloring.
Courtesy of Julia Burke

10-1/2"-18"	$400-$500
24"-31"	$600-$700

*Add $200-$400 for groom (boy version with lamb's wool wig) or authentically costumed character dolls such as Annie Oakley or Alice.

Tiny Tears: all jointed vinyl; rooted or molded and painted hair; sleep eyes with lashes; nicely molded fingers and toes; open nurser mouth; tiny holes for tear ducts; typically marked "American Character Doll/Pat."

13"	$300
17"	$500
22"	$600

Toodles: all vinyl chubby, bent-limb baby body; "rolling joint" at elbows and knees; rooted or molded hair; sleep eyes; open nurser mouth; older toddler version with molded teeth and open smiling mouth; typically marked "AM," "Amer-9," "American Char.," "Toodles," or unmarked.

American Character 13" Tiny Tears, **$300**.
Photo courtesy of James D. Julia Inc.

14"-21"	$300-$375
23"-25"	$400-$450
30"	$500

Whimsies: one-piece vinyl body; face with elf-like quality; rooted hair; very large eyes; full, smiling, closed mouth; typically marked "Whimsies/1960/American Doll & Toy."

22"	$275

Annalee Mobilitee Dolls, Inc.

Barbara Annalee Davis began making puppets and dolls in 1933 that she sold at various New England craft shops. Davis married Charles Thorndike in 1941, and settled in Meredith, New Hampshire, where they soon concentrated on making cloth dolls and animal characters full time. Annalee Thorndike stepped down from the day-to-day activities at the end of 1997.

Hair and labels may help to determine the production date of an early Annalee doll. From 1934 to 1960, yarn was used for hair; from 1960 to 1963 orange or yellow feathers adorned the tops of heads; and since 1963 synthetic fur has been used. Tags may prove to be even more definitive in determining age. From 1930-1950, there were either white tags with black lettering or light green tags with dark green lettering; in 1954, white tags with red lettering; in 1955, "Pat. Pending" and "Meredith NH"; in 1960, "C" & "R" were added; in 1963, the production year "1963/1964" was added; in 1970, tags were glued to the bottom of the doll (a practice quickly abandoned); in 1973, embroidered; in 1976, Tyvek® labels included contents and material; in 1980, less expensive poly-non-woven; in 1983, addition of logo head; in 1987, the actual year of production was added.

Annalee Mobilitee 30" Santa and Mrs. Claus, **$400.**
Courtesy of Jennifer Herlocher

Special museum collection of 10" Annalee Mobilitee adult dolls, **$350 for the pair.**
From the collection of Maribeth Herlocher. Photograph courtesy of Julia Burke, www.juliaburke.com

Prices listed are for originally costumed dolls with no damage.

10" child:
  1950s $2,600
  1960s $1,800
  1970s $500
  1980s $300
7"-10" adult:
  1950s $4,500
  1970s $1,500
  1990s $250
7"-8" Baby/Angels:
  1960s $500
  1970s $450
  1980s $400
7"-10" Disney characters:
  1990s $350-500
26"-30" Mr./Mrs. Santa:
  1960s $600
  1970s $450
  1980s $400
24" Motorized Santa:
  1972 ....$550
8" Elephant:
  1976......................$350
18" Frog Bride & Groom:
  1980......................$650
8" Pig Ballerina:
  1981 ....$185
18" Bear Ballerina
  1985 ....$325
5" Duck with Umbrella:
  1986 ....$75
10" Stork with three babies in a basket:
  1987 ....$450
10" Golfer:
  1992 ....$100

Arranbee Doll Company

The Arranbee Doll Company was founded in New York in 1922 and operated until 1959. Miss Ruby Hopf, Georgene Averill's sister, was Arranbee's principal designer. Vogue acquired Arranbee in 1959 but continued to use the "R & B" marking until early in 1961.

Bisque

Prices listed are for appropriately costumed dolls in good condition.

My Dream Baby: bisque flange neck; cloth body or socket head; composition, bent-limb baby body; lightly spray-painted hair; small, glass sleep eyes; open mouth (mold 351) or closed mouth (mold 341); typically marked "AM Germany/341/3/1/2K," "Germany/Arranbee," or "AM 351/4 Germany Arranbee."

Open mouth/cloth body:
9"-12" ....$300-$500
15"-18" ....$700-$800
20"-24" .... $900-$1,100

Open mouth/composition body:
9"-12" ....$350-$550
15"-18" ....$775-$875
20"-24" .... $975-$1,200

Closed mouth/cloth body:
9"-12" ....$375-$575
15"-18" ....$800-$900
20"-24" .... $1,00-$1,250

Closed mouth/composition body:
9"-12" ....$450-$650
15"-18" ....$875-$975
20"-24" .... $1,100-$1,400

Dolly Face: bisque socket head; jointed composition body; good wig; glass eyes; open mouth; typically marked "Simon & Halbig/Arranbee/Patent/Germany."
18" $950
20" $1,000
24" $1,200

Composition

Prices listed are for appropriately costumed dolls in good condition.

Nursery Rhyme*: all jointed composition; molded and painted hair; painted eyes; closed mouth; original character costume; typically marked "R & B Doll Co." or "R & B."
9" $375

*Add $400 for dolls with the original elaborate suitcase-style box.

Mama or Character Baby*: composition shoulder or socket head; cloth or composition body; molded and painted hair; painted or tin sleep eyes; closed or open mouth; typically marked "R & B," "Arranbee," or "Little Angel R & B."

  7" $250
  14"-16" ....$375-$450
  18"-21" ....$500-$525
  *Add $50 for Botteltot with attached celluloid bottle.

Child Dolls: (Nancy, Nancy Lee, Debu-Teen, Girls From the Southern Series, Nancy Jean, and Princess Betty Rose) older child or teenager; all jointed composition; molded and painted hair or good wig; painted or sleep eyes; closed mouth; typically marked "Nancy/Arranbee/Dolls," "R & B," or "Debu-Teen."

  12"-14" ....$400-$500
  17" $600
  18"-21" ....$650-$750

Kewty: all jointed composition; molded hair with swirl across forehead and deep part; sleep eyes; open or open/closed mouth; typically marked "Kewty." (Due to similarities to the Nancy Doll, it is generally accepted that Kewty is an Arranbee doll, though some believe Kewty is a carnival doll produced by Domec.)

  14"-16" ....$400-$500

Arranbee 18" Debu-Teen, marked "R&B," a beautiful, apparently mint condition all original doll with her box, which is a rare treasure. Expect a doll in this condition to be valued at **$1,200 or more.**
Courtesy of McMasters-Harris Auction

Magic Skin/Latex

Arranbee made a few rubber-type dolls in the late 1940s. Collectors often referred to this type of doll as "Magic Skin," perhaps because it can seem to deteriorate and vanish right before your eyes. When considering the purchase of a Magic Skin doll, remember that the rubber will get sticky and rot. The process may be slowed by regularly rubbing cornstarch into the doll. Eventually, however, age will triumph and the doll will deteriorate. A rubber doll is only a temporary addition to your collection.

Child or Baby: all Magic Skin or vinyl head on Magic Skin body; molded and painted hair or wig; painted or plastic eyes; closed mouth; typically marked "A & B," "Arranbee," "210 Pat/Pen," or "Made in USA."

10"	**$95**
14"-18"	**$125-$150**
22"-25"	**$175-$200**

Hard Plastic/Vinyl

Production of hard plastic dolls began in the 1940s. Prices listed are for dolls in near-mint, original condition.

Little Dear: socket-head baby; vinyl baby body; rooted synthetic hair; sleep eyes with molded lashes; open/closed mouth; typically marked "R & B" or "Arranbee."

8"-12"	**$75-$125**

Nancy Lee: older child socket head; vinyl body, saran wig; sleep eyes with molded lashes; distinctive "S" eyebrows; closed mouth; typically marked "Arranbee" or "R & B."

14"	**$550**
17"-20"	**$700-$900**

Susan: older child socket head; vinyl body; synthetic wig; sleep eyes with molded lashes; open/closed mouth; typically marked "Arranbee" or "A & B."

14"-16"	**$200-$250**

Angel Baby: socket head; vinyl baby body; curly, rooted synthetic hair; sleep eyes; open drink and wet mouth; typically marked "R & B" or "Arranbee."

20"-24"	**$200-$300**

My Angel Walking Doll: socket head; jointed vinyl walker body; rooted straight hair; sleep eyes with molded lashes; smiling mouth; typically marked "Arranbee," "R & B" or "Made in USA."

20"	**$400**
36"	**$600**

Littlest Angel: all hard plastic, jointed walker body; synthetic wig; sleep eyes with molded or real lashes; closed mouth; typically marked "R & B," "Arranbee," or "Made in USA."

10"	**$250**

Nanette and Nancy Lee: all jointed hard plastic; long, thin legs; synthetic wig; sleep plastic eyes with molded or real lashes; closed mouth; typically marked "R & B," "Arranbee," "210 Pat/Pen," or "Made in USA." (Teenage-style dolls: Angeline; Dream Bride; Taffy [caracul wig], Prom Queen, Francine.)

14"-17"	**$550-$650**
21"-23"	**$750-$850**

Coty Girl: shapely jointed all vinyl; high heel feet; sleep eyes, molded lashes; small closed mouth; synthetic rooted hair; typically marked "P."

10"	**$250**

Artist Dolls

Individually designed, crafted, and produced works of art, the high investment potential of the artist doll encourages a relatively safe existence, as few are purchased as toys. Do not confuse the original artist dolls listed here with the more commonly found, moderately priced, commercially produced dolls designed by many of the same artists.

Many of the artists listed are members of either the National Institute of American Doll Artists (N.I.A.D.A.) or Original Doll Artists Council of America (O.D.A.C.A.). Material, workmanship, subject matter, and visual or decorative appeal are all contributing aspects that assure a wise investment rather than a speculative acquisition.

Prices listed are for dolls in original, mint condition.

Artist Original Doll Value Comparisons

Adair-Kertzman, Linda:
   Porcelain; magical miniature fairies ....$600-$900
Adams, Christine:
   Oilcloth; painted-featured tiny tots...$200-$350
Angel, Cindy:
   Porcelain; child or portrait with vintage accessories............................$300-$700
Aprile, Paulette:
   Wax or porcelain; detailed lady or child portrait............................ $3,000-$4,500
Armstrong-Hand, Martha:
   Porcelain; expressively adult, child, or baby .... $2,800-$3,500
Barrie, Mirren:
   Cloth; historical characters ....$200-$500
Beckett, Bob and June:
   Wooden; smiling impish child...$300-$600
Bello, Yolanda:
   Porcelain; one of a kind or limited edition .... $1,500-$3,500
Blakely, Halle:
   Porcelain; historical portrait; authentic costumes .... $1,500-$3,500
Brahms, Abigail:
   Wax or porcelain; child or adult .... $1,000-$3,000
Brandon, Elizabeth:
   Porcelain; child ....$400-$700

Bringloe, Frances:
  Wooden; small early American child ....$400-$600
Brouse, Mary:
  Porcelain; original designed child or adult...$200-$250
Bruns, Nancy:
  Wooden; child with detailed facial features ....$700-$900
Bruyere, Muriel:
  Molded; cloth; hand-painted facial features .... $700-$1,200
Bullard, Helen:
  Wooden; adult or child...$300-$500
Burnell, Patricia:
  Clay-based composition characters; period costumes...................... $900-$1,500
Cameron, Beth:
  Santa .... $1,200-$1,700
Campbell, Astry:
  Porcelain; child; finely modeled and costumed .... $900-$1,500
Clear, Emma:
  Porcelain, bisque, or china; original design; adult .... $700-$1,500
Crees, Paul:
  Wax; portrait dolls with magnificent costumes .... $1,200-$3,000
Dengel, Dianne:
  Cloth; child or baby stitched and painted features............................$250-$500
Deval, Brigette:
  Wax or porcelain; one of a kind or limited edition......................... $3,500-$5,500
Ellis, Cathy:
  Super Sculpey; charming character face child.....................................$300-$600
Fisher, Ruth:
  Porcelain; Oriental child ....$300-$500
Fox, Madelaine:
  Clay-like composition; historical costumed portrait...................... $1,200-$2,500
Goodnow, June:
  Porcelain; American Indian tribal costuming................................... $1,200-$2,800
Green, Evelyn:
  Baked composition; beautiful historical figures .... $550-$1,200
Gunzel, Hildegard:
  Porcelain or wax over porcelain; lifelike children .... $1,500-$3,000
Hale, Patti:
  Wooden; charming in their simplicity ....$400-$600
Heighton, Jean:
  Cloth, latex, or porcelain; fantasy costumed folks ....$400-$700
Heiser, Dorothy (Heizer):
  Cloth; stitch-sculptured portrait, wonderful costumes.................. $2,500-$6,000
Helm, Anne:
  Gesso over wood; painted facial features..$200-$400
Hesner, Dorothy:
  Porcelain; "Fruit Head" characters with comic appeal ....$100-$350
Holmes, Barbara:
  Sculpey, porcelain, or wax; characters...$300-$500
Johnson, Sharon:
  Porcelain; child ....$200-$300
Kane, Maggie Head:
  Porcelain; character portrait adult or child..$400-$700
Koerling, Cindy:
  Native American babies in authentic costume..................................$600-$800

Lafitte, Desirat:
Wax; portrait with exquisite period
costumes.. $1,000-$1,500
Ling, Tita:
Wooden; oriental child or adult.............$800-$1,000
Little, Virginia:
Wooden; carved; historically significant
character...$400-$700
Mark, Suzanne:
Porcelain; miniature suggest movement ...$250-$400
McLean, Jan:
Porcelain; child; artist-designed
costumes... $3,000-$5,000
Motter, Jennifer Berry:
Cloth; three-dimensional hand-painted
features ....$500-$1,500
Nelson, Bill:
Modeled character faces; wire armature
bodies.. $2,500-$4,500
Oldenburg, Mary Ann:
Porcelain; child ....$400-$800
Park, Irma:
Wax; tiny characters posed in delightful
settings...$300-$500
Parker, Ann:
Wax or wax over; miniature costumed
portrait ....$400-$900
Port, Beverly:
Porcelain, cloth, wax, or composition;
huminals..$500-$750
Price, Jeanette:
Porcelain or Sculpey; Santa Claus and
gnomes ....$300-$700
Randolf, Patricia Gene:
Porcelain or ceramics; artsy characters ..$600-$1,200
Ray, Jean:
Composition children ....$500-$750
Redmond, Kathy:
Porcelain; portrait; fine attention to
detail.. $1,500-$3,500
Robinson, Pat:
Porcelain; lifelike; articulated adult, figures $400-$900
Sandreuter, Regina:
Wooden; child; delicate features and
natural finish .... $1,500-$2,500
Saucier, Madeline:
Cloth.. $400-$600
Scattolini, Laura:
Cernit; pensive child; appropriately
costumed...$700-$1,800
Smith, P. D.:
Composition; child with expressive facial
modeling... $2,800-$3,700

15" Queen Victoria holding 6"
Edward, marked "R" within a
cat, **$3,000**,
by Kathy Redmond.
Courtesy of McMasters-Harris Auction

22" artist doll, **$3,000**, by P. D.
Smith of Santa Cruz, California.
Courtesy of McMasters-Harris Auction

24" wax Gibson Girl, **$2,000**, by Lewis Sorensen.
From the collection of Julia Burke. Courtesy of Julia Burke, www.juliaburke.com

21" Princess Margaret Rose artist doll by Martha Thompson, **$1,700.**
Photo courtesy of James D. Julia Inc.

4" girl with a wagon, artist doll by Eunice Tuttle, **$700.**
Photo courtesy of James D. Julia Inc.

Smith, Sherman:
Wooden; Grodnertal-type; artistic body construction .... **$400-$1,000**

Sorensen, Lewis:
Gibson Girl, less than 12" .... **$500-$800**
Wax, porcelain or papier- mâché; character portrait .... **$1,500-$3,500**

Stafford, Joyce:
Porcelain; small child .... **$200-$400**

Thanos, Charleen:
Porcelain; beautifully sculptured children .... **$2,000-$3,500**

Thompson, Martha:
Hand-pressed porcelain or cultured glass .... **$1,000-$3,000**

Treffeisen, Ruth:
Porcelain; child .... **$2,000-$3,000**

Tuttle, Eunice:
Porcelain or wax; miniature child, angel, or character.. **$700-$900**

Wallace, Shelia:
Wax; historically costumed portrait; inserted hair .... **$3,000-$5,000**

Walters, Beverly:
Porcelain; miniature; fashion portrait ..... **$700-$1,400**

Walters, Helen:
Cloth; folk art; painted and embroidered characters .... **$600-$900**

Webster, Mary Hortence, assisted by Loredo Taft:
Composition; character with whimsical costume.. **$400-$700**

Wick, Faith:
Porcelain; historic or fictional character .**$700-$1,500**

Wilson, Lita:
Porcelain; beautifully designed petite portrait .... **$600-$1,200**

Witherspoon:
Cloth; painted studio characters from New Orleans .... **$2,500-$4,000**

Wright, Phyllis:
Porcelain; child with expressive hand-painted eyes .... **$400-$800**

Wyffels, Berdine:
Porcelain; child .... **$250-$300**

Zeller, Fawn:
Porcelain; one of a kind .... **$2,500-$3,500**

Averill Manufacturing Company

Averill Manufacturing Company was located in New York, New York, from 1913 until 1965. Headed by the husband and wife team of Georgene and James Paul Averill, Georgene's brother, Rudolph A. Hopf, served as president.

Georgene and James Averill branched out in 1923, forming Madame Georgene, Inc., and later went on to form Georgene Novelties, Inc.

Georgene Averill also did design work for George Borgfeldt (her most popular doll was the Bonnie Babe) and served as superintendent of Borgfeldt's toy department.

Madame Hendren is a trademark used by Averill Manufacturing Company.

Bonnie Babe

Prices listed are for appropriately costumed dolls in good condition.

Bonnie Babe resembles a one-year-old baby; bisque or celluloid head; cloth body with composition limbs, or composition bent-limb baby body; molded and painted hair; sleep eyes; open, smiling, slightly crooked mouth with two lower teeth; typically marked "Copr. By/Georgene Averill/Germany/1005-3653/1386" (or "1402").

Bisques head/cloth body:
    14"-18" .... $1,600-$2,000
    22"-24" .... $2,000-$2,700
Composition body:
    14"-16" .... $2,300-$3,000
    22"-24" .... $3,700-$4,000
Celluloid head:
    14"-18" .... $600-$950
    22" .... $1,000-$1,100

Composition

Prices listed are for appropriately costumed dolls in good condition.

Dolly Record: composition head; metal eyes; phonograph mechanism housed in body; typically marked "Madame Hendren/Averill."

24"-26" .... **$1,500-$1,600**

Mama Doll: composition head and limbs; cloth body; molded and painted hair or good wig; painted or tin sleep eyes; closed or open/closed mouth with teeth; typically marked "Genuine Madam Hendren Doll 1717 Made in USA."

10" **$200**
15"-17" .... **$400-$450**
22"-24" .... **$600-$650**

Bobby and Dolly Dolls: composition head and limbs; cloth body; molded and painted hair, Chocolate Drop with yarn pigtails; painted, side-glancing eyes; pug nose; closed, smiling, single-lined, painted mouth; typically marked "G.G. Drayton"; neither Averill nor Hendren names appear on this doll.

14"-16" .... **$600-$650**

Whistling Dolls*: (Nell, Black Rufus, Dan, or Sailor) composition head; cloth body; molded and painted hair; painted, side-glancing eyes; puckered mouth with hole for whistling; cloth-covered spring legs are part of whistling mechanism; whistling sound is made when feet are pushed; typically marked "USA" or unmarked; hangtag "I whistle when you dance me on one foot/and then the other/Patented Feb. 2, 1926. A Genuine Madame Hendron Doll."

14" **$500**
*Add 100 for Black Rufus.

Costumed Character: composition head and lower limbs; cloth body; molded and painted hair or mohair wig; painted eyes; closed mouth; tagged; appropriate felt character costume; typically marked "Madame Hendren" or unmarked.

10"-14" .... **$300-$500**

Body Twist: (Dimmie and Jimmie) all

Averill 14" composition Dimmie marked "Madame Hendron/Patent Pending" and "Dimmie, Jimmie's Girl Friend" hangtag, **$650**, with a mohair bear on wheels.
Courtesy of David Cobb Auction

jointed composition; large ball joint at waist; molded and painted hair; painted eyes with large pupils and eye shadow; typically unmarked; wrist tag "Dimmie/Jimmie, Another Madame Hendren Doll/Made in USA" or "Jimmie/Dimmie's Boy Friend/Another Madame Hendren Doll/Made in USA."

14" **$650**

Val-Encia: composition shoulder head and limbs; slim body with voice box; low center of gravity allows the doll to walk; face flocked to resemble felt; mohair wig; big, painted eyes surrounded by dark eye shadow; typically stamped "Genuine/Madame Hendren/Doll/1714 Made in U.S.A."

15"-19" .... **$600-$750**

Harriet Flanders: all jointed composition; molded tufts of hair; painted eyes; three eyelashes above each eye; open mouth with painted tongue; typically marked "Harriet Flanders/1937."

12"-16" ....$400-$500

Child: (Peaches, Little Cherub) all jointed composition; molded and painted hair or mohair wig; painted or tin sleep eyes; closed mouth; typically marked "Madame Hendren Dolls Patent Pending, Madame Hendren."

14"-15" ....$500-$600

Celluloid

Prices listed are for appropriately costumed dolls in good condition.

Sunny Boy or Sunny Girl: celluloid head; composition arms and legs; slender cloth body; molded hair; glass eyes; marked "Sunny Girl" with a turtle and a sunburst; wrist tag "Sunny/Girl [Boy]/the doll with the/beautiful bright eyes, Averill Manufacturing Co. USA."

14"-17" ....$550-$575
19"-22" ....$600-$700

Cloth

Prices listed are for appropriately costumed dolls with good color.

Grace G. Drayton*: (Dolly Dingle, Chocolate Drop, Happy Cryer, Sis, Baby Bunny, Mah-Jongg Kid, Kitty Puss, and Susie Bear) cloth doll; movable limbs; painted face; large, round, side-glancing eyes; pug nose; single line, smiling mouth; typically marked "Dolly Dingle/Copyright By/G. G. Drayton."

11"-14" ....$850-$750
16" $950

*Add $100 for Chocolate Drop or tu-faced.

Maud Tousey Fangel: (Snooks, brunette, and Sweets, blonde) painted face; painted or yarn hair; big eyes with long lashes; closed, smiling mouth; printed clothing and flesh-colored body; typically marked "MTF" at seam on side of head or unmarked; hangtag "Soft Baby Doll/Created Exclusively for us by/Maud Tousey Fangel/America's Foremost Baby Painted/Georgene Novelties, Inc. New York, N.Y."

12"-14" .... $900-$1,000
16"-18" .... $1,100-$1,200
22" $1,500

Averill 12" Maude Tousey Fangel "Sweets," **$900.**
Courtesy of McMasters-Harris Auction

Child or Baby Doll*: (Bridesmaid, Ring Bearer, Flower Girl, Mary Had a Little Lamb, Girl Scout, Brownie, and International Dolls) mask face; cloth body; yarn hair; painted features; all sateen; applied facial decoration and elaborate costuming; typically unmarked.

    Sateen:
        12" $350
        16"-22" ....$500-$600
    International/mask face:
        12"-15" ....$225-$275
        24" $350
      *Add $100 for originally costumed Girl Scout or Brownie.

Comic Character Doll: (Alvin, Little Lulu, Nancy, Sluggo, Tubby Tom, and Becassine) swivel head; mask face; yarn hair; painted eyes; applied ears; closed mouth; character costumes; typically unmarked; hangtag character name "Georgene Novelties, Inc. New York City, Exclusive Licensed Manufacturers Made in U.S.A."

    12"-14" $1,500

Character Doll: (Nurse Jane and Uncle Wiggily) all cloth; shaped face and body; painted features; typically unmarked; hangtag "Georgene Averill."

    18"-19" ....$800-$900

Vinyl

Prices listed are for dolls in near-mint, original condition.

Aver Baby: vinyl head and hands; cloth body; molded hair; painted eyes; wide open, smiling mouth; typically marked "Averill."

    18" $400
    24"-26" ....$450-$500

Baby Dawn: all vinyl; chubby baby body; rooted hair; large sleep eyes; dimpled cheeks; open/closed, smiling mouth; typically marked "AVERILL."

    20" $500

Pair of Averill 12" cloth Holland International Georgene Novelty dolls in mint condition with wrist tags, **$250 each.**
Photograph courtesy of Ty Herlocher

Bähr & Pröschild

Bähr & Pröschild was a porcelain factory in Ohrdruf, Germany. Founded in 1871, it continued operating until 1910.

Dating a Bähr & Pröschild doll is relatively easy. The earliest dolls were marked with only a mold number. In 1988, "dep" was added. Around 1895, the initials "B & P" were included. In 1900, a crossed swords symbol was added. Finally, in 1919, when Bruno Schmidt purchased the business, Bähr & Pröschild dolls adopted a heart as a trademark and incorporated it into the markings.

Some of the many Bähr & Pröschild mold numbers identify specific dolls. For example, 217 is a black doll, 220 is Oriental, 244 is an Indian character, and 678 is a closed-mouth googly. Other mold numbers are not so definitive. The same mold number may be found with either open or closed mouth and open pate or Belton-style dome head.

12" Bähr & Pröschild #604 open-closed mouth with molded teeth and flirty eyes, **$750.**
Courtesy of David Cobb Auction

13" Bähr & Pröschild dolly face, **$900.**
From the Pat and Bill Tyson Collection.

Prices listed are for appropriately costumed dolls in good condition.

Belton-Type Doll: bisque solid dome or flat top, two or three holes; jointed composition, wooden body; good wig; paperweight eyes; pierced ears; closed mouth; typically marked in 200 series.

10"-12"	**$2,400-$3,000**
18"-20"	**$4,000-$4,300**
24"	**$5,200**

Closed Mouth Child Doll: bisque shoulder or socket head; kid or jointed straight wrist composition body; good wig; glass eyes; pierced ears; closed mouth; typically marked in 200 or 300 series.

Socket head:

12"	**$1,400**
16"-20"	**$1,900-$2,600**
24"	**$3,200**

Shoulder head:

12"	**$1,100**
14"-20"	**$1,500-$2,000**
24"	**$2,500**

Dolly Faced*: bisque shoulder or socket head; kid or jointed composition body; good wig; glass eyes; pierced ears; open mouth; typically marked in 200 or 300 series.

Socket head:

10"-12"	**$750-$800**
18"-22"	**$1,200-$1,500**
24"	**$1,600**

Shoulder head:

10"	**$350**
16"	**$750**
20"-22"	**$800-$900**

*Add $300-$500 for early square cut teeth.

Character Babies: bisque socket head; composition bent-limb baby body; solid dome or good wig; sleep eyes; open mouth; typically marked "585," "587," "604," "619," "620," "624," and "678."

10"-14"	**$700-$900**
18"-20"	**$1,400-$1,500**
22"-24"	**$1,750-$2,100**

Character Dolls*: bisque socket head; jointed composition body; solid dome; painted hair or good wig; sleep or painted eyes; open/closed or closed mouth; typically marked "244," "520," "536," "562," and possibly others.

244/closed mouth/glass eyes:

12"	**$3,250**
14"	**$3,850**

520/closed mouth/painted eyes:

14"	**$4,600**
18"	**$6,000**

536/closed mouth/painted eyes:

14"	**$6,900**

562/closed mouth/glass eyes:

12"	**$6,700**

*Add $500 for jointed toddler body.

Barbie® & Friends

The Barbie era began in 1958 when Ruth Handler, wife of the co-founder of Mattel, decided that a fashion doll with an expensive wardrobe would be a wonderful idea.

Barbie has changed with the times. There have been at least three instances in which Mattel has instigated a trade-in program. The first was in May 1967. A new Twist 'N Turn Barbie could be had in exchange for $1.50 and a used Barbie doll in any condition. More than 1.4 million Barbies were traded that month. The second trade-in program was for Living Skipper in 1970, and most recently the politically incorrect talking Barbie that said, "Math is tough," which some found offensive.

When examining a Barbie doll, check condition carefully. Any doll in less than perfect condition will quickly drop in value. To command mint value, a Barbie must have her original box, have beautiful facial coloring, have her hair in its original set, retain all accessories, and never have been played with.

Barbie Wedding Party Gift Set in mint condition, **$4,000**, including Skipper in #1904 Flower Girl costume, Ken in #787 Tuxedo, Titian Bubble-Cut Barbie wearing #947 Bride's Dream costume, and Midge in #987 Orange Blossom costume.
Courtesy of McMasters-Harris Auction

Barbie #1 with box, **$9,900.**
Courtesy of McMasters-Harris Auction

Barbie #1 in good condition,
$3,000.

Barbie #1*: 1959; vinyl heavy, solid body; soft, silky floss blond or brunette hair, styled in ponytail with curly bangs; highly arched (upside down V-shaped) eyebrows; painted black and white eyes with heavy black eyeliner and a thin line of blue on the eyelid; holes in balls of feet with copper tubes; wearing one-piece black and white striped swimsuit, gold hoop earrings, and black high heel plastic shoes with holes in the soles. Marked "Japan" on the arch of the foot; marked on the hip:

Barbie T. M.
Pats. Pend.
©MCMLVIII
by
Mattel Inc.

The #1 doll stand is a round, black plastic base with two prongs. It is marked "Barbie T.M." The fashion booklet has Barbie's profile on the cover and is marked "Barbie T.M." The box is marked "Barbie T.M." and "850."

Mint condition .... $9,900.
Fair to good condition................................. $3,000.
Poor condition .... $700.

Barbie #2*: made for three months in 1959-1960; identical in appearance to Barbie #1, but without holes in the feet, and most have pearl stud earrings. The Barbie #2 stand is a round, black plastic base with a "T" wire support placed one inch from the edge. Barbie #2 is marked the same as #1. Most fashion booklets and boxes were also marked the same, although a few #2 have been found with the "Barbie®" mark.

Mint condition .... $9,500.
Fair to good condition................................. $2,500.
Poor condition .... $600.
Add $1,000 for brunette.

Barbie #3: 1960; rounded and tapered eyebrows, blue eyes, most with dark brown eyeliner, some with blue eyeliner on upper eyelid; marked in the same manner as #1 and #2. The major differences between Barbie #1 and #2 and the 1960 Barbie #3 are the eyebrows and eyes. Barbie #3 was the first to have real eye color.

Mint condition .... $2,500.
Fair to good condition................................. $1,100.
Poor condition .... $150.

Barbie #4: 1960; solid body retains its nice flesh-tone color. The vinyl used for Barbie #4 has a tendency to turn green at the earring holes. Marked "Barbie®" on fashion booklet and box. Barbie #4 is marked in the same manner as #1, #2, and #3.

Mint condition .... $1,200.
Fair to good condition................................. $250.
Poor condition .... $100.

Barbie #5: 1961; hollow-body; blond, brunette, or red firm textured saran hair; longer eyebrows; smaller pupils show more blue eye color; blue eyeliner; fashion booklet and box marked "Barbie®"; gold-colored wrist tag with "Barbie" written in script across the front; first box to offer red hair. Barbie #5 is marked in the same manner as #1, #2, #3, and #4, or may have T.M. replaced with ®.

   Mint condition $700
   Fair to good condition...................................... $200
   Poor condition... $60

Barbie #6: Hollow body; dark royal blue eyes until 1963, then more aqua; blond, brunette, red, ash blond, or platinum hair; with box $400

Bubble Cut: hollow body; saran hair, bubble-cut style brunette, light brown, blond...................................... $750

Fashion Queen: Egyptian-style gold and white swimsuit and head covering; three interchangeable wigs and wig stand $700

Miss Barbie: Open/close eyes; three interchangeable wigs; lawn swing, swimming cap, pink swimsuit.. $2,000

Swirl Ponytail: Rooted hair, long sweeping bang crosses forehead; one-piece red swimsuit...................... $900

Bendable leg, center part: Four different hairstyles; swimsuit with striped top, teal green bottom $3,200

Bendable leg, side part: Specially rooted hair .. $7,500

Color Magic: Blond hair changes to scarlet red; swimsuit changes color (add $300 for brunette)......... $2,500

Color Magic: Midnight black hair changes to ruby red; swimsuit changes color (hair fails to return to black) $3,500

Twist 'N Turn "TNT": Real rooted eyelashes......... $600

"TNT": Must be in original Trade In Box $1,000

Talking Spanish: Ponytail to one side; pull-string at back $600

Truly Scrumptious (talking): Pink gown; pull-string at back $1,000

Truly Scrumptious (non-talking): Pink gown; hair pulled straight back... $1,400

Living: Jointed wrists, bendable elbows and ankles . $400

Malibu: Tanned-tone vinyl $65*

Live Action: Battery operated stage moves Barbie in a dancing motion.. $400

Growing Pretty Hair: Pink dress; hair piece, hair ornaments... $600

Hair Happening: Red-haired Twist 'N Turn, several hair pieces to add; wearing pink skirt, white blouse .. $1,700

Walk Lively: Red jumpsuit; Miss America; battery operated walker stand.. $350

Bubble Cut Barbie, **$750.**
Courtesy of McMasters-Harris Auction

Twist 'n Turn Barbie with pivoting waist, 1967, in "played with" condition, **$200-$250.** If perfect, **$600.**

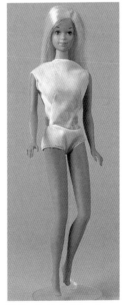

Malibu Barbie in "played with" condition, **$40-$45.**

Midge marked "Midge TM © 1962/Barbie © 1958 by Mattel, Inc." in original box with booklet, **$500.**
Courtesy of McMasters-Harris Auction

Busy Holding Hands: Hands open and close to hold things, five accessories for holding **$400**
Ward's Anniversary: Montgomery Ward exclusive; copy of Barbie #5 or #6 .... **$600**
Quick Curl: **$150**
Sun Valley: Mint on card; no box **$450***
Gold Medal Sports: **$250**
Beautiful Bride: **$400**
Ballerina: Hair pulled back, stands on toes **$150**
Super Star: Wear and Share accessories **$400**
Le Nouveau: Theatre de la Mode by Billy Boy **$750**
Feelin' Groovy: Designed by Billy Boy **$600**
Mardi Gras: 1st American Beauty Series **$250**
Pink Jubilee: 1st Jubilee Series **$2,700**
My Size: 36" tall **$250**
Evergreen Princess: From Winter Princess LE **$200**
  With red hair LE/Disney Convention **$400**
Peppermint Princess: From Winter Princess LE **$150**
Snow Princess: 1st Enchanted Season **$175**
Snow Princess: brunette hair color **$450**
Gold Jubilee: 2nd in Jubilee Series/celebrate 35 years **$800**
Christian Dior: 1st in series **$125**
Christian Dior: 2nd in series **$100**
International Barbie: Eskimo, Scottish, Canadian, Greek, Irish, Indian, Japanese .. **$100**
  German, Hawaiian, Parisian, Peruvian, Swiss **$45**
  Italian **$300**
Porcelain: Blue Rhapsody, Enchanted Evening, Benefit Performance, Wedding Party **$400**
Porcelain: Solo in the Spotlight, Sophisticated Lady, Gay Parisian, Royal Splendor, Star Lilly **$275**
Porcelain: Plantation Bell **$325**
Happy Holiday: Red gown with silver trim **$500**
  White gown with fur trim **$250**
  Fuchsia gown with silver trim **$250**
  Green velvet gown with sequins **$200**
  Silver gown with beading **$150**
  Red gown with gold **$150**
  Gold gown with fur **$150**

Bob Mackie: Gold.............................$700
    Platinum.......................................$600
    Starlight Splendor......................$600
    Empress Bride.............................$750
    Neptune Fantasy $600
    Masquerade Ball........................$400
    Queen of Hearts.......................$300
    Goddess of the Sun...................$250
    Moon Goddess...........................$200
    Madame du Barbie....................$300
Classique Line: Benefit Ball by Carol Spencer...$200
    Opening Nite by Janet Goldblatt $125
    City Style by Janet Goldblatt $150
    Uptown Chic by Kitty Black Perkins $100
    Evening Extravaganza by Kitty Black Perkins $125
    Midnight Gala by Abbe Littleton $125
    Starlight Dance by Cynthia Young...$100
FAO Schwarz: Golden Greetings ..$225
    Winter Fantasy...........................$200
    Night Sensation $175
    Rockettes...................................$195
Little Debbie: Little Miss Debbie.....$75
Bloomingdale's: Nicole Miller $100
Hallmark: Victorian Elegance.........$110
FAO Schwarz: Silver Screen $175
Wal-Mart: Tooth Fairy $50
Spiegel: Shopping Chic $125
FAO Schwarz: Jeweled Splendor ..$200
    Circus Star...................................$125
Bloomingdale's: Donna Karan.......$125
Airport/Duty Free: Traveler.............$75
Bloomingdale's: Calvin Kline $85
Bloomingdale's: Ralph Lauren.......$125
J. C. Penney: Royal Enchantment....$60
FAO Schwarz: Statue of Liberty.....$250
Toys-R-Us: Pink Ice.........................$125
Stars and Stripes: Air Force...........$175
    Navy or Marine $150
    Marine Gift, Army Gift (93), Air Force Gift (94) Set $250

#60 Titian Hair Happening Barbie in original box, **$1,700**, and #45 Blonde Bendable Leg Francie in original box, **$400**.
Courtesy of McMasters-Harris Auction

Great Eras: Gibson Girl or 1920s Flapper...$150
    Egyptian Queen or Southern Bell.$150
    Medieval Lady or Victorian Lady$100
    Grecian Goddess.........................$90
    Chinese Empress $75
    No original box.

Gift Sets

Mix and Match: Barbie $2,000
Sparkling Pink Gift: Barbie.........$1,700
Party Time Gift: Skipper $900
Round the Clock: Gift Barbie......$1,800
Wedding Party Gift: Barbie in Bride's Dream, Ken in Tuxedo, Midge in Orange Blossom, Skipper as Flower Girl.$4,000
Cut 'N Button: Skooter...................$700
On Parade Gift: Barbie, Ken, and Midge..$4,000
Little Theatre: Barbie and Ken with production costumes......................$12,000

Belton-Type

Although Belton-type dolls are generally regarded as French, the beautiful bisque dolls were probably manufactured in Germany after 1870. A distinguishing characteristic of the Belton doll is the uncut pate section with one, two, or three small holes. The top of the head may be concave, flat, or convex. Other common factors include a good wig; closed mouth; quality paperweight eyes; long painted lashes; pierced ears; straight wrist jointed composition or kid body; typically unmarked or marked with a size or mold number only. There are variations in the faces along with the quality of bisque and decoration. Evaluate dolls carefully.

19" French Look Belton-type marked with size number only "11," **$4,000.**
Courtesy of David Cobb Auction

15" Belton-type marked "N7," often called an "Owl Faced Belton," **$2,300.**
Courtesy of David Cobb Auction

Prices listed are for appropriately costumed dolls in good condition.

French Look 137/183/163 and possibly others:
9"-14" .... $2,700-$3,500
18"-22" .... $3,900-$4,300
24" $5,200
German wide-eye owl look:
9" $1,400
12"-18" .... $1,900-$2,700
20"-24" .... $3,000-$3,700

22" French Look Belton-type, **$4,800.**
Courtesy of David Cobb Auction

16" German Look Belton-type often referred to as "owl faced" with hint of molded teeth, **$2,400**, and 13" French Look Belton-type, **$3,500.**
Courtesy of David Cobb Auction

C. M. Bergmann

C. M. Bergmann, Waltershausen, Germany launched his company in 1888 with just two employees. He specialized in ball-jointed composition bodies with bisque heads from the factories of Armand Marseilles, Simon & Halbig, Alt, Beck & Gottshalck, William Gobel, and perhaps other German companies. Bergmann filed for bankruptcy in 1931.

Prices listed are for appropriately costumed dolls in good condition.

Standard Quality Dolly Face: bisque socket head by Armand Marseilles or other German manufacturer; composition body; good wig; glass eyes; open mouth; typically marked "C. M. Bergmann Waltershausen Germany 1916"; "A. M. Columbia."

10"-18"	$500-$600
24"-28"	$750-$1,000
32"-32"	$1,500-$1,900
36"-38"	$2,400-$2,800
40"-42"	$3,000-$3,300

Better Quality Dolly Face: bisque socket head by Simon & Halbig and others; jointed composition body; good wig; glass eyes; open mouth; typically marked "C. M. B. Simon & Halbig":

10"-18"	$750-$950
24"-28"	$1,200-$1,500
30"-34"	$1,550-$2,000
36"-38"	$2,500-$3,500
40"-42"	$4,200-$4,700

Marked "Eleonore":

16"-22"	$1,000-$1,200
24"-28"	$1,400-$1,600
34"	$2,500

Standard Quality Character Baby*: bisque socket head by Armand Marseilles or other German manufacturer; composition bent-limb baby body; good wig; glass eyes; open mouth; typically marked "A. M. C. M. B."

14"	$750
20"	$975
24"	$1,350

29" C. M. Bergmann, mold "1916" dolly face $1,300.

Courtesy of Susan Miller

Better Quality Character Baby*: bisque socket head by Simon & Halbig, William Goebel, and possibly others; composition bent-limb baby body or stockinet torso with composition limbs (may have rubber hands); good wig; glass eyes; open mouth; typically marked "C B Bergmann B 4,""134," or "S H C M B."

    14" **$1,400**
    20" **$2,500**

612 Character Baby*: bisque socket head by Simon & Halbig; composition bent-limb baby body; smiling mouth with laugh lines and dimples modeling around mouth and eyes; typically marked "Simon & Halbig/612/C M Bergmann."

    14" **$2,900**
    18" **$3,200**

*Add $500 for jointed toddler body.

20" C. M. Bergmann/Simon Halbig, **$1,000.**
Courtesy of Susan Miller

George Borgfeldt & Co.

George Borgfeldt & Co., located in New York City from 1881 through the 1950s, was an international importing company, not a doll manufacturer. Borgfeldt was responsible for importing thousands of dolls into America.

Before World War I, Borgfeldt had exclusive American and Canadian rights to many German and American doll companies. Borgfeldt was responsible for commissioning two of the most successful dolls ever made—Rose O'Neill's Kewpie and Grace Putnam's Bye-Lo.

Bisque

Prices listed are for appropriately costumed dolls in good condition.

Dolly Face Shoulder Head: bisque shoulder head; kid, cloth, or imitation kid body; good wig; glass eyes; open mouth; typically marked "G. B.," "Florodora," "My Playmate," or "Alma."

12"	$375
16"-18"	$425-$450
20"-24"	$500-$600

Dolly Face Socket Head: bisque socket head; jointed composition body; good wig; glass eyes; open mouth; nicely painted or haphazardly applied features; typically marked "My Dearie," "Pansy," "My Girl," "Florodora," "My Playmate," or "G.B."

Judge quality objectively whether standard or better quality.

Standard quality:

12"-18"	$525-$600
22"-26"	$700-$900
30"-32"	$900-$1,300
34"-36"	$1,700-$2,000

Better quality:

12"18"	$650-$775
22"-26"	$950-$1,400
30"-32"	$1,600-$2,000
36"	$2,800

24" George Borgfeldt, **$750.**
From the collection of Gerrie Harvey.

12-1/2" George Borgfeldt, marked "251/GB/Germany/ DRMG 248/1," **$2,300.**

Courtesy of McMasters-Harris Auction

18" rare bisque Gladdie character child, marked "Gladdie Copyriht by Helen W. Jensen/ Germany," **$4,950.**

Courtesy of David Cobb Auction

Character Baby: bisque socket head; composition bent-limb baby body; good wig; glass or painted eyes; open or open/closed mouth; typically marked "251/248," "326," "327," "329," or "G.B."

12"-14"	**$550-$650**
18"	**$900**
22"-24"	**$1,100-$1,200**

Mold "251/248" is a charming character with open/closed mouth and molded tongue. The mold number is 251, and 248 is the German registration number.

Mold "251/248":

12"	**$2,300**
20"-22"	**$3,400-$3,700**

Bye-Lo Baby (a.k.a. Million Dollar Baby)*: specially designed cloth "frog" body with celluloid hands or five-piece bent-limb baby body; solid dome; painted hair; tiny glass eyes; closed mouth; typically marked "1923 Grace S. Putnam/Made in Germany" or "1369 Grace S. Putnam."

Cloth body:

12"-14"	**$700-$900**
16"-18"	**$1,100-$1,700**
20"-26"	**$1,900-$2,300**

Composition body:

14"-16"	**$1,400-$1,800**
20"	**$2,500**

Rare painted eyes/smiling mold "1415":

12"-14"	**$4,700-$5,000**
18"	**$7,500**

*Add $100 for black version.

Fly-Lo (a.k.a. Baby Aero): bisque flange neck; cloth body; molded and painted hair; glass sleep eyes; closed, slightly smiling mouth; may have non-removable satin suit with wings, wire is attached from wing to doll's wrist; typically marked "Grace S. Putnam Germany 1418/#."

12"-14"	**$4,700-$5,000**
18"	**$7,500**

Baby Bo-Kaye: bisque baby head; sweet, wistful, almost pouting expression; cloth body; composition limbs; molded and painted hair; glass, oval sleep eyes; open/closed full mouth with two lower teeth; typically marked "Copr. by J. L. Kallus, Germany 1394," "1407."

12"	**$2,300**
20"-23"	**$3,400-$3,700**

Gladdie: biscaloid (imitation bisque composition) or bisque flange head; cloth body; composition limbs; deeply molded and painted hair; glass eyes; open/closed, laughing mouth with molded upper teeth; typically marked "1410 Germany" or "Gladdie Copyriht by

Helen W. Jensen/Germany." The word "copyright" may be misspelled as "copyriht."

Bisque:
18"	$4,950
22"-24"	$6,000-$6,900

Biscaloid:
18"-22"	$1,300-$1,600
24"	$2,500

Composition

Prices listed are for appropriately costumed dolls in good condition.

Many composition dolls, both German- and American-made, were distributed by George Borgfeldt. Examples include: Mamma's Angel Child, Hollikid, Com-A-Long, Daisy, Bye-Lo, Fly-Lo, and Baby Bo-Kaye. Most have cloth bodies. Characteristics and markings are identical to those of their bisque counterparts; typically marked "My Playmate," "Borgfeldt," or "G.B."

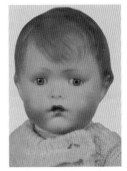
18" Baby Bo-Kaye, marked "Corp by J. L. Kallus Germany 1394/38," **$3,400.**
Courtesy of McMasters-Harris Auction

Character babies:
12"-17"	$450-$550
20"	$700

Bye-Lo:
10"-14"	$400-$525
17"-20"	$725-$750

Fly-Lo:
12"	$1,300
14"	$1,800

Baby Bo-Kaye:
12"-14"	$900-$1,200

Tin

Prices listed are for appropriately costumed dolls in good condition.

Juno: tin shoulder head; cloth body; molded and painted hair, or mohair wig; painted or sleep eyes; closed mouth; typically marked "Juno" in an oval.

Borgfeldt 20" Bisque Bye-Lo Baby, **$1,900.**
Photograph courtesy of Julia Burke, www.juliaburke.com

Molded hair/painted eye:
12"-15"	$165-$210
20"	$240

Molded hair/glass eye:
12"-15"	$220-$245
20"	$300

Wig/glass eye:
12"-15"	$300-$335
20"	$345

Jne Bru & Cie

Jne Bru & Cie was located at Paris and Montreuil-sous-Bois, France, from 1866 to 1899. There is no doubt that the delicately molded, limpid-eyed bébés produced by Bru during the last quarter of the 19th century are among the most treasured prizes of the doll world.

After 1899, S.F.B.J. made Bru Dolls and Bébés. In fact, S.F.B.J. renewed the trademark for Bru in 1938 and again in 1953.

12-1/2" smiling Bru fashion doll with a rare articulated wooden body, **$6,300.**
Courtesy of James Julia Auction, Inc.

Prices listed are for appropriately costumed dolls in good condition.

Fashion Lady

Poupée de Modes (Fashion Ladies)*: bisque swivel head; shoulder plate; gusseted kid lady body with pinking around top of leather; human, mohair, or skin wig; paperweight or painted eyes; pierced ears; small, closed, somewhat-smiling mouth; beautifully dressed; shoulder plate occasionally marked "B. Jne & Cie"; typically marked with incised number (oval face) of letter size (smiling mouth).

Oval face/numbered:
11"-14"	**$3,000-$3,900**
18"-22"	**$5,000-$6,800**
25"-28"	**$7,500-$8,700**
36"	**$12,000**

Smiling/lettered:
11"-14"	**$3,500-$4,400**
17"-22"	**$6,000-$7,500**
25"-28"	**$8,400-$9,200**
36"	**$14,000**

*Add $2,500 for original jointed wooden body.

Bébé Bru

Brevete Bébé*: bisque socket head; kid-lined bisque shoulder plate; kid body pulled high on shoulder plate and straight cut (leather pinked where cut); bisque lower arms; skin wig; cork pate; paperweight eyes; delicately shadowed eyelids; long lashes painted on upper and lower lids; lightly feathered brows; pierced ears; full cheeks; closed mouth with white space between lips; typically marked with size number only; body stamped "Bébé Brevete SGDG Paris."

11"-14"	$16,000-$22,000
17"-22"	$25,000-$30,000
26"-30"	$35,000-$36,000

*Add $7,500 for Bébé Modele with articulated all-wood body, pin and dowel joints at shoulder, elbows, waist, hip, knees, and ankles.

Circle Dot: bisque socket head; kid-lined bisque, deep shoulder plate with molded breasts; kid gusseted body; bisque lower arms with no joints at the elbows; fine mohair wig; cork pate; paperweight eyes, finely lined in black; somewhat heavier feathered brows; pierced ears; plump cheeks; closed mouth with slightly parted lips and suggestion of molded and painted teeth; typically marked with a dot within a circle or crescent over a dot.

11"-18"	$17,000-$25,000
24"-28"	$32,000-$38,000
36"	$39,000

Black Circle Dot:

14"-17"	$30,000-$35,000
22"	$40,000

Jne Bébé*: bisque socket head; kid-lined, deep shoulder plate with molded breasts; kid body with scalloped edge at shoulder plate; bisque lower arms with graceful hands; kid-over-wood upper arms, hinged elbows; may have wooden lower legs; good wig; cork pate; paperweight eyes, finely lined in black; long lashes; pierced ears; closed mouth with suggestion of molded tongue; typically marked "Bru Jne" and a size number; body labeled "Bébé Bru" and "BTE SGDG."

12"-18"	$20,000-$27,000
22"-28"	$29,000-$37,000

*Add $700 for a wooden jointed body, provided the markings are not that of Bru Jne R. If there is an "R" in the marking, a wooden body is appropriate.

26" Circle Dot Bru Bébé, **$36,000.**
Courtesy of McMasters-Harris Auction

19" Bru Jne Bébé, **$28,000.**
Courtesy of James Julia Auction, Inc.

Bru Jne R Bébé: bisque socket head; wood-and-composition jointed body; good wig; paperweight eyes; pierced ears; open or closed mouth; quality of bisque ranged from beautiful with fine decoration to less attractive standard quality, which greatly affects the value; typically marked "Bru Jne R" and size number, stamped "Bébé Bru."

Closed mouth/Jue R:
11"-14"	$4,500-$6,700
16"-22"	$7,500-$9,700
25"-28"	$11,600-$15,600
33"	$22,300

Open mouth/Jue R:
13"	$2,100
20"-22"	$4,200-$5,400
26"	$6,600
35"	$8,200

Bébé Teteur (Bru Nursing Bébé): bisque socket head; kid-lined bisque shoulder plate; kid body with bisque lower arms; kid-covered, metal upper arms and legs; carved wooden lower legs or jointed wood-and-composition body; skin wig; paperweight eyes; mouth opened in an "O" with hole for nipple; mechanism in head sucks liquid as key is turned; typically marked "Bru June N T."

13"	$9,800
15"	$11,000
16"	$11,300

After the 1899 formation of S.F.B.J., dolls are generally of lesser quality.

Later Nursing:
13"	$6,000
16"	$7,000

15" Early Bébé Teteur or Bru Nursing Bébé, **$11,000.**
Courtesy of James Julia Auction, Inc.

27" Bru Jne R #12 Bébé, **$13,500.**
Courtesy of David Cobb Auction

Cameo Doll Company

The Cameo Doll Company operated in Port Allegheny, Pennsylvania, from 1922 until 1970. In 1970, the entire Cameo Doll Company, including equipment, was acquired by the Strombecker Corporation of Chicago.

Doll collectors are fascinated with dolls produced between World War I and World War II. Cameo dolls are among the most avidly sought. They are not only charming, but in terms of artistry and construction, among the finest quality American dolls made in the 20th century.

It is common for early Cameo dolls to be unmarked or have only a wrist tag. Later dolls were usually well marked and, after 1970, "S71" was added.

Composition

Prices listed are for appropriately costumed dolls in good condition.

Scootles*: all jointed composition; deeply molded, wavy hair; painted side-glancing eyes; closed, smiling, watermelon mouth; typically marked with "Scootles" wrist tag only.

8"-10"	$550-$600
14"-13"	$650-$750
16"-20"	$1,100-$1,400

Black Scootles:

10"-13"	$900-$1,100

*Add $250 for sleep eyes.

Dog (Ginger, Bones, and Streak): composition dog head; wooden, jointed body; typically marked with paper label "Des & Copyright by J. L. Kallus."

8"-10"	$500-$600

Pete the Pup: composition character dog head; segmented wooden body; ball hands; side-glancing eyes; round nose; wide, smiling mouth; typically marked "Pete the Pup" label on chest, "Cameo" on foot.

8"-10"	$500-$550

Joy/Pinkie: composition head and hands; segmented body; molded and painted hair; side-glancing eyes; tiny pug nose; closed, smiling mouth; typically marked "Joy" or "Pinkie" label on chest.

10"	$425
15"	$650

Margie: composition head; attached by hook to 18-piece wood-segmented body; painted hair and head band; side-glancing eyes, upper lashes; open, smiling mouth with four teeth; typically marked "Margie" label on chest.

10"-15"	$400-$600

Cameo 13" composition Scootles in mint condition with original box, marked "Scootles Designed and Copyright by Rose O'Neill/A Cameo Doll" hangtag. In this condition, the value is **$1,250.**
Courtesy of Masters-Harris Auction

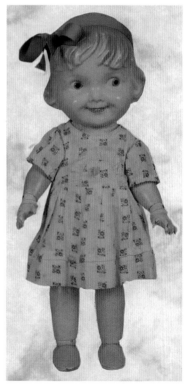

Cameo 15" Margie, apparently redressed, **$450.**
Courtesy of Masters-Harris Auction

Betty Boop: composition head, hands, upper torso, and skirt; segmented body; molded and painted black hair; side-glancing eyes; molded and painted red swimming suit; typically marked "Betty Boop/Des & Copyright by Fleischer/Studios" label.

12"-18" .... **$900-$1,000**

Pretty Bettsie: all composition head; one-piece body; molded and painted bobbed hair and facial features with side-glancing eyes; molded and painted flapper-style dress, socks, and shoes; typically marked "Pretty Bettsie Des. & Copyright by JL Kallus" on chest sticker.

12"-18" .... **$900-$1,000**

Champ: composition freckled-face boy; molded and painted hair falling across forehead; large eyes; closed, smiling mouth; original jersey with "CHAMP" printed across front.

12"-16" .... **$500-$750**

Giggles: starfish hands; painted hair with bun in back and bangs in front; side-glancing eyes; closed, smiling mouth; typically marked "Giggles/Designed and copyrighted/Rose O'Neill/Cameo Doll Co." wrist tag.

12"-15" .... **$900-$1,000**

Marcie: all composition; painted hair; side-glancing eyes, closed slightly; puckered mouth; dressed in original young girl's French-style outfit; molded and painted socks and shoes; typically unmarked or wrist tag only.

10"-15" .... **$400-$600**

Sissy: all jointed composition; balanced to stand alone; painted hair; painted eyes; smiling mouth; typically unmarked or wrist tag only.

12"-16" .... **$500-$750**

Little Annie Rooney: all composition; one-piece head and torso; long, thin legs with molded shoes; orange yarn hair; big oval painted, side-glancing eyes; small nose; closed, smiling mouth; wearing original green dress and felt jacket tagged "Little Annie Rooney/trademark/copyright 1925 by Jack Col-

lins/pat applied for."

15" **$900**

R.C.A. Radiotrons/Hotpoint Man: composition head; attached by hook to wood-segmented body; molded and painted top hat in shape of radio tube; boots and facial features; marked "R.C.A. Radiotrons" across the hat and on a band across the chest.

16"-18" .... **$1,000-$1,200**

Pop-Eye: faithful reproduction of cartoon Popeye; composition head; wooden, segmented body finished in bright colors; molded sailor cap; no hair; small eyes; very full cheeks; wooden pipe in closed mouth; wood painted to represent clothing; marked "King Features/Syn, Inc. 1932" on foot.

15"-18" .... **$800-$950**

Bandmaster/ Drum Major or Bandy: composition head; wooden, segmented body (20 segments assembled with coil spring); molded high shako head; cheerful, painted facial features; red and white painted drum major's uniform; carries wooden baton; medal molded around neck; marked "G.E." (General Electric trademark); "Mfg. Cameo Prod. Inc./Port Allegany, Pa./Des. & by JLK."

16"-18" .... **$1000-$1,200**

Crownie: composition head; wooden, segmented body; molded and painted long, wavy hair with crown; painted, closed eyes; jolly, laughing open/closed mouth; brightly painted body, representing clothing; wearing felt cape; holding wooden baton; typically marked "Mfg. Cameo Prod. Inc./Port Allegany, Pa./Des. & by JLK."

15"-18" .... **$800-$950**

Baby Blossom: composition head and limbs; cloth body; molded and painted hair in short style with lock coming down over forehead; side-glancing or sleep eyes; dimpled, fat cheeks; typically marked "Baby Blossom" hangtag, and appropriately "Des. & Copyright/by I. L. Kallus/Made in USA."

20" **$900**

Vinyl

Prices listed are for near mint original condition.

Scootles: all vinyl; fully jointed; molded and painted hair and eyes; closed, smiling, watermelon mouth; typically marked "R7234 Cameo JLK."

14" **$250**
19" **$400**
27" **$800**

Miss Peep: all vinyl; pin-hinged joints at shoulder and hip; painted hair; inset, good-quality plastic eyes; nurser/open mouth (drink and wet baby); typically marked "CAMEO."

15" **$250**
18"-21" ....**$300-$400**

Baby Mine: all vinyl; pin-hinged, jointed at shoulder and hip; painted hair; sleep eyes; open/closed mouth with molded tongue; typically marked "CAMEO."

16"-19" ....**$250-$300**

Plum: one-piece latex body; two squeakers, one in bottom for spanking, one in tummy for hugging; painted hair; sleep eyes; open/closed mouth; typically marked "Cameo."

18"-24" ....**$200-$275**

Margie: all vinyl; ball-and-socket universal joints at neck, shoulder, hip, elbows, and waist; rooted hair; sleep eyes; slightly parted lips; typically marked "Cameo T.M." or "9093/60" or "9013/60."

15" **$225**
18"-21" ....**$300-$400**

Cameo 20" Baby Blossom with collection
of vintage toys, **$900.**
Courtesy of McMasters-Harris Auction

Campbell Kids

Various manufacturers have produced Campbell Kids. Grace Drayton originally designed the Kids in 1909 for Campbell's advertising cards. Within a year, dolls were being manufactured not only as premiums, but also for over-the-counter sales.

Composition

Prices listed are for appropriately costumed dolls in good condition.

All composition Campbell Kids share a similar face with molded and painted, bobbed hair; round, side-glancing eyes; chubby cheeks; pug nose; and closed smiling mouth. Distinguishing characteristics are body types and markings that include:

Premium Kid: flange neck; cloth body; stub hands; unmarked; offered as magazine subscription premium.

    10" $400

Early Horsman: flange neck; cloth body; composition arms; marked "E. I. H. © 1910."

    10" $425
    12"-14" ....$500-$600

Horsman: all composition; jointed at neck, shoulder, and hip; unmarked.

    12" $850

Dee & Cee: (Canadian company) all composition; similar to Horsman *except* lesser quality composition; eyelashes heavier and thicker; hair color slightly orange.

    12" $750

American Character: all composition; jointed at neck, shoulder, and hip; marked "A Petite Doll."

    12" $850

Modern

Prices listed are for dolls in near mint, original condition.

Magic Skin: latex body; marked "Campbell Kid/made by Ideal Toy Corp."

    10"-12" ....$75-$100
    14" $125

12" Horsman Campbell Kids, **$600-$800** each, depending on condition and originality of costuming, with 11" Truette Little Pigs.
Courtesy of David Cobb Auction

Bicentennial Kids: all vinyl; molded and painted features; colonial costume.

    10" $200/set

Porcelain: in a soup can; military costumes; Happiness and Joy; sequence costumes; wrist tag "1998 T.M. Collectible Concepts."

    12" $100

Happy & Joy: Version of the Horsman issued as a 1997 reproduction.

    10" $110

Catterfelder Puppenfabrik

Catterfelder Puppenfabrik manufactured dolls in Walterhaussen, Germany, from 1894 until the 1930s. Kestner supplied most of the heads for Catterfelder, generally representing babies, although child dolls were also produced.

Catterfelder Puppenfabrik 20" #200 character baby, **$1,100.**
Courtesy of David Cobb Auction

Catterfelder Puppenfabrik 16" #220 character child, **$12,000,** holding small mohair bear.
Courtesy of McMasters-Harris Auction

Bisque

Prices listed are for appropriately costumed dolls in good condition.

Dolly Face: bisque socket head; jointed wood-and-composition body; good wig; glass eyes; short, painted lashes; feathered brows; open mouth with teeth; typically marked "Catterfelder Puppenfabrik," "270," "264," and probably "1100," "1200," and "1357."

16"-22"	**$900-$1,100**
24"-26"	**$1,300-$1,800**
36"	**$3,000**

Character Baby: bisque socket head; composition bent-limb baby body; molded and painted hair or good wig; painted or glass eyes; open or open/closed mouth; typically marked "CP 200," "201," "208," "262," "263/ Depoiert," or "Catterfelder Puppenfabrik."

200/201/208:

10"-14"	**$500-$650**
20"-24"	**$1,100-$1,500**

262/263:

10"	**$850**
16"-20"	**$1,450-$1,700**
22"-24"	**$2,100-$2,700**

Character Child: bisque socket head; jointed wood-and-composition body; good wig; painted eyes with line indicating eyelid; small pug nose; closed, slightly pouting mouth; typically marked "207" or "219."

18"	**$6,400**

Character Child: bisque socket head; jointed wood-and-composition body; good wig; painted or sleep eyes; open/closed mouth with two molded teeth; typically marked "210," "215,""220" or "217."

16"	**$12,000**
20"	**$15,000**

Celluloid

Prices listed are for appropriately costumed dolls in good condition.

Child: all celluloid; molded and painted hair; painted eyes; molded and painted socks and shoes; typically marked with mermaid in shield.

8"-12"	**$125-$175**

Celluloid Dolls

Celluloid was produced in Germany, France, United States, Japan, England, Poland, and other countries from 1869 until about 1950.

Markings may include an embossed stork (Parsons-Jackson), turtle (Rheinische Gummi/Schutz), Indian head (American), mermaid (Cellba), beetle or ladybug (Hernsdorfer-Germany), star (Hollywood), SNF (Société Nobel Francaise), ASK (Zast of Poland), or others. For additional marks, refer to *Antique Trader's Doll Makers & Marks*.

Production of celluloid became illegal in the United States during the 1940s because it burned or exploded if placed near an open flame or high heat.

Celluloid dolls are grouped into several categories rather than by manufacturer. When considering a celluloid doll, check condition carefully and evaluate quality critically. Discoloration is considered damage.

Prices listed are for appropriately costumed dolls in good condition.

All Celluloid: molded in one piece or jointed at shoulders only; molded and painted hair and facial features; undressed or molded clothing; often pink in color; marked or unmarked.

4"-6"	$30-$40
8"	$50
10"-12"	$55-$65

All Celluloid*: jointed at neck, shoulder, and hip or bent-limb baby body; molded hair or good wig; painted eyes; dressed or undressed; marked or unmarked.

Painted eye:

4"	$95
8"-12"	$125-$175
16"-20"	$275-$295

11" French Petitcolin celluloid painted eye character baby, marked with embossed eagle, **$150.**

Courtesy of Susan Miller

18" German Schultz celluloid glass eye child with fully jointed celluloid body. When a celluloid doll is found in this original mint condition, expect a value of **$900 or more**.

Courtesy of McMasters-Harris Auction

15" German Rheinische Gummi/Schutz celluloid glass eye character child, original costume marked with embossed turtle, **$450**.

From the collection of Julia Burke. Courtesy of Julia Burke, www.juliaburke.com

Glass eye character:

12"-14"	$300-$350
18"-22"	$450-$500

Add $200 for black version.

Celluloid, Shoulder Head: cloth or kid body; celluloid or composition arms; molded and painted hair or good wig; glass or painted eyes; closed mouth or open mouth with teeth; marked or unmarked.

Painted eyes:

12"-18"	$200-$250
20"-22"	$275-$300

Glass eyes:

12"-18"	$265-$310
20"-22"	$335-$350

Better Quality, Socket Head*: dolly, character, or baby face; composition-and-wood body; mohair or human hair wig; glass eyes; applied lashes and brows; closed or open mouth with teeth; typically marked by various manufacturers, such as Franz Schmidt, Käthe Kruse, Kämmer & Reinhardt, and others.

12"-14"	$550-$575
16"-20"	$675-$875
24"	$1,100

Add $200 for black version.

Käthe Kruse Type: celluloid child doll; socket head; jointed at neck, shoulder, and hip; molded and painted hair or good wig; painted or sleep eyes; closed mouth; typically marked with turtle.

16"	$750
20"	$950

Flocked: socket head flocked to resemble felt; flocked jointed body; mohair wig; painted, side-glancing eyes; closed mouth; marked or unmarked.

8"	$400
16"	$60

12" German black celluloid glass-eye character doll with pierced ears. If this character doll had its original native costume, it would have a value of **$500**. In its present undressed condition, its value is **$350**.

Courtesy of Susan Miller

Chad Valley, Ltd.

Chad Valley, Ltd. was located in Harbonne, England, and manufactured toys as early as 1897. The company began producing dolls in 1917 and continued into the 1940s. Various types of cloth dolls were made, the earliest predominately with stockinette faces. Around 1924, the company began producing hand-painted felt faces on dolls made of velvet or velveteen.

Prices listed are for originally costumed dolls in good condition.

Character Dolls: velvet face and body; plush wig; glass or painted side-glancing eyes; painted facial features; typically labeled "Hygienic Toys/Made in England by/Chad Valley Co. Ltd.," "Chad Valley/Hygienic/Toys/Made in/England/The Seal of Purity"; hangtag "Chad Valley Hygienic Fabric Toys."

Chad Valley 18" Princess Elizabeth, marked "The Genuine Princess Elizabeth British Made Doll" hangtag, and "Made in England" cloth label. When found in this pristine, near mint condition with hangtag, expect the value to be **$2,300**.
Courtesy of McMasters-Harris Auction

Painted eye:
10"-12" ....$300-$400
14"-16" ....$550-$650
18" $900

Glass eye:
12" $800
14"-16" .... $1,200-$1,400
18"-20" .... $1,800-$2,300

Child Dolls: felt mask; velvet body; good wig; double thickness of felt for ears; glass eyes or painted, side-glancing eyes; molded and painted facial features; typically labeled "Hygienic Toys/Made in England by/Chad Valley Co. Ltd.," and celluloid button "Chad Valley/British/Hygienic Toys," hangtag "Chad Valley Hygienic Fabric Toys."

Painted eye:
10"-12" ....$425-$550
14"-16" ....$700-$850
18" $950

Glass eyes:
14"-16" ....$850-$900
18" $1,100

Royals: felt mask; velvet body; mohair wig; glass eyes; nicely modeled features in portrait likeness; typically marked "HRH (Name)/British made Doll/By permission of/Her Majesty The Queen/Sole makers/The Chad Valley Co. Ltd./Harbonne/England."

16"-18" ....$1,700-$1,900

Martha Chase

Martha Chase dolls were made in Pawtucket, Rhode Island, from about 1880 to 1938. They were made of stockinette fabric stretched over a mask with raised features. The head and limbs were sized with a coating of glue and paste, dried, and painted with oils. Features were hand-painted, the rough brush strokes of the hair providing a realistic texture. Ears and thumbs were applied separately.

Rare 27" George Washington character doll, marked "Chase Stockinet Doll Trademark" stamped on hip, with original box. The extraordinary condition, in addition to the original box, adds to this doll's value of **$12,500.**
Courtesy of McMasters-Harris Auction

Prices listed are for appropriately costumed dolls in good condition.

Adult: stockinette adult face; cloth body; heavily oil-painted head, arms, and legs; molded and painted hair; painted eyes; thick lashes; closed mouth; typically marked "Made by Martha Chase" under arm, "Chase Hospital Doll," or hangtag "Made by hand/Chase Stockinette Doll."

Female:
14"-16" .... $1,700-$1,800
18"-22" .... $2,300-$2,700
Male:
14"-16" .... $3,400-$3,600
18"-22" .... $3,800-$4,200

Baby: stockinette baby face; cloth body; heavily oil-painted head, arms, and legs; molded and painted hair; painted eyes; chubby cheeks; slightly smiling mouth; typically marked with paper label "The Chase Stockinette Doll/Made of Stockinette and Cloth/Stuffed with cotton/Made by Hand/Painted by Hand/Made by Especially Trained Workers" or stamped "Made by Martha Chase" or "Chase Hospital Doll."

14"-18" .... $750-$850
22"-26" .... $950-$1,200

Child: stockinette child face; cloth body; heavily oil-painted head, arms, and legs; molded and painted hair; attached ears; painted eyes, thick lashes; slightly smiling mouth; typically marked "Chase Hospital Doll" or "Made by Martha Chase."

16"-20" .... $1,700-$2,200
24"-26" .... $2,800-$3,000
30" $3,400

Hospital Doll: all stockinette; entire body and head are heavily oil-painted; molded and painted hair and facial features; typically marked "Chase Stockinet Hospital Doll/Pawtucket, R.I./Made in USA."

20" $950
62" $1,600

Portrait Character: stockinette, cloth body; character features raised and heavily oil-painted; good wig or molded and painted hair; painted eyes, attached ears; closed mouth; typically marked "The Chase Stockinette Doll/Made of stockinette and cloth."

Duchess/Mad Hatter $7,100
Tweedle Dee/Dum....... $7,600 (each)
Frog Footman......................... $9,300
Alice in Wonderland $9,200
George Washington $9,700
Black Ethnic
characters .... $12,000-$16,000

28", 16", and 20" Martha Chase stockinette dolls, **$3000**, **$1,700**, and **$2,200**, respectively.
Courtesy of David Cobb Auction

China Heads

China heads of glazed porcelain were made primarily in Germany from 1840 to the 1940s. Identifying china heads according to manufacturer is nearly impossible. China heads characteristically have painted eyes; a red line, indicating eyelids; full cheeks; and a small, closed, smiling mouth.

Very rare early china heads were attached to commercially made, jointed, wooden bodies with china limbs. Most china heads, however, were sold separately. The consumer either purchased a body or made one.

Several terms are used to describe china heads. The most commonly found models are named for their hairstyle. Occasionally, unique characteristics suggest additional classification. Glass-eyed china head dolls are referred to as "French china." Flesh-colored or pink luster china heads with wigs, rather than painted hair, are known as "English china." "Kinderkopf" is applied to any style of china head representing a child. A "china socket"-style head attached to a china shoulder plate is very rare and desirable.

Familiar to collectors are the "Pet Name" dolls with painted gold letters across the molded yoke.

In deference to space, we have included two or three price ranges for each type of china head, but please remember that a wide range of sizes can be found, and you should use your good judgment and common sense to interpose the value of additional sizes.

Prices listed are for appropriately costumed dolls in good condition.

Adelina Patti: elaborate hairstyle with center part and rolled curls; 1860s.

    6" **$300**
    14"-16" ....**$600-$650**
    22"-24" .... **$950-$1,000**

Alice (in Wonderland): hair styled with molded headband; 1850s.

    14" **$750**
    20"-22" .... **$1,200-$1,500**
    36" **$3,800**

Biedermeier: bald or solid dome head, some with top of head painted; good wig; 1840s.

    12"-14" .... **$1,500-$1,700**
    18"-20" .... **$1,900-$2,200**
    24" **$2,500**

17" KPM German china head, **$7,000.**
Courtesy of James Julia Auction, Inc.

Bun China Head*: hair styled in bun, braid, or roll in back; 1840s.

    8" **$1,000**
    14"-16" .... **$2,900-$3,200**
    20"-24" .... **$5,000-$6,200**
    Add $500 for fancy bun.

Countess Dagmar: pierced ears; various finely decorated, elaborate hairstyles; 1840s.

    14" **$800**
    18" **$1,200**
    22" **$1,700**

Covered Wagon*: hair styled flat on top with sausage curls around head; 1840s.

    12" **$700**
    14"-16" ....**$850-$950**
    20"-24" .... **$1,200-$1,600**
    Add $500 for brown eyes.

Curly Top: hair styled with ringlet curls over entire head; 1850s.

    8" **$700**
    16"-18" .... **$1,000-$1,200**
    22"-23" .... **$2,200-$2,300**

24" Countess Dagmar china head, **$1,800.**
Courtesy of McMasters-Harris Auction

Currier & Ives: hair styled with long bangs and molded headband; 1860s.

    14"-18" ....**$750-$900**
    20"-22" .... **$1,200-$1,500**
    36" **$3,800**

Dolly Madison: all-over curls with molded ribbon; 1870s.

    6" **$300**
    14"-16" ....**$600-$650**
    22" **$950**

31" modified Dolly Madison china head, **$1,200**; 26" curly hair china head, **$2,300**; 26" flat top china head, **$750**; 25" Highbrow, **$750**; and 22" Highland Mary china head, **$750.**
Courtesy of David Cobb Auction

22" English pink-tint china head, rare large size with beautifully detailed painted eyes and original extended mohair wig, **$3,800.**

Photo courtesy of James D. Julia Inc.

14" French glass eye china head, **$4,000.**

Courtesy of McMasters-Harris Auction

English China Head: flesh-tinted china; solid dome head or small slit to insert wig; 1840s.

12"-14"	**$2,200-$2,600**
16"-20"	**$2,800-$3,200**
24"	**$4,200**

Exposed Ear: hair pulled back from face in curly bun; molded exposed ears; 1850s.

16"	**$4,500**
22"	**$7,000**

Flat Top or Civil War: hair styled with part in middle and short curls around head; 1850s.

8"-12"	**$325-$375**
20"	**$650**
30"-36"	**$1,100-$2,000**

French China Head: glass or beautifully painted eyes; feathered brows; open crown with cork pate; good wig; shapely kid body; 1850s.

12"-14"	**$3,800-$4,000**
18"	**$4,600**
20"-22"	**$5,300-$5,800**

Glass Eyed: painted hair with exposed ears; glass eyes; 1870s.

16"	**$5,500**
22"	**$8,000**

Greiner Style: high forehead; hair styled with middle part, wavy sides, and comb marks; exposed ears; 1850s.

12"-14"	**$1,500-$1,700**
18"-20"	**$1,900-$2,200**
24"	**$2,500**

Highbrow: very round face and high forehead; hair styled with center part, flat top, and sausage curls around head; 1870s.

12"-18"	**$375-$475**
20"-24"	**$650-$750**
36"	**$2,000**

Highland Mary: hair styled with straight top and curls at sides; 1860s.

14"-18"	**$500-$600**
20"-24"	**$650-$850**
28"	**$1,000**

Jenny Lind: high forehead, hair parted in middle and pulled back into bun; 1860s.

6"	**$950**
16"-20"	**$1,800-$2,100**
24"	**$2,800**

K.P.M.: delicate, fine Meissen porcelain; marked "KPM" or crossed swords; handwritten mold number inside shoulder pate; 1840s.

16"	$6,500
20"	$8,000
24"	$12,000

Kinderkoff: obvious childlike modeling; 1840s.

12"	$2,400
20"	$3,000
24"	$3,800

Lowbrow: common, wavy, painted blond or black hairstyle; 1890s.

8"	$200
16"	$350
22"-24"	$500-$550
36"	$1,800

Man or Boy: masculine-styled china head; 1840s.

12"	$1,200
18"-20"	$2,000-$2,700
28"	$4,000

Mary Todd Lincoln: hair snood; decoration at the crown with flowers or ruffles; 1860s.

12"	$1,200
18"-20"	$1,600-$1,800
22"	$2,500

Morning Glory: high forehead; exposed ears; flowers molded at nape of neck; 1860s.

20"	$9,000
24"	$14,000

Pet Name China Head: common hairstyle; name printed in gold on shoulder plate (names include Agnes, Bertha, Daisy, Dorothy, Edith, Esther, Ethel, Florence, Helen, Mabel, Marion, Pauline, and Ruth); 1905.

14"	$375
20"-22"	$500-$600
28"	$900

Sophia Smith: hair styled with straight sausage curls, not curved to head; 1860s.

16"	$2,900
20"	$4,000
22"	$4,500

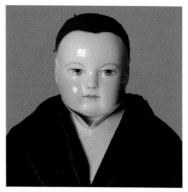

16-1/2" French china head man with nicely decorated facial features and wearing a close-cropped mohair wig, **$4,500.**

Photo courtesy of James D. Julia Inc.

20" Spill Curl china head, **$1,600.**
Courtesy of McMasters-Harris Auction

Spill Curl: individual curls over forehead and shoulders; 1870s.

6"	$750
16"-20"	$1,200-$1,600
30"	$3,700

Add $300 for pierced ears, $1,000 for glass eyes, $1,000 for unusual or elaborate decoration, $300 for molded necklace, or $1,500 for wooden articulated body with china lower limbs to any doll.

Cloth Dolls

From the earliest pioneering days until the present, cloth dolls of all types have been produced in the United States. The two most popular types are pillow or rag dolls and vintage folk art dolls.

Pillow or rag dolls were early printed or lithographed dolls designed to be cut, sewn, and stuffed at home.

Vintage folk art dolls were handmade by known or unknown artists. There are vast differences in quality, depending on the talent and skill of the maker. Uniqueness makes general pricing difficult. Several sample listings are provided in order to help gauge the current market. Charm and appeal is often a more crucial factor than condition.

14" printed child with yarn hair, **$225.**

Courtesy of Susan Miller

Printed and lithographed vintage pillow or rag dolls: 14" wide-eyed puppy, **$350**; 16" bunny, **$350**; 12" child, **$200**; and 8" black child, **$250.**

Courtesy of McMasters-Harris Auction

11" vintage folk art doll with drawn facial features and human hair wig, **$1,000.**

Courtesy of McMasters-Harris Auction

Prices listed are for dolls with good color.

Vintage Pillow or Rag Doll (1880-1930)

Child: (American Beauty, Columbian Sailor, Crackles, etc.)
8" $160
12"-18" .... $200-$275
20"-24" .... $300-$350

Ethnic Character: (Darky Dolly, Tommy Trim, etc.)
8" $250
15"-18" .... $350-$450
20"-24" .... $500-$600

Character: (Little Red Riding Hood, Santa, etc.)
16" $350
20" $400
24" $500

Animals: (Baby the Elephant, Beauty the Cat, etc.)
12" $300
14" $350
15" $400

Uncut sheets are valued at twice the amount listed.

Flat characters: (Live Long Toys heavy oilcloth dolls in profile)
12" $150
15" $200
17" $250

17" Live Long flat oilcloth Orphan Annie character doll, **$250.**

Courtesy of Julia Burke, www.juliaburke.com

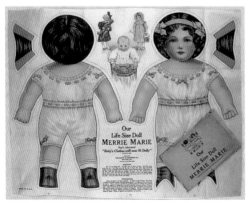

22" Merrie Marie by Selchow & Righter, uncut with original envelope. When found in uncut mint, pristine condition with wonderful bright coloring and original package, expect the value to be **$750.**

Courtesy of McMasters-Harris Auction

Complete lithographed cloth Aunt Jemima Family by Davis Milling Company in wonderful unplayed-with condition with bright coloring, featuring Aunt Jemima, Uncle Mose, Diana Jemima, and the rarely found Wade David, **$1,200.**

Courtesy of McMaster-Harris Auctions

14" mid-20th century golliwog by unknown artist, **$750.**

Photograph courtesy of David Cobb Auction

Collectible and Contemporary Printed Cloth Dolls (1940-1980)

Advertising: various characters styled for marketing products as varied as toothpaste to cupcakes to car parts. ....**$75-$200**, depending on appeal

Archie: orange hair; dark, thick eyebrows; wide open eyes; freckles across nose; printed red shirt; orange and black bell bottom pants; marked "Archie" (c. 1960). . **$200**

Beatles Forever: John, Paul, George, and Ringo; 21"; printed; instruments; signature stands; wrist tag "Applause." **$900/set**

Campbell Kids: lifelike character with familiar red and white outfit (c. 1980). **$40**

Petite Bébé: various sweet child or doll face "by the yard to sew at home"; marked "circa 1860" (c. 1980). **$30**

Snow White and the Seven Dwarfs: dwarfs with character faces; Snow White with black hair and red ribbon; the 8" doll set (c. 1970). **$175**

Hallmark: 7" printed historical or holiday character dolls; most with a piece of removable clothing; typically marked with cloth tag "Hallmark c 1976" in original lithographed boxes appropriately designed. **$55**

Vintage Folk Art Dolls (before 1920)

Black Lady: all cloth; handmade, black stockinette limbs; stockinette head shows considerable skill in its making; hand-stitched, molded features; red painted lips; black shoe-button irises on painted white eyes; black wool wig with red ribbons; brass rings sewn to side of head as earrings; wearing original printed cotton dress with apron; none of the typical "mammy doll" qualities found on many black dolls (late 1800s). **$1,200**

Child: all cloth; handmade, one-piece; rather naive ink-drawn features; touches of red on lips and cheeks; horsehair sewn to head for hair; wearing original brown cotton dress; feather-stitched red satin insert at bodice; white apron, hand-knitted stockings, straw hat (mid-late 1800s). **$1,500**

Child: all cloth; handmade, two-piece head and torso (front and back) joined at side seams; legs attached to body at hips; stub hands; painted head, arms, and booted legs; nicely done features; dressed in cotton dress with ruffled trim (early 1900s). **$900**

Couple: all cloth; mask-pressed and heavily oil-painted facial features; shaped ears; well-made pilgrim- or Quaker-style costumes; pair (1920s).....................**$1,800**

14" black vintage (1940) folk art doll, **$600.**

Courtesy of Susan Miller

Family: all black cotton; stitch jointed body; fleeced yarn hair; embroidered and painted facial features; well detailed; "salt-of-the-earth" costuming; mother, father, sister, and brother (c. 1900). **$3,200**

Gentleman: all cloth; artistically handmade man doll; cotton stuffed body; very long limbs; stitched fingers; oil-painted head, arms, and booted feet; extremely well-done facial features, shading, and accents giving great charm; original finely made blue wool suit, brocade vest, white shirt, and red tie; carrying black top hat (late 1800s)... **$1,500**

Photo Doll: all cloth; handmade; face is picture-cut from paper and covered with gauze; poorly proportioned body with long arms and short legs; rather large bosom; wearing original print cotton dress, net and lace bonnet (c.1930s). **$200**

Pouty Baby: stockinette; stitched-shaped face with well-defined eyes; shoes; button eyes; painted brown lashes; pouty mouth; yarn hair; home-spun dress and shoes (turn of the century). **$1,200**

Toddler: all cloth; handmade, cotton stuffed, one-piece; hands and head completely painted over; facial features embroidered in red and black thread; twisted thread hair knotted to head; original old woolen clothes; hand knitted stockings; appealing face, sweet smile (c. 1920s). **$700**

Collectible Folk Art Dolls (1920-1970)

Little People: Xavier Roberts' original Cabbage Patch dolls, hand-stitched at his home in the mountains of Georgia, so popular at craft shows that he borrowed $400 on his Visa card and started Babyland Hospital, which eventually led to the Cabbage Patch craze a few years later. All cloth with stitched facial features; dressed in real baby clothes. **$750**

Dolly: 15"; all cloth; stuffed body, attached head, arms and legs jointed to allow movement; yarn hair styled in braids; felt and embroidered facial features; handmade pink dress with rows of lace; white socks, white leather handmade shoes with pink bows; unmarked.. **$300**

Nancy and Her Doll: Marla Florio; 12"; all cloth; one-of-a-kind; stiff cloth legs; clutching armful of cloth mini babies; yarn hair; needle-sculptured features; blue sweater, print slacks, white socks, blue shoes. **$500**

Native American: Unknown craft person; 18" all muslin; shaped neck and torso; attached limbs; embroidered facial features; floss hair; detailed costume with bead trim, necklace and headband. **$1,050**

Nursing African Doll: Ann Fisher; 24"; brown cloth doll; large head; long arms attached to body; well developed bosom; black yarn hair tied up in a big red bow; felt eyes, large, round white circles with black centers; wide, red felt mouth; brass rings sewn on sides of head as earrings; removable twin babies attached to bosom with snaps; bright costume. **$200**

Topsy Turvy Doll: Mamie Tyson; 16"; all cloth; head at both ends, attached at mid-section; one head is white with yellow yarn hair, beautifully embroidered wide awake facial features, nicely stitched fingers; pink flowered dress with eyelet trim; doll flips over and dress falls to reveal black doll with black yarn hair, embroidered sleeping facial features, nicely stitched fingers, and white gown with eyelet trim; exceptional quality and workmanship. **$750**

Dewees Cochran

Dewees Cochran began creating dolls in New Hope, Pennsylvania around 1934. Her first dolls were sold at local gift shops. Later, she traveled to New York City to peddle her dolls at fashionable shops such as Saks. Dewees eventually created meticulously sculpted and beautifully dressed living portrait dolls. Orders poured in within days of their introduction. The early portrait dolls featured carved balsa wood heads, perfectly proportioned stuffed silk bodies, and beautiful costumes.

Following the success of her portrait dolls, Dewees and husband Paul moved to New York and set out to produce quality dolls. In 1936, she developed six basic face shapes, believing that, given the proper eye and hair color, any child could be captured in a portrait doll using one of six basic shapes. A customized portrait doll could be likened to nearly any child.

The war years all but brought an end to Dewees Cochran doll production. Dewees became art director for the R. H. Donnelley Corporation, and later design director for the School of American Craftsmen. When the war ended and materials were once again available, she formed a small doll company—Dewees Cochran Dolls, Inc.—and in 1947, the Cindy doll was introduced. After less than a year and fewer than 1,000 Cindy dolls, production stopped.

In 1951-1952, Dewees developed the famous Grow-Up series of dolls. In 1957, two little boys joined the Grow-Up family. For the next five years, a new version of each doll was produced with features representing various stages of development. A child of five could watch her doll progress through ages 5, 7, 11, 16, and 20 over the span of five years. Grow-Up dolls matured from childhood to adulthood in face and figure, growing from 12-1/2 to 18 inches.

Prices listed are for appropriately costumed dolls in near mint condition.

Cindy: all latex; jointed at neck, shoulder, and hip; human hair wig; painted eyes; human hair or painted lashes; closed, slightly smiling mouth; marked "Dewees Cochran Dolls" within oval; production number written above mark.

15" $1,250

Grow-Up Series Dolls: (Stormie, Angel, Bunnie, Peter, or Jeff, ages 6-20) all latex; jointed at neck, shoulder, and hip; human hair wig; painted eyes, human hair or painted lashes; beautifully dressed; marked "DC" and signed around initials on back; typically marked: "DC/BB-54 #9," "DC/SS 58/1," and "DC/JJ 60/2."

12-1/2" $2,500
15-1/2" $2,700
18" $2,900

Look-Alike Portrait Dolls: one of six faces; custom order portrait doll; all latex; joined at neck, shoulder, and hip; human hair wig; painted eyes; human hair or painted lashes; open/closed mouth; beautifully dressed; marked "Dewees Cochran Dolls 19" in script on small of back.

17" $2,900

Individual Portrait: carved or sculptured face; silk body; human hair wig; beautifully painted facial features; nicely costumed; typically marked "Dewees Cochran" signature under arm or behind ear. .... **$4,000-$6,000**

14" and 11" Kim of Kimport dolls, **$2,700** and **$2,500**, respectively, a Grow-Up exclusive for Kimport Dolls, marked "DC Dewees Cochran 1962."
Courtesy of McMasters-Harris Auction

15-1/2" Susan Stormalong in beautiful original condition, by Dewees Cochran, **$2,700.**
Photo courtesy of James D. Julia Inc.

Composition Dolls

Composition dolls were made by countless manufacturers in various countries from 1912 until about 1940. Many are unmarked and/or unidentified.

When World War I halted imports, American doll makers seized upon the opportunity to market dolls without foreign competition. Hundreds of small companies began production, and after a year or two, quietly went out of business. Thousands of these composition dolls with no marks or unknown marks were produced and sold.

27" Russian composition, marked "MODEDA," with inappropriate new shoes and apparently redressed, **$375**; 28" German #3066 with flirty eyes and replaced baby shoes, **$400**; 23" Italian composition in original costume, **$500**; and 21" redressed French composition, marked "Jumeau," **$350.**

Courtesy of David Cobb Auction

Prices listed are for appropriately costumed dolls in good condition.

Flange Neck Child: cloth body; composition limbs; painted features; typically unmarked or marked by a small or unknown manufacturer.

13"-14"	$275
17"-20"	$400-$425
21"-22"	$500
25"-26"	$750

Novelty character: all composition; various body joints; painted features; foreign costumes; fairy tale or wedding attire; intended as display dolls, not as toys; typically unmarked or marked by small or unknown manufacturer.

11"-12"	$250
15"-16"	$300

Mama Type: cloth body; composition limbs; good wig; glass, tin, or glassine eyes; open mouth with teeth; typically unmarked or marked by a small or unknown manufacturer.

11"-12"	$350
15"-20"	$425-$450
21"-24"	$525-$550

Baby/Infant*: composition bent-limb baby body; molded hair or wig; sleep or painted eyes; open or closed mouth; typically unmarked or marked by a small or unknown manufacturer.

11"-14"	$500
15"-16"	$550
17"-20"	$600-$650

*Add $100 for black doll.

24" early composition with straw-stuffed cloth body holding an American Eagle lithograph bank box. The outstanding original condition, in addition to the ever-important visual appeal of early dolls, dictates a value of **$1,400.**
Courtesy Ty Herlocher

18" composition with glass flirty eyes, **$600.**
Courtesy of Sandra Lee Products, Inc., sandralee.com

20" composition baby with glass eyes, **$650.**
Courtesy of Sandra Lee Products, Inc., sandralee.com

24" unmarked composition child resembling Shirley Temple in mint condition, **$850.**
Courtesy of David Cobb Auction

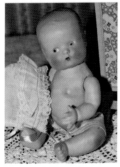

11" all composition character baby with original box and accessories, **$500** in mint condition with accessories and box.
Courtesy of Susan Miller

Child Type*: (may resemble Shirley Temple, Madame Alexander, or other popular characters) dolly face; composition jointed body; good wig; sleep or flirty eyes; open mouth with teeth; typically unmarked or marked by a small or unknown manufacturer.
Exceptional:
11"-14" ....$450-$550
17"-22" ....$650-$750
24" $850
Standard:
11"-14" ....$200-$250
17"-22" ....$300-$350
24" $375
*Add $100 for black doll.

Teen-type*: (may resemble Nancy, Debu-teen, Suzanne, Madame Alexander, or other popular characters) teen face; composition jointed body; good wig; sleep eyes; open or closed mouth; typically unmarked or marked by a small or unknown manufacturer.
13"-16" ....$400-$450
17"-20" ....$500-$550
21"-22" $600
*Add $100 for black doll.

Molded Hair Loop Type: molded loop for hair bows; composition body jointed at shoulder and hip, or tightly stuffed cloth torso with composition limbs; painted facial features; typically unmarked or marked by a small or unknown manufacturer.
11"-12" $250
13"-14" $300
15"-16" $350

Patsy-Type: all composition; jointed at neck, shoulder, and hip; slightly bent right arm; long, thin legs; molded and painted bobbed hair; painted or sleep eyes; typically unmarked or marked by a small or unknown manufacturer.
13"-16" ....$400-$450
19"-20" $500

Character Dolls

Buddy Lee: 13"; all composition; molded and painted features; large, side-glancing eyes; originally dressed in one of the several different advertising costumes; typically unmarked or marked "Buddy Lee."

Lee Jeans, Cowboy, or John Deere $750
Coca-Cola (tan suit with red stripes) $950
Coca-Cola (white suit with red stripes) or Gas Station $900
Other soft drink outfits or Engineer $650

Burgarella: Italian; excellent quality heavy composition jointed at neck, shoulder, hip, and maybe elbow and knee; human hair wig; beautifully painted facial features with dramatic eyes; typically marked only with cloth label sewn into clothing, "Burgarella Made in Italy."

17" $900
22" $1,200

Carmen Miranda: 14"; all jointed composition; mohair wig; sleep eyes; original red taffeta and black lace gown with mantilla; typically unmarked or wrist tag only (Uneeda) $750

Also a similar version by Eegee

15"-20" .... $450-$650

Dennie Dimwit or Bobbi Mae: 11"; all composition; molded head mounted on stick fastened to top of legs, attached to hollow body with metal rod; when doll is touched, it sways; typically marked "Pat. Pending" inside dress (Toy Craft Inc.). $250

12" composition Buddy Lee in "Union Made Lee" costume, **$750.**
Courtesy of McMasters-Harris Auction

Above: Beautifully expressive 17" all original Italian Burgarella composition with painted eyes, **$900.**
Courtesy of David Cobb Auction

Left: 11" Dennie Dimwit and Bobbi Mae swinging and swaying composition dolls, **$250 each.**
Courtesy of Maribeth Herlocher

Famlee Doll: 16"; "A Whole Family of Dolls in One"; set of body and several interchangeable heads; matching costumes; typically unmarked (Berwick Doll Co.). **$1,400**

Gene Carr Kids*: 14"; (Blink, Jane, Mike, Skinny, and Snowball) character faced; cloth body; composition hands; typically unmarked (Horsman). **$600**

Add 300 for black Snowball

Jackie Robinson: black; socket head; jointed at shoulder and hip; molded and painted hair; black side-glancing eyes; open/closed mouth with teeth; wearing Dodgers uniform; typically unmarked (Allied Grand).

14"-20" .... **$1,200-$1,600**

Johnny: composition head; cloth body with felt-stitched finger hands; modeled characterization with large open, downcast eyes; wide open/closed "Call for Phillip Morris" mouth with molded teeth; dressed in bellhop uniform and cap; typically unmarked **$1,500**

Kewpie-Type: 12"; jointed at neck, shoulder, and hip; star-shaped hands; no wings; molded hair in topknot; painted side-glancing eyes; closed mouth; typically unmarked... **$300**

Lone Ranger or Tonto: 21"; composition socket head, hands, and feet; cloth body and limbs; molded and painted black hair; painted brown eyes; closed mouth; original costume; typically unmarked or hangtag "The Lone Ranger and Tonto/Manufactured by Dollcraft Novelty Co./Sole Licensees/New York City," "Lone Ranger" in rope script, "Official Doll copyright T.L.R. Co., Inc."

Lone Ranger **$1,800**
Tonto **$1,500**

Ming Ming: 11"; all jointed composition; painted, suggested Oriental facial features; solid dome painted or yarn hair; original taffeta Oriental costume and painted shoes; unmarked (Quan Quan). **$350**

Monica Studio Doll: exceptional quality; all jointed composition; implanted human hair with widow's peak; beautifully painted features; original costume; typically unmarked or wrist tag "Monica Doll Hollywood."

17" **$750**
19" **$900**
21" **$1,000**

Pinocchio: 12"; all jointed composition; molded and painted hair; round eyes; large nose; closed, smiling mouth; unmarked (Crown). **$600**

Puzzy, Sizzy: 15"; "Good Habit Kids"; all composition; character faces with full cheeks; painted hair; marked "H of P USA," "Sizzy H of P USA" (Herman Cohen)..................... **$600**

Tony Sarg's Brown Mammy with Baby: 17"; flange neck and lower limbs; substantial cloth body; stereotypical painted facial features; wide beaming smile; red dress, white apron; holding all composition baby; painted features; wrapped in blanket; typically unmarked, hangtag "Tony Sarg's Mammy Doll sole Distributors Geo. Borgfeldt Corp." **$1,500**

Trudy: 15"; composition head and arms; cloth body; three faces, smiling, sleeping, and crying; knob at top of head turns head; painted features; unmarked (Three In One Doll Corp.) **$450**

Two Face: 16"; composition head; cloth body; one face laughing and one crying; molded and painted hair and features; unmarked **$400**

Group of all original early American composition: 16" Effanbee Baby Brother, **$400**; 16" Madame Alexander McGuffy Ann, **$700**; 12" Effanbee Baby Sister, **$350**; 14" Madame Alexander Alice, **$800**.
Courtesy of David Cobb Auction

Danel & Cie

Danel & Cie was located in Paris and Montreuil-sous-Bois, France, from 1889 until at least 1895.

In 1890, Jumeau sued Danel for infringement, claiming that Danel had "borrowed" molds and tools from his factory and had enticed workers to "leave the employment of Jumeau and join Danel & Cie." Danel denied the charges, but the courts ruled in favor of Jumeau.

In 1892, Jumeau began using the names "Paris Bébé" and "Français Bébé," both previously used by Danel. In 1899, Danel & Cie became a charter member of the Société de Fabrication de Bébés & Jouets (S.F.B.J.).

Perhaps the most important contribution Danel & Cie made was the introduction of exquisite mulatto and gorgeous black dolls.

Prices listed are for appropriately costumed dolls in good condition.

Early Paris Bébé: (before 1892, appears very similar to a Jumeau Bébé) bisque socket head; wood-and-composition French body; good wig; paperweight eyes, finely lined in black; heavy feathered brows; pierced ears; closed mouth; typically marked "Tête Déposé/Paris Bébé," also may have the Eiffel Tower trademark.

    13"-15" .... **$4,200-$5,000**
    22"-27" .... **$5,900-$6,500**
    33" **$7,500**

Black Paris Bébé:
    15" **$6,200**
    19" **$7,000**

Later Paris Bébé: (after 1892, narrow face with aquiline nose) bisque socket head; wood-and-composition French body; good wig; paperweight eyes, finely lined in black; feathered brows; pierced ears; closed, slightly smiling mouth; typically marked "Tête Déposé/Paris Bébé," also may have the Eiffel Tower trademark.

    17"-19" .... **$6,700-$7,100**
    24" **$8,000**

Bébé Français: (occasionally attributed to Ferte of Paris) bisque socket head; wood-and-composition French body; good wig; paperweight eyes, finely lined in black; feathered brows; pierced ears; closed mouth; typically marked "B (size number) F."

    15"-19" .... **$5,400-$6,200**
    24" **$7,200**
    31" **$8,500**

Danel 29" later Paris Bébé, **$10,000.**
Courtesy of David Cobb Auction

Danel 19" early Paris Bébé, **$5,600.**
Courtesy of David Cobb Auction

Dean's Rag Book Company

Dean's Rag Book Company of England has made cloth books, toys, and dolls since its conception in 1903. In 1920, the company introduced the first molded, pressed, and painted three-dimensional dolls called "Tru-To-Life" rag dolls.

14" Dean's English cloth doll. If in good, clean condition, this doll would have a value of **$800**, however, showing age and appearing worn and disheveled results in a value of **$500**.

Courtesy of Susan Miller

20" Dean's rag doll, holding a smaller identical rendition, **$1,400**.

Courtesy of David Cobb Auction

Prices listed are for appropriately costumed dolls with good color.

Child Doll: all cloth; felt head and arms; dark pink cloth body, long slender legs; mohair wig; painted eyes; white highlight dot at upper eye pupil; two-tone, closed mouth; marked "Hygenic Al Toys"/picture of two dogs having a tug-of-war over a book/"Made in England/Dean's Rag Book Co. Ltd." within an oval on bottom of foot.

    10" $600
    14"-15" ....$800-$850
    17"-20" $1,200-1,400

Printed Flat Face Doll: stuffed cotton bodies; marked "Hygenic Toys/Dean's Rag/Made in England" within an oval.

    9"-15" ....$200-$275
    17"-20" ....$350-$400

Other Dean's Dolls

Wolley Wally: Dean's Golliwog.

    12" $500
    16" $700

Dancing Boy and Girl: hugging; bobs up and down on a golden string.

    12" $600

Filly on a Trike: velvet arms, legs, and dress (which is part of the body); mohair wig; beautifully painted eyes; attached to metal tricycle.

    12" $1,400

Mickey Mouse: brown velvet; brown velvet pants with buttons on front; large, white felt hands.

    16" $2,900

Minnie Mouse: brown velvet; large, white felt hands.

    16" $2,700

Peter Pan: molded felt face; velvet body; wearing gold velvet suit.'

    17" $2,700

Wendy: molded felt face; velvet body; wearing white nightgown.

    17" $2,500

Denamur, Etienne

Denamur produced lovely French bébé dolls in Paris from 1857 to 1899. Take time to examine Denamur dolls. Many bébés were produced with creamy pale bisque and large paperweight eyes, well defined with black lining the undercut, with long lashes and fully feathered, nicely arched brows. Smaller and later dolls unfortunately are often found with rather coarse bisque and heavily applied, at times splotchy decoration. The word "Deposé" must be incised under the E. D. initials, along with a size number.

Prices listed are for appropriately costumed dolls in good condition.

Bébé: bisque socket head wood-and-composition French or five-piece papier-mâché body; good wig; paperweight eyes, finely lined in black; feathered brows; pierced ears; closed or open mouth; typically marked "E. D. (size number) Deposé."

Closed mouth/exceptional:
11"	$2,700
18"-22"	$3,700-$4,600
26"-28"	$5,300-$6,000

Closed mouth/standard:
11"	$1,600
18"-22"	$2,500-$3,100
26"-28"	$3,800-$3,900

Open mouth:
11"	$1,500
15"-22"	$2,000-$2,500
28"	$3,100

Le Bambin: 18"-20" ....$2,700-$3,100

Etienne Denamur 30" open mouth, size number 14 bébé, **$3,500**, and 19" closed mouth, size number 8 bébé, **$2,700**.
Courtesy of David Cobb Auction

Exceptional quality 24" Etienne Denamur closed mouth, size number 10 bébé, **$5,000**.
Courtesy of David Cobb Auction

DEP Dolls

DEP dolls originated in the 1880s. These bisque dolls should not be confused with dolls commonly found with the addition of the letters "DEP" to a registered mold number. The DEP dolls described here are incised only "DEP" along with a size number.

The early, closed-mouth DEP dolls were made with exceptionally fine bisque and delicately applied decoration, showing great artistry. Later open-mouthed models, although generally of good quality, lack the beauty of the earlier dolls.

Typical 22" DEP open mouth doll, **$1,500.**
Courtesy of Susan Miller

Prices listed are for appropriately costumed dolls in good condition.

Closed Mouth: bisque socket head; composition-and-wood jointed body; good wig; paperweight eyes; heavy feathered brows; long, thick eyelashes; pierced ears; closed mouth; typically marked "DEP" and size number.

12"	**$2,400**
16"-18"	**$3,200-$3,800**
20"-22"	**$4,000-$4,800**
24"	**$5,200**

Open Mouth: bisque socket head; composition-and-wood jointed body; good wig; deeply molded eye sockets; glass or paperweight eyes often appearing askew; painted lower and real upper lashes; feathered brows; pierced ears; open mouth with upper teeth; typically marked "DEP" and size number.

12"-18"	**$1,000-$1,300**
24"-28"	**$1,800-$2,500**
30"-34"	**$2,900-$3,400**

Black:

16"	**$2,900**
24"	**$4,400**

Door of Hope Dolls

Door of Hope dolls were made from 1901 to 1949 in Shanghai and Canton, China, at the Protestant mission called Door of Hope.

A woman working five days a week could make only one doll a month. The head, hands, and arms to the elbow were carved of pear wood. The hair, eyes, and lips were painted. A few of the dolls had fancy buns or flowers carved into their heads. Most have hands with rounded palms and separate thumbs, although some have only cloth stub hands. Cloth bodies were stuffed with raw cotton. The elaborate handmade costumes are exact copies of clothing worn by the Chinese people.

Condition and costuming are important factors when determining value. Prices listed are for undamaged dolls in original costume.

Door of Hope: wooden head; cloth body with wood or cloth lower limbs; painted facial features; painted or carved hair; perfect examples of Chinese costuming; typically unmarked.

Door of Hope 11" Cantonese Amah with baby, **$2,250**, and 12" farmer complete with paty-wrake, **$2,000**.
Courtesy Roberta and Ziggy of Roberta's Doll House

Child/Adult*:
    6"..**$2,500**
    7-1/2".....................................**$2,200**
    11-1/2"..................................**$2,000**
Amah with baby:
    10-1/2"..................................**$2,250**
Bride/Manchu lady:
    10-1/2"..................................**$2,500**
    16"...**$2,700**
Priest:
    11-1/2"..................................**$2,300**
    Add $300 for specially carved hair ornamentation.

Cuno & Otto Dressel

The Dressel family operated a toy business in Sonneberg, Germany, from the 1700s until 1942. The company purchased bisque doll heads from Armand Marseille, Simon & Halbig, Ernst Heubach, and Gebrüder Heubach.

Trademarks registered by Cuno & Otto Dressel include Holz-Masse (wooden composition), Admiral Dewey, Admiral Sampson, Bambina, Die Puppe de Zukunft (Doll of the Future), Fifth Ave. Doll, Jutta, Jutta-Baby (named for Countess Jutta, the Patroness of Sonneberg), McKinley, M. Miles, Poppy, Uncle Sam, and Victoria.

Original 23" Cuno & Otto Dressel flirty eye child on a flapper body, **$1,400.**
Courtesy of James Julia Auction, Inc.

Bisque

Prices listed are for appropriately costumed dolls in good condition.

Dolly Face*: bisque socket or shoulder head; kid body or jointed composition body; good wig; glass eyes; feathered brows; open mouth; typically marked "COD 93DEP," "AM 1893COD," "1896," "1898," "1776," or "COD1912."

Shoulder head:
12"-18" .... $450-$550
22" .... $700-$900
Socket head:
14"-18" .... $550-$700
22"-26" .... $850-$950
40" $2,800

Jutta Child*, **: bisque head by Simon & Halbig; jointed composition body; good wig; glass eyes; pierced or unpierced ears; open mouth; marked "1349/Jutta/S & H," "S & H/1348/Jutta," or "1348 Dressel." (Simon & Halbig Jutta dolls must be marked 1348 or 1349.)

14"-20" .... $800-$1,000
24"-30" .... $1,400-$1,800
36"-40" .... $3,500-$4,200

Character Baby*: bisque shoulder or socket head; bent-limb baby or cloth body; molded and painted hair or good wig; painted or glass eyes; typically marked "COD341" or "Heubach Koppelsdorf 1922/Jutta Baby/Germany."

12"	$475
14"-20"	$600-$900
22"-24"	$1,000-$1,200
28"	$1,800

Jutta Character Baby*: bisque socket head by Simon & Halbig; bent-limb baby body; good wig; glass eyes; open mouth; marked "Jutta 1914" or "Jutta 1920." (Simon & Halbig Jutta babies must be marked 1914 or 1920.)

12"-14"	$750-$900
18"-24"	$1,200-$2,000

*Add $500 for jointed toddler or high jointed flapper body.
**Add $200 for black version.

Prominent German manufacturers such as Gebrüder Heubach and Simon & Halbig produced Cuno and Otto Dressel's character dolls. They can be whimsical and charming or simply beautiful. Their three main categories include:

Character Portrait: modeled to represent military, political, or legendary figures; bisque socket head; jointed composition body; painted or glass eyes; typically marked "S," "D," "R," or "A."

Uncle Sam/Admiral Dewey:

12"-14"	$2,000-$2,200
16"	$2,400
20"	$3,500

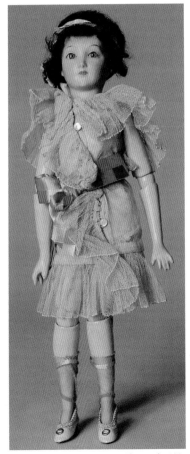

Original 14" Cuno & Otto Dressel flapper, **$4,600.**
Courtesy of James Julia Auction, Inc.

13" Cuno & Otto Dressel's authentically presented Uncle Sam, **$2,100.**
Photo courtesy of James D. Julia Inc.

Original 18" Cuno & Otto Dressel Father Christmas (using Uncle Sam head), **$3,300.**
Courtesy of James Julia Auction, Inc.

Old Rip/Farmer/Buffalo Bill:

   12"-14" .... **$1,700-$2,000**

   22" **$5,500**

Character Child*: bisque socket head; jointed composition body; molded and painted hair or wig; painted or glass eyes; open or closed mouth; typically marked "Germany," "C.O.D.," "C.O.D./ S.H.," and perhaps a size number.

  Painted eye:

   12"-14" .... **$3,300-$3,600**

   16"-18" .... **$3,900-$4,200**

   20" **$4,600**

  Glass eye:

   12"-14" .... **$3,500-$3,900**

   16" **$4,500**

   22" **$5,200**

   24" **$5,700**

Character Lady**: lovely, slim young woman; bisque socket head; shapely, jointed-composition lady's body with graceful arms and legs; feet molded for high heel shoes; good wig; glass eyes; closed mouth; typically marked "1469/ C O Dressel Germany," "1468 COD," "SH1468," or "S & H/COD/1469."

   14" **$4,600**

   *Add $500 for jointed toddler body.
   **Add $200 for black version.

Composition

Prices listed are for appropriately costumed dolls in good condition.

Character Lady: composition limbs and shoulder head; cloth body; good wig; glass eyes; closed mouth; typically marked "C.O.D."

   14"-18" .... **$1,500-$2,000**

Character Child: composition socket head; jointed composition body; painted hair with brush marks; glass or painted eyes; closed, puckered mouth; typically marked "C.O.D."

   18"-20" .... **$2,400-$2,700**

   24" **$3,000**

Dolly Face: composition socket head; jointed composition body; good wig;

glass eyes; open mouth; typically "M & S.," "C.O.D.," or "Jutta."

    14"-18"............................$450-$475
    24".. $600

Papier-Mâché

Papier-mâché was made from powdered or torn bits of paper and paste. Prices listed are for appropriately costumed dolls in good condition.

Shoulder Head: papier-mâché shoulder head and limbs; cloth body; molded and painted hair or good wig; painted or glass eyes; feathered brows; closed mouth; entire head and shoulder plate with varnish-like coating; typically marked with winged helmet and "HOLZMASSE."

    Painted eye:
       14"-20".........................$600-$700
       24"-26".........................$800-$900
    Glass eye:
       18"....................................... $750
       20"-24".........................$800-$900
       26"..................................... $1,100

Wax

Prices listed are for appropriately costumed dolls in good condition.

Reinforced Wax: rare, usually poured and reinforced with plaster or composition; wax shoulder head; cloth body; wax over composition arms; good wig; glass eyes; typically marked with winged helmet and "ED"; body stamped "HOLZMASSE" or "Dressel."

    14"-18".................... $900-$1,200
    20"-24".................. $1,700-$1,800
    28"..................................... $2,000

Wax-Over Composition: composition shoulder head coated with layers of wax; cloth body; wax-over composition limbs; good wig; painted or glass eyes; closed mouth; typically marked "ED Patent DE HOLZ-MASSE" inside back shoulder plate and "XXXVIII" painted in gold.

    18"....................................... $600
    24"....................................... $750

Early original 19" Cuno & Otto Dressel papier-mâché with glass eyes, **$800.**
Courtesy of David Cobb Auction

22" bisque open mouth Eden Bébé, **$2,800.**
Courtesy of David Cobb Auction

14" composition character, **$1,200.**
Courtesy of Busy and Company Doll Auctions

Eden Bébé
(Fleischmann and Bloedel)

Eden Bébé, a trade name, is more familiar than the manufacturer, Fleischmann and Bloedel Doll Factory. The company was established in 1873 in Fürth, Bavaria, and Paris, France. In 1899, Saloman Fleischmann formed and became director of the Societe Francaise de Febrication de Bébés & Jouets (S.F.B.J.) The firm changed directors and ownership many times and eventually filed for bankruptcy in the early 1920s.

Prices listed are for appropriately costumed dolls in good condition.

Eden Bébé: bisque socket head; five-piece or jointed wood-and-composition body; good wig; cork pate; paperweight eyes, finely lined in black; feathered brows; long eyelashes; pierced ears; open or closed mouth with a hint of a molded tongue; typically marked "Eden Bébé" or "Eden Bébé Paris."

Closed mouth:
11"-14"	$2,600-$3,000
22"-26"	$3,900-$4,400
28"	$5,000
30"	$5,600

Open mouth:
11"-14"	$1,800-$2,000
20"-24"	$2,600-$3,100
30"	$4,000
34"	$4,400

Black:
16"	$4,100

Composition Character: Composition head; five-piece cloth body; artistically or exaggerated painted features; mohair wigs; typically marked "Fleischman & Bloedel."
14"	$1,200
18"	$1,500

Eegee

Mr. and Mrs. E. Goldberger founded the famous Eegee doll company in 1917 in Brooklyn, New York. The trademark EEGEE was adopted in 1923. Early dolls were marked "EG," followed by "E. Goldberger," and finally "Eegee" or occasionally "Goldberger."

Eegee is one of the longest-running, continuously operating manufacturers of dolls in the United States. Although the company never achieved the level of fame acquired by many other doll companies, Eegee constantly produced innovative and appealing quality dolls.

Composition
Prices listed are for appropriately costumed dolls in good condition.

Child: composition socket head; jointed composition body; molded and painted hair or good wig; painted or sleep eyes; open/closed mouth; typically marked "EEGEE," "E. Goldberger," or "E.G."

16"	$650
18"-20"	$700-$750

Baby: composition limbs and flange neck; cloth body; molded and painted hair or good wig; tin sleep eyes; open/closed mouth with molded teeth; typically marked "E. Goldberger," "E.G.," or "EEGEE."

14"	$325
16"-18"	$400-$425
22"	$500

Early Latex
Early latex was a synthetic material that looked and felt like human skin. Over time it becomes unstable and deteriorates, becoming badly discolored. The process may be slowed by regularly rubbing cornstarch into the doll.

Prices listed are for appropriately costumed dolls in good condition.

Child: early latex head with wooden plug neck flange; one-piece latex body; molded and painted hair; sleep eyes; open/closed mouth; typically marked "EEGEE" or "EE-GEE."

14"-17"	$125-$175

Hard Plastic & Vinyl

Prices listed are for dolls in near mint, original condition.

Gigi Perreaux (child actress): vinyl head; jointed, hard plastic body; dark brown synthetic wig; brown sleep eyes; feathered brows; open/closed mouth with molded teeth; typically marked "E.G."

18"-20" .... $900-$1,100

Beautiful 22" fully jointed, hard plastic and vinyl Eegee ballerina in mint condition with original box. A lovely doll in mint condition with original box is a rare find, giving this example a value of **$800**.

Courtesy of Julia Burke, www.juliaburke.com

Child*: socket head; jointed or walker hard plastic body; rooted saran hair; sleep eyes; closed mouth; typically marked "E.G." or "EEGEE."

14"-18" ....$300-$400
22"-28" ....$500-$600

*Add $100 for tagged "Barbara Cartland" (romance novelist) in royal blue satin gown with feather trim.

Baby: vinyl socket head; molded plastic body; rooted hair; painted or sleep eyes; closed mouth; typically marked "Eegee."

10"-14" ....$50-$95
18"-22" ....$100-$125

Teen: all vinyl; jointed at neck, shoulder, and hip; rooted hair; painted or sleep eyes; closed mouth; typically marked "20/25M," "EEGEE," or "20 HH."

12"-18" ....$100-$150
28"-36" ....$185-$200

Musical Dimples: vinyl head and hands; cloth body containing music box; rooted hair; painted eyes; open/closed mouth; body and clothing as one; typically marked "14 BD/Eegee Co."

12"-18" ....$75-$100

Dolly Parton: vinyl head; jointed plastic woman's shapely body; painted eyes; open/closed mouth with molded teeth; original gown; marked "DOLLY PARTON/EEGEE CO./HONG KONG/Goldberger Mfg. Co."

12" $150
18" $300

Gemmette: vinyl socket head; vinyl and plastic jointed, adult bodies; rooted hair; nicely painted facial features; elaborate costumes; typically marked "1963 Eegee."

12"-18" ....$100-$150
28"-36" ....$185-$200

Granny: plastic and vinyl; rooted long gray hair pulled into bun; painted facial features; closed mouth; original cotton "homespun" dress; typically marked "Eegee/3."

14" $200

Effanbee Doll Company

Effanbee is an acronym for Fleischaker & Baum, who founded this prolific doll company in New York City around 1910. The standards set by the early Effanbee company will continue, thanks to the Robert Tonner Doll Company, which rescued Effanbee from bankruptcy in 2002.

Composition

Prices listed are for appropriately costumed dolls in good condition.

Character Doll*: (Chubby Boy Bud, Billy Boy, Marietta, Betty, Baby Grumpy, Pouting Bess, Coquette, Harmonica Joe, Katie Kroose, and Whistling Jim) cloth body; sewn-on shoes; painted facial features; typically marked "Effanbee," "176," "Deco," "172," "174," "Baby Grumpy," "166," "162," "462," or "116."

7"-10"	$400-$450
12"-16"	$500-$600

*Add $200 for black or Oriental version.

Child and Baby: (Baby Dainty, Sweetie Pie, Mickey, Baby Bright Eyes, Lovums, Rosemary, and Marilee) composition limbs and shoulder head; cloth body; molded hair or good wig; painted or tin sleep eyes; open/closed mouth; typically marked "Effanbee/Lovums/c Pat No.," "Effanbee/Rosemary Talks Walks Sleeps," "Effanbee/Baby Dainty," "Effanbee/Marilee/CopyR/Doll," or possibly others.

12"-16"	$450-$550
17"-20"	$600-$700
24"-27"	$750-$850

Dolly Face: (Mary/Ann/Jane/Lee) composition socket head; jointed wood-and-composition body; good wig; sleep eyes; open mouth; typically marked "Effanbee," "MaryAnn," or possibly others.

16"	$500
18"-20"	$550-$650
24"	$750

Mama: (Bubbles and Lambkin) composition head and limbs; cloth body; molded hair or good wig; sleep eyes; open/closed mouth, most say "mama"; typically marked "Effanbee/Bubbles/Corp 1924/Made in U.S.A.," "Effanbee/Dolls/Walk, Talk, Sleep/Made in U.S.A.," "1924/Effanbee/Dollys/Walk, Talk, Sleep/Made in USA," or "EFFANBEE."

10"-12"	$350-$450
16"-22"	$600-$750
25"-27"	$850-$900

Ventriloquist Doll*: (Charlie McCarthy, W. C. Fields, Lucifer) composition and cloth; pull string activates mouth; typically marked "Lucifer/V. Austin/EffanBEE," "Fleischaker & Baum," "W. C. Fields/EffanBEE," or "EDGAR BERGEN CHARLIE McCARTHY EFFANBEE."

18"	$2,500

*Add $200 for black or Oriental versions.

American Children: composition socket head; jointed composition body; human hair wig; beautifully detailed painted eyes; closed mouth; original, well-made outfit; typically marked "Effanbee/American Children" or "Effanbee/Ann Shirley."

17"-20"	$2,500-$2,900

Child/Lady: (Suzanna, Tommy Tucker, Ann Shirley, Amish, and Little Lady) all composition; jointed at neck, shoulder, and hip; good wig; sleep eyes; closed mouth; typically marked "EFFANBEE USA" or "EFFANBEE/ANN SHIRLEY."

12"	$325
14"-20"	$400-$550
22"-27"	$700-$800

Open Mouth American Children: (Barbara Joan, Barbara Ann, Barbara Lou, and Peggy Lou) all composition; jointed at neck, shoulder, and hip; human hair wig; sleep or painted eyes; open mouth; original well-made outfit; typically marked "EffanBEE/Ann Shirley" or unmarked.

14"	$700
17"	$1,000
20"	$1,300

Historical/Historical Replica Dolls*: 20" with Ann Shirley body and American Children head with painted eyes. Original costumes were made from satins, velvets, and silks; 14" version known as a Historical Replica Doll, an accurate representation with beautifully painted eyes and historically correct cotton costumes; typically marked "EffanBee American Children."

14"	$800
20"	$2,500

*Add $200 for black or Oriental versions.

Doll House Doll: 6"; composition head and hands; cloth-covered wire armature body; molded and painted shoes; molded and painted hair; painted blue eyes; closed mouth; original detailed costume; typically marked "EFFanBEE." **$100**

Tu-Face: (Johnny or Susie) 16"; composition head and hands; cloth body; painted facial features on front and back of head, one crying, the other smiling; molded and painted hair; typically marked "Effanbee New York." **$600**

Button Nose*: 8"; all jointed composition; molded and painted hair; painted, round, side-glancing eyes; closed, slightly smiling mouth; typically marked "Effanbee." **$400**

*Add $200 for Oriental facial features.

Little Sister and Big Brother: 12" and 16"; composition socket head; shoulder plate and hands; cloth body; floss hair; painted eyes; small closed mouth; original Little Sister's pink and white and Big Brother's blue and white outfits; typically marked "Effanbee."

12" Little Sister	$350
16" Big Brother	$400

14" Effanbee historical replica dolls, **$800 each.**
Courtesy of James Julia Auction, Inc.

Candy Kid: 13"; all jointed composition; chubby child figure; molded and painted hair; painted eyes; pointed eyebrows; closed mouth; original gingham outfit; holding small stuffed monkey; typically marked "EFFANBEE." **$600**

Mae Starr: 28" phonograph doll; composition head and limbs; cloth body. **$1,500**

Patsy's and Patsy Family*: all jointed composition; painted and molded hair or good wig; painted or sleep eyes; closed mouth; typically marked "EFFANBEE PATSY DOLL," "EFFANBEE PATSY BABY," or with other variations of the Patsy family.

6" Wee Patsy	$750
7" Baby Tinette	$450
8" Tinette Toddler	$500
9" Patsy Babyette	$500
9" Patsyette*	$550
10" Patsy Baby/Babykins*	$600
10" Patsykins/Patsy Jr.*	$650
14" Patsy	$800
15" Patricia	$750
16" Patsy Joan*	$750
19" Patsy Ann*	$800
22" Patsy Lou	$800
27" Patsy Ruth	$1,800
30" Patsy Mae	$1,900

19" Patsy Ann, **$800**; 11" Patsy Jr. with trunk, **$650**; 16" Patsy Joan, **$750**; and 15" Patricia, **$750**. All dolls appear in original costumes but with replaced shoes.
Courtesy of David Cobb Auction

Group of Effanbee composition dolls: 22" Patsy Lou, **$800**; 19" Patsy Ann, **$800**; 15" Patricia, **$750**; 11" Patsy Jr., **$650**; 6" Wee Patsy, **$750**; and an 8" Button Nose, **$400**.
Courtesy of David Cobb Auction

14" Skippy, **$750**.
Courtesy of Susan Miller

Skippy*: 14"; newspaper character drawn by Percy Crosby and produced as playmate for Patsy; all composition or composition head and limbs; cloth body; molded and painted hair; painted, round, side-glancing eyes; closed mouth; typically marked "Patsy Pat./Pending" or "Effanbee Skippy/P.L. Crosby"; original pin "I am Skippy The All American Boy." **$750**

*Add $500 for black or Oriental versions.

Hard Rubber

Prices listed are for appropriately costumed dolls in good condition.

Dy-Dee Baby: hard rubber; drink-and-wet doll; hard rubber or plastic socket head; hard rubber body; jointed at shoulder and hip; attached soft rubber ears; molded and painted hair; sleep eyes; open nurser drink and wet mouth; marked "Effanbee/DyDee Baby/U.S. Pat.

11" Klumpe clown, **$250.**
Courtesy of Susan Miller

1-857-485/England-880-060/France-723-980/Germany-585-647/Other Pat. Pending." The rubber heads (and eventually bodies) were replaced with hard plastic.

9"	**$450**
12"-16"	**$425-$475**
18"-20"	**$550-$575**
24"	**$750**

Cloth

Gaining in popularity are the charming cloth display or souvenir-type dolls made in Spain by Klumpe, imported and distributed by Effanbee. Prices listed are for dolls in near mint, original condition.

Klumpe: 10"-12"; all firmly stuffed cloth; wire armature body; felt or floss hair; amusing pressed and painted caricature facial features; wide-open eyes; expressive mouth; authentically designed, sewn-on costumes; typically marked with hangtag or wrist tag only, "I am a Klumpe doll/hand made in Spain//distributed by EFFANBEE," "Klumpe Made in Spain," "Klumpe/Patented Barcelona"; may also have a production or style number......... **$175-$350**, depending on characterization

Hard Plastic/Vinyl

Prices listed are for dolls in near mint, original condition.

Howdy Doody: hard plastic character head and hands; cloth body; molded and painted hair; sleep eyes; open/closed mouth; original cowboy costume with scarf printed "Howdy Doody"; marked "Effanbee."

    18"-19" **$550**
    23"-24" **$650**

Honey: all jointed hard plastic; synthetic wig; sleep eyes; closed mouth; typically marked "Effanbee," hangtag "I am Honey An Effanbee Durable Doll."

    14"-19" ....**$425-$525**
    20" **$575**
    23"-24" **$650**
    27" **$850**

Cinderella or Prince Charming:

    18"-19" **$850**

Madame Schiaparelli-designed, elaborately costumed:

    18"-19" **$750**

Vinyl

Mickey the All American Boy: 11"; all jointed vinyl; molded hat and hair; painted eyes; closed smiling mouth; freckles; typically marked "Mickey/Effanbee." **$200**

Patsy Ann: 15"; all jointed vinyl; rooted hair; sleep eyes; closed smiling mouth; typically marked "Effanbee Patsy Ann/1959." **$250**

Miss Chips: 18"; all jointed vinyl; rooted hair, full bangs; very large, side-glancing sleep eyes; closed mouth; typically marked "Effanbee/19©65/1700." **$125**

Rootie Kazootie: 19"; vinyl hands and character flange neck; cloth body; molded and painted hair, long curl coming down forehead; round, painted eyes; open/closed laughing mouth; typically marked "Rootie/Kazootie/Effanbee." **$350**

Joel Ellis

Joel Ellis operated the Co-Operative Manufacturing Company in Springfield, Vermont, from 1873 to 1874. Ellis patented and manufactured wooden dolls and employed about 60 people, most of them women. The Joel Ellis doll is considered one of the earliest commercially made American dolls. It embodies many technical innovations. The doll's unique mortise-and-tenon construction allowed a complete range of movement. Although most Joel Ellis dolls are unmarked, their mortise-and-tenon joint construction, metal hands, and distinct facial features make them easy to identify. Joel Ellis dolls tend to age rather poorly. They are particularly prone to peeling and flaking. As a result, collectors are a bit more tolerant of worn or age-stricken dolls. The desirability rests in the doll's design and historical significance rather than any artistic decoration.

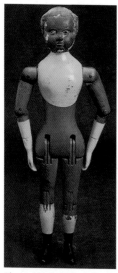

Above: 12" Joel Ellis doll with worn face, **$1,400.**
Courtesy of James Julia Auctions, Inc.

Prices listed are for dolls in fair to good original condition with normal wear.

Joel Ellis Doll: wooden head and body; painted metal hands and feet; molded and painted hair; heavily painted facial features; closed mouth; undressed; typically unmarked or marked "1873" on paper band around waist.

12"	**$1,900**
15"-18"	**$2,400-$2,800**

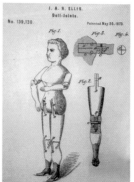

Left: Patent application showing unique mortise-and-tenon construction.
Courtesy of Patent Archive

French Bébés

There are many French socket-head bébés found in the marketplace today that were produced by small or unknown manufacturers or not attributed to any specific maker.

Prices listed are for beautifully dressed dolls in good condition.

Bébé: fine quality bisque, socket head; wood-and-composition French body; good wig; paperweight or good enamel eyes, finely lined in black; pierced ears; closed mouth; marks are listed below. The # indicates a size number.

A L #:
  20"-22" ....$38,000-$40,000
A # V:
  20"-22" ....$8,500-$10,000
B. F.:
  20"-22" ....$6,500-$6,900
B.L./B # L:
  20"-22" ....$6,800-$7,400
BM Black:
  20"-22" ....$36,000-$40,000
C.P.:
  20"-22" ....$67,000-$69,000
F.R.:
  20"-22" ....$29,000-$34,000
J:
  20"-22" ....$14,500-$16,000
J M:
  20"-22" ....$27,000-$34,000
PAN:
  20"-22" ....$17,500-$19,000
P.D.:
  20"-22" ....$25,000-$28,000
R # R:
  20"-22" ....$6,400-$7,500

22" Petit & Denontier closed mouth, size number 4 French Bébé, **$28,000.**
Courtesy of David Cobb Auction

20" French Bébé marked with size number 8 only, **$9,000.**
Courtesy of James Julia Auctions, Inc.

French Fashion-Type

French fashion-type dolls, known as Poupée de Mode, were manufactured between 1860 and 1930. Whether produced in France, Germany, or Austria, collectors use the term "French fashion" or "fashion doll" for a lady doll with a fashionably formed cloth, kid, and/or wooden body.

Smiling 20" Bru with articulated wooden body, **$8,400**, and 14" kid-bodied **Poupée** marked with size number 1 only, **$3,500**.
Courtesy of David Cobb Auction

Gorgeous 24" kid-bodied portrait Poupée de Mode, elegantly costumed in vintage satin with matching chapeau, **$5,200**.
From the collection of Debbie Recksiek. Courtesy of Julia Burke, www.juliaburke.com

17" Poupée de Mode on kid body with fine bisque hands, **$4,000**. Carrying lunettes (glasses) and Ombrelles et En-tou-cas (umbrella or parasol) accessories valued at **$1,100-$1,500**.
Courtesy of James Julia Auctions, Inc.

Prices listed are for beautifully dressed dolls in good condition.

Wooden Body Poupée de Mode: pale, fine bisque swivel head; kid-lined bisque shoulder plate; attached with kid to fully articulated wooden body; wooden peg joints; good wig; paperweight eyes, finely lined in black; painted, long lashes; softly feathered brows; pierced ears; small, closed mouth; typically marked with size number only or unmarked.

12"-15"	$6,000-$7,000
16"-20"	$7,500-$8,500
22"-24"	$10,000-$11,000
30"	$15,000
34"	$22,000

Black:

15"	$15,000
24"	$28,000

Kid Body Poupée de Mode: pale, fine bisque swivel head; kid-lined bisque shoulder plate; fine gusseted kid body; bisque or kid arms with stitched fingers; good wig; exquisitely painted or paperweight eyes, finely lined in black; painted lashes; feathered brows; pierced ears; closed mouth; typically marked with size number only or unmarked.

12"-15"	$3,200-$3,700
16"-20"	$3,800-$4,500
22"-24"	$4,800-$5,200
30"	$6,500
34"	$9,000

Rochard Jeweled Stanhope: bisque shoulder plate; kid body; bisque lower arms; photographic scenes of Paris and religious figures can be seen through the glass jewels of the necklace, known as a Stanhope Bodice, when doll is held to the light; good wig; stationary eyes, finely lined in black; short lashes; thin, feathered brows; closed mouth; marked "Ed. Rochards Brevete S.G.D.G. France Patented 1867." Note: Only 12 examples have been documented and are known to exist to date.

18"	$50,000

18" unmarked swivel head Poupée de Mode, **$4,200.**
Courtesy of David Cobb Auction

Large collection of accessories for a well-appointed Poupée de Mode. Prices range from **$100** for a locket to **$300** for leather gloves to **$1,500** for a fancy outfit.
Courtesy of Susan Miller

French Fashion Type Accessories

Accessories to complete the Poupée de Mode's wardrobe include tiny parasols, reticules, kid gloves, toilette sets, opera glasses, embroidered handkerchiefs, corsets, stationery, watches, tea sets, and even miniature all-bisque French dolls of her very own are collectibles in their own right.

Fulper Pottery Company

The Fulper Pottery Company, founded in 1805 and located in Flemington, New Jersey, is well known for its art pottery and utilitarian wares. Due to import shortages caused by World War I, Fulper produced bisque dolls and doll heads from 1918 to 1921. The quality of Fulper dolls ranges from very poor to very good. Their historical value is perhaps more significant than their aesthetic value.

Prices listed are for appropriately costumed dolls in good condition.

Dolly Face Socket Head: bisque socket head; jointed composition body; good wig; glass eyes; open mouth with molded teeth; typically marked "Fulper Made in USA."

Exceptional quality:
13"-15" ....$700-$800
24"-26" .... $1,000-$1,500
Standard quality:
13"-15" ....$450-$500
24"-26" ....$700-$900

Dolly Face Shoulder Head: bisque shoulder head; kid body, bisque or composition lower arms; good wig; glass eyes; open mouth with molded teeth; typically marked "Fulper Made in USA."

Exceptional quality:
13"-15" ....$500-$650
24"-26" .... $1,000-$1,200
Standard quality:
13"-15" ....$350-$450
24"-26" ....$750-$850

Character Baby*: bisque character socket head; composition body; good wig; celluloid, metal, or glass sleep eyes; open mouth with molded teeth; typically marked "Fulper Made in USA."

Exceptional quality:
15" $800
18" $950
22"-24" .... $1,400-$1,700

Standard quality:
13"-15" ....$400-$600
18" $700
22"-24" .... $1,000-$1,300
Add $500 for jointed toddler body.

Fulper 29" socket head child, body stamped "Amberg," **$1,000.**
Courtesy of David Cobb Auction

Francois Gaultier

The 1860 Francois Gaultier factory was located in St. Maurice and Charenton in the province of Seine, on the outskirts of Paris, France. Francois Gaultier produced dolls until at least 1916, the later years as a part of Societe Francaise de Fabrication de Bébé & Jouets (S.F.B.J.). Gaultier produced doll heads for several well-known doll companies including Gresland, Jullien, Rabery & Delphieu, Simonne, and Thiller.

Gaultier 17" shoulder head, painted eyes, Poupée de Mode, **$2,400.**
Courtesy of Susan Miller

Gaultier 18" swivel head with glass eyes, **$3,400,** and 11" swivel head Poupée de Mode, **$2,400.**
Courtesy of David Cobb Auction

Gaultier 13-1/2" early block
closed mouth bébé, **$5,100**,
and 10-1/2" later scroll mark
bébé, **$3,700**.
Courtesy of David Cobb Auction

Prices listed are for beautifully dressed dolls in good
condition.

French Fashion Poupée de Mode*: bisque swivel
head, lower arms; kid-lined shoulder plate; kid lady
body; good wig; paperweight or painted eyes, finely
lined in black; long lashes; feathered brows; pierced
ears; closed mouth; marked "F.G."

Painted eyes:

8" $1,000
12-1/2"-13-1/2" ....$1,300-$1,800
15"-17" ....$2,000-$2,400

Glass eyes:

8" $1,500
10-1/2"-13-1/2" ....$2,100-$2,600
15"-20" ....$2,900-$3,700
23"-25" ....$4,000-$4,600
31"-35" ....$7,200-$8,700

*Add $2,500 for fully articulated wooden body.

Block Letter Bébé: bisque socket head; jointed composition, straight-wrist body or kid-lined shoulder plate
kid body; good wig; paperweight eyes, finely lined in
black; delicately shadowed eyelids; pierced ears; slightly parted closed mouth; marked with early block letters
"F.G."

Socket head:

10-1/2"...$5,000
13-1/2"-19" ....$5,100-$6,000
20"-25" ....$6,500-$7,700
27"-31" ....$7,900-$8,500
35" $9,600

Scroll Mark Bébé: bisque socket head; composition
jointed body; good wig; paperweight eyes, finely lined
in black; long lashes; feathered brows; pierced ears;
closed mouth; marked "F.G." within a scroll.

Exceptional quality:

11-1/2"-17" ....$3,900-$4,700
20"-27" ....$5,000-$6,100
31"-35" ....$6,900-$7,200

Standard quality:

8" $1,500
11-1/2"-17" ....$2,300-$3,400
20"-25" ....$3,700-$4,300
27"-35" ....$4,500-$5,200

Open Mouth Bébé: bisque socket head; composition
jointed body; good wig; paperweight eyes; long lashes;
feathered brows; pierced ears; open mouth with teeth;
marked "F.G." within scroll.

13-1/2"-20" $2,400
25"-31" ....$3,300-$3,800
35" $4,200

Exceptional Gaultier 20" scroll
mark bébé, **$5,000**.
Courtesy of David Cobb Auction

German Bisque Dolls

Various small or unknown German doll manufacturers, operating after 1880, produced bisque dolls. The questions and mysteries concerning a doll can be endless. Who made it? What does the mark mean? Where does it come from? How old is it? What is it worth? Hundreds of dolls were produced with little or no documentation, making is virtually impossible to answer all the questions or solve all the mysteries. When you encounter a bisque doll with no markings or with an unidentified mark, the following may help you place a value on unidentified or unlisted German bisque dolls. Evaluate the quality, workmanship, and condition. Many of the markings listed are identifiable companies not covered in this pocket guide; to learn more about them and hundreds of others, consult *Antique Trader Makers and Marks* (Antique Trader 1999).

Prices listed are for appropriately costumed dolls in good condition.

Dolly Face: bisque socket or shoulder head; jointed composition or kid body; good wig; glass eyes; open mouth; typically marked "444," "478," "422," "457," "495," "G. B.," "L. H. K.," "GS," "BJ," "Girlie," "K," "CK701," "PR," "DK," "EUSt," "PSch," "WD" "ROMA," "2210," "TR," and surely others.

27" #478 German bisque, **$800.**
Courtesy of McMasters-Harris Auction

Shoulder head standard quality:
12"-18"	$250-$450
24"-28"	$600-$700
30"-34"	$750-$1,000

Shoulder head exceptional quality:
12"-18"	$400-$650
24"-28"	$600-$800
30"-34"	1,000-$1,200

Socket head standard quality*:
12"-18"	$300-$450
24"-28"	$700-$800
30"-34"	$850-$1,000

Socket head exceptional quality*:
6"-10"	$750-$850
12"-18"	$900-$1,100
24"-28"	$1,250-$2,000
30"-36"	$2,700-$3,400

Deduct $200 for a five-piece body.

Beautiful 20" German bisque
#495 lady on a slim waist lady's
body, which adds about **$500**
to the total value of **$1,650**.
Courtesy of David Cobb Auction

Unmarked, fine quality 31"
closed mouth German bisque,
$5,500.
Courtesy of McMasters-Harris Auction

13" German bisque "5" closed
mouth socket head on a separate kid-lined shoulder plate,
kid body, pierced ears, **$1,700**.
Courtesy of David Cobb Auction

Closed Mouth: bisque socket or shoulder head; jointed composition or kid body; good wig; glass eyes; finely painted lashes; feathered brows; pierced or unpierced ears; closed mouth may have white space between lips; delicate coloring; typically marked "R 806," "503," "506," "WD," "TR," "104," "HL," "510," "ELISA," "100," "121," "300," "101," "G.L.," "B," "N," "86," "120," "126," "162," "179," "183," "6," "5," and surely others.

Shoulder head:

12"-14"	**$1,400-$1,800**
16"-18"	**$2,100-$2,500**
22"-24"	**$3,000-$3,400**

Socket head:

14"-14"	**$2,800-$3,200**
18"-22"	**$3,600-$4,300**
24"-26"	**$4,900-$5,200**

Sonneberg Bébé: group of exceptionally beautiful bisque socket head dolls circa 1885; Sonneberg-style composition and wooden jointed body; good quality paperweight or spiral threaded eyes; dramatic black-lined eye undercut; feathered brows; closed mouth with molded white space between the shaded and accented lips; pierced ears; typically marked "132," "137," "183," "124," "136," "182," and possibly others or with a size number only.

14"-18"	**$4,000-$4,700**
22"-25"	**$5,700-$6,500**
26"-27"	**$7,000**

Character Baby*: bisque socket or shoulder head; composition bent-limb baby or cloth body; molded and painted hair or good wig; glass eyes; typically marked "Made in Germany," "44611," "HVB," "PM," "800," "SAH," "TH," "EB," "Sweet Baby," and surely others.

10"-14"	**$500-$700**
18"-20"	**$800-$1,000**
24"	**$1,500**

*Add $500 for jointed toddler body.

Character Child: bisque socket head; jointed composition body; molded and painted hair or good wig; glass or painted eyes, may have line above lid to indicate lid; closed mouth; typically marked "HJ 1," "GK 223," "216," "230," 820," "660," "500," "WSK," "130," and surely others.

10"	**$2,400**
16"	**$3,500**
20"-24"	**$6,000-$7,800**

Molded Bonnet: bisque shoulder head; cloth body; painted or glass eyes; closed mouth; typically unmarked or marked with size number only.

Painted eye:

8"-12"	**$350-$500**
14"-16"	**$750-$850**

Glass eye:

    10"-12" ....$800-$850

    14"-16" .... $1,100-$1,200

    18" $1,400

Molded Hair Shoulder Head: (American School Boy) bisque shoulder head; cloth or kid body; molded and painted hair; painted or glass eyes; closed mouth; typically marked "Germany," size number or unmarked.

Painted eye:

    10" $450

    16" $600

Glass eye:

    10" $700

    16" $1,000

    20" $1,400

Nicely decorated 22" shoulder head German bisque, **$1,400.**

Courtesy of David Cobb Auction

Other Notable German Bisque Dolls

De Fuisseaux: freckled bisque socket or shoulder head with extended plate; composition, cloth, or kid body; bisque hands or lower limbs; stunning, cameo-shaped character face; elongated neck; artfully sculptured nose and throat hollow; good wig; painted blue or gray eyes; defined eyelids; closed, solemn mouth; typically marked "DF/B/F," "F," or "B" along with a size number.

    15" $2,200

    18"-20" .... $2,500-$2,700

Nursing Baby: 19"; bisque socket head; early eight-ball jointed wood and composition body; good wig; glass eyes, finely lined in black; feathered brows; open "O" mouth with nursing mechanism extending to the back of the head; marked "86." **$4,900**

18" De Fuisseaux painted eyes, closed mouth, solid dome shoulder head, **$2,500.**

Courtesy of Mrs. Adam Condo

F. Bierschenk 616 Character: 22"; slender-faced bisque socket head; five-piece composition body; good wig; intaglio eyes; detailed, eye-corner modeling; open/closed mouth with tiny upper beaded teeth; marked "F B 616." **$19,500**

Other more easily found Fitz Bierschenk character dolls:

    20"-22" .... $2,300-$2,700

WSK 130 character: 25"; solid bisque dome socket head; jointed wood-and-composition body; molded and painted hair; painted eyes; molded lids; soft brows; prominent nose; open/closed mouth; protruding ears; typically marked "WSK 130."................................. **$8,500**

B & D 213 Lady: 21"; bisque socket head; kid lined shoulder plate; kid body; beautifully molded slender lady face; sleep eyes; closed mouth; typically marked "BD 213 Germany."... **$8,500**

23" German bisque F. Bierschenk character doll marked "FB." Nicely molded, rare large size character with great appeal, **$3,700.**

Photo courtesy of James D. Julia Inc.

E. Gesland

Gesland produced, exported, distributed, and repaired bisque dolls from about 1860 until 1928. Gesland purchased bisque heads from F. Gaultier, Verlingue, Rabery & Delphieu, and possibly others. Gesland dolls had outstanding body features. The body and limb frame was steel; joints were riveted; the framework was wrapped with kapok or cotton and covered with stockinette or fine lambskin. Hands and feet were either bisque or painted wood. Most were marked with the Gesland stamp or label.

Prices listed are for appropriately costumed dolls in good condition.

Poupée de Mode: bisque swivel head; kid-lined bisque shoulder plate; Gesland body; bisque or wooden hands and feet; good wig; paperweight eyes, finely lined in black; long lashes; feathered brows; pierced ears; closed mouth; typically marked "F.G.," "R.D.," and stamped "E. Gesland Bte F.G.," "E. Gesland Bte S.G.D.G./Paris" on body.

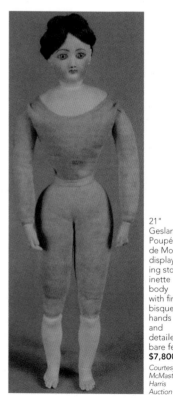

21" Gesland Poupée de Mode displaying stockinette body with fine bisque hands and detailed bare feet, **$7,800.**
Courtesy of McMasters-Harris Auction

Early beautiful*:
13"-15"	$5,400-$6,300
21"-27"	$7,800-$8,800
31"	$9,500

Later familiar:
13"-17"	$4,000-$5,100
23"-27"	$5,900-$6,500
31"	$7,800

Double the amount for man with molded derby and masculine features.

Left: Outstanding 31" F.G. Gesland bébé with a familiar face, **$7,800.**

From the collection of Susan Roberts.

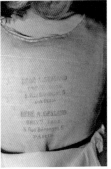

Above: Gesland mark found stamped on back of the previous 31" bébé.

Courtesy of Susan Roberts

Bébé: bisque socket head; jointed composition or Gesland body; bisque or wooden hands and feet; good wig; paperweight eyes; long lashes; feathered brows; pierced ears; closed mouth; typically marked "R. # D.," "F. G.," "A. Gesland Fave De Babes/& Tetes incassables, Bte S.G.D.G./Reparations en tous genres/5 & 5 Rue Beranger/En Boutique/Paris."

10"-15"	$3,900-$4,300
19"-23"	$4,800-$5,700
27"-31"	$6,900-$7,800
Exceptionally beautiful:	
14"-15"	$6,500-$7,400
21"	$8,000
25"	$9,000

William Goebel

In 1876, Franz D. Goebel and his son, William, built a porcelain factory in Oesleau, Bavaria. William Goebel became sole owner in 1893, changing the name to William Goebel.

Early Goebel bisque objects were marked with a triangle and a quarter moon. After 1900, a crown above an intertwined "W & G" was introduced.

26" Goebel crown mark, moon face, smiling character toddler, **$1,200**, and 12" molded hair, crown mark character child, **$500**, holding 7" Cabinet doll marked "K," **$475**.
Courtesy of David Cobb Auction

Prices listed are for appropriately costumed dolls in good condition.

Dolly Face: bisque shoulder or socket head; jointed composition or kid body with bisque arms; good wig; glass eyes; feathered brows; open mouth; appropriately dressed; typically marked with Goebel trademark and "36," "350," "521," "120," "89," "330," "80," and possibly others.

Shoulder head:

12"-16"	$500-$700
18"-20"	$750-$800

Socket head:

14"-18"	$700-$800
20"-22"	$900-$950
24"-26"	$1,000-$1,200

Character Baby*: bisque character baby socket head; composition bent-limb baby body; good mohair wig; glass eyes; open mouth; molded teeth; appropriately dressed; typically marked with trademark, "B/Germany," "120," "123," or "124."

14"-16"	$650-$750
20"-22"	$1,000-$1,200
24"	$1,500

Add $500 for jointed toddler body.

Cabinet Character Doll: bisque character socket head; five-piece papier-mâché body; molded and painted hair; may have molded ornamentation; painted eyes; closed or open/closed mouth; appropriately dressed; typically marked with trademark "73," "84," or "34." The letters "S," "B," "A," "K," "M," "C," "H," "SA," "G," or "T" may appear alone or with a mold number.

7"-8"	$500
14"	$600
18"	$700

Googly-Eyed Dolls

Most early 20th century doll manufacturers produced googly-eyed dolls between 1912 and 1938. The term "googly-eyed" is probably from the German "Guck Augen," meaning eyes ogling to one side. The impish little characters demonstrate their youthful exuberance with pugged noses, rounded faces, and wide alert eyes.

Prices listed are for appropriately costumed dolls in good condition.

Googly-Eyes: bisque socket head; composition or papier-mâché body; molded and painted hair or good wig; round, googly, painted or glass eyes; smiling watermelon mouth; typically marked with mold number and/or manufacturer.

For googly-eyed characters, 8"-14" were used as a comparison base, but please remember the dolls actually came in a wide range of sizes from 7"-20", and you should use your good judgment and common sense to interpose the value of additional sizes:

Armand Marseille:
200 Glass eyes:
  8"-10" .... $2,200-$2,500
200 Painted eyes:
  8"-10" .... $1,800-$2,100
210 Painted eyes:
  8"-10" .... $2,300-$2,600
240 Painted eyes:
  8"-10" .... $2,100-$2,400
240 Glass eyes:
  8"-10" .... $2,700-$3,000
241 Glass eyes:
  8"-10" .... $3,600-$3,900
252 Painted eyes:
  8"-10" .... $1,800-$2,000
253 Glass eyes:
  8"-10" .... $3,000-$3,400
254 Painted eyes:
  8"-10" .... $1,300-$1,500
257 Glass eyes:
  8"-10" .... $1,700-$2,000
310 Glass eyes:
  8"-10" .... $2,200-$2,600
324/322 Painted eyes:
  8"-10" .... $1,200-$1,400
323 Glass eyes:
  8"-10" .... $2,300-$2,600
325 Glass eyes:
  8"-10" .... $1,300-$1,600

Bahr & Proschild:
    686 Glass eyes:
        8"-10" ....$4,200-$4,700

Butler:
    179 Glass eyes:
        8"-10" ....$1,600-$1,900

Demalcol:
    Demalcol, glass eyes:
        8"-10" ....$900-$1,100

Max Handwerk:
    "Bellhop," glass eyes:
        12"-14" ....$3,500-$3,700
    Elite 1 Molded helmet, glass eyes:
        12"-14" ....$3,200-$3,400
    Elite 2 Two face, glass eyes:
        12"-14" ....$3,800-$4,000
    Elite Molded hat, glass eyes:
        12"-14" ....$3,500-$3,700
    Elite Uncle Sam, glass eyes:
        12"-14" ....$3,300-$3,500

Hertel, Schwab & Co.:
    163 Glass eyes:
        12"-14" ....$5,400-$5,700
    165 Glass eyes:
        12"-14" ....$5,400-$5,750

    172 Glass eyes, toddler:
        12"-14" ....$7,900-$8,200
    173 Glass eyes, baby:
        12"-14" ....$7,000-$7,300
    175 Glass eyes, winking:
        12"-14" ....$5,300-$5,500
    178 Glass eyes, open mouth:
        12"-14" ....$6,100-$6,600
    222 Painted eyes:
        12"-14" ....$3,000-$3,200
    222 Glass eyes:
        12"-14" ....$3,400-$3,700

Gerbruder Heubach:
    Elizabeth, glass eyes:
        8"-10" ....$3,400-$3,600
    3823 Einco, glass eyes:
        8"-10" ....$5,800-$6,200
    8589/9141 Painted eyes:
        8"-10" ....$1,300-$1,500
    8606/8729 Painted eyes:
        8"-10" ....$1,200-$1,400
    8995 Painted eyes:
        8"-10" ....$3,400-$3,500
    9056/9081 Painted eyes:
        8"-10" ....$1,600-$1,800

16" Hertel Schwab #165 Googly, **$7,200.**
Courtesy of McMasters-Harris Auction

9085 Painted eyes:
   8"-10" ....$1,500-$1,700
9141 Glass eyes:
   8"-10" ....$1,800-$2,200
9513/9572/9573/8678 Glass eyes:
   8"-10" ....$2,700-$2,900
9578 Tiss Me, glass eyes:
   8"-10" ....$2,100-$2,300
9594 Glass eyes:
   8"-10" ....$1,000-$1,200
10542 Glass eye:s
   8"-10" ....$3,400-$3,700

Ernest Heubach:
322 Glass eyes:
   8"-10" ....$2,600-$2,900
219/260/261/262/263/264 Painted
eyes:
   8"-10" ....$1,000-$1,100
255/274/289 Painted eyes:
   8"-10" ....$1,200-$1,300
318 Painted eyes:
   8"-10" .... $1,200-$1,400
319 Tearful, painted eyes:
   8"-10" .... $1,700-$1,900

310 Glass eyes:
   8"-10" .... $3,900-$4,300
Kammer & Reinhardt:
131 Glass eyes:
   12"-14" .... $13,000-$15,000
Kestner:
111/122/208 glass eyes:
   12"-14" .... $3,200-$3,500
221 Glass eyes:
   12"-14" .... $9,300-$9,600
Kley & Hahn:
180 Glass eyes:
   12"-14" .... $3,600-$4,000
Morimura Brothers:
MB copy of Hertel, Schwab 173,
glass eyes:
   12"-14" .... $3,500-$3,750
Porzellanfabrick Mengersgeruth:
255 PM, glass eyes:
   8"-10" .... $2,900-$3,200
950 Glass eyes:
   8"-10" .... $4,600-$4,900
Schieler, August:
Schieler Glass eyes:
   12"-14" .... $3,000-$3,200

13" Kammer & Reinhardt/Simon & Halbig "131"
Googly, **$12,000.**
Courtesy of McMasters-Harris Auction

12" composition Hug-Me, **$1,300.**
Courtesy Roberta and Ziggy of Roberta's Doll House

12" Samstag & Hilder "Hug Me Kiddy" composition mask face (a 1912 McCall premium) Googly eye character, **$1,300**, and a 14" Kammer & Reinhardt #131 bisque Googly eye character, **$14,000.**
Courtesy of David Cobb Auction

8" SFBJ #245 Googly, **$6,000.**
Courtesy of James Julia Auctions, Inc.

Rechnagel:
43/44/45/47/50 Painted eyes:
8"-10" .... **$1,500-$1,700**
S. F. B. J.:
245 Glass eyes:
12"-14" .... **$6,500-$8,000**
Herm Steiner:
133 Glass eyes:
8"-10" .... **$1,400-$1,600**
223/242/247 Disc Pupils:
12"-14" .... **$1,700-$1,900**
Strobel & Wilkin:
250/405 Glass eyes:
8"-10" .... **$2,000-$2,600**
Composition Googly Eye: composition head; cloth or composition body; molded hair or good wig; round, googly glass or disc eyes; smiling watermelon mouth; typically unmarked or with mold number and/or manufacturer.
Hug Me Glass eyes:
10"-12" .... **$900-$1,300**
94-7/323 Glass eyes:
10"-14" .... **$1,000-$1,400**
LaPrialyline Hansel/Gretel Painted eyes:
10"-12" .... **$2,800-$3,100**
Black Disc pupils*:
10"-12" .... **$1,500-$1,700**
954647 Disc pupils*:
10"-12" .... **$2,750-$2,900**
Disc Pupils–Insert Movable Disc Pupils Under Glass

Heinrich Handwerck

Heinrich Handwerck Sr. and his wife, Minna, started producing dolls in Gotha, near Waltershausen, Thüringia, Germany, in 1876. They managed to build one of the most prolific firms in Germany before closing in 1930. They developed a working relationship with Simon & Halbig, which produced fine quality bisque doll heads designed by Handwerck. When Heinrich Handwerck Sr. passed away in 1902, the business was purchased by Kämmer & Reinhardt.

Left: Beautiful pristine 26" Heinrich Handwerck with matching size number 5 marked on head, body, and shoes, **$1,500.**
Courtesy of Susan Miller

Prices listed are for appropriately costumed dolls in good condition.

Shoulder Head Dolly Face: bisque shoulder head; kid body; bisque arms; good wig; glass eyes; open mouth with teeth; typically marked "Hch H Germany" or "139."

> 16"-18" ....$525-$575
> 20"-22" ....$625-$675

Dolly Face: bisque socket head; jointed composition body; good wig; glass eyes; feathered brows; pierced ears; open mouth with teeth; typically marked "Heinrich Handwerck," "W," "HAND-WERCK," "H," "HHW," "HH," "Hch H" "HW," /99," "109," "89," "79," "69," "119," or "W."

> 10"-14" ....$700-$850
> 22"-26" ....$1,000-$1,600
> 36"-42" ....$3,600-$4,700

> Black Dolly Face:
> 20" $2,500
> 24" $3,600

Closed Mouth: bisque socket head; jointed composition body; good wig; glass eyes; feathered brows; pierced ears; closed mouth with slight space between lips; typically marked "89" or "79."

> 18"-20" ....$3,000-$3,200
> 22"-24" ....$3,700-$4,000

Character Baby: bisque socket head; composition bent-limb baby body; good wig; glass eyes; open mouth; typically marked "Germany HW," "LaBelle," or "Baby Cut."

> 16"-18" ....$1,200-$1,500
> 22" $2,200

Heinrich Handwerck 36" #79, **$3,600.**
Courtesy of David Cobb Auction

28" Heinrich Handwerck child doll in pristine condition, **$1,900.**
From the collection of Mr. and Mrs. Adam Condo

Heinrich Handwerck 28" #109, **$1,700.**

Max Handwerck

The firm of Max Handwerck, located in Walterhausen, Thüringia, Germany, was originally owned by Heinrich Vortmann and Max Handwerck in 1899. Henrich Vortmann left in 1902 and, after Max Handwerck's death, the business was owned by his widow, Anna.

Prices listed are for appropriately costumed dolls in good condition.

Bébé Elite Character*: bisque socket head; composition, bent-limb baby body; good wig; glass eyes; finely painted lashes; feathered brows; open mouth with two upper teeth; typically marked "Max Handwerck Bébé Elite Germany" and triangle within a half moon trademark.

16"-18"	$800-$900
20"-22"	$1,100-$1,300
24"-26"	$1,600-$1,800

Add $500 for jointed toddler body.

Dolly Face: bisque socket head; jointed composition body; good wig; glass eyes; painted lashes; feathered brows; open mouth with teeth; typically marked "283 Max Handwerck Germany," "285," "297," "286," and "287."

16"-24"	$500-$700
28"	$850
30"-34"	$1,200-$1,800
38"-40"	$2,500-$2,700

Max Handwerck 21" child doll, **$600.**
Courtesy of McMasters-Harris Auction

Hasbro®, Inc.

Hasbro®, Inc., originally known as Hassenfeld Bros., was founded by Henry and Hillel Hassenfeld in Pawtucket, Rhode Island, in 1923. The family-owned and -operated toy business adopted the familiar Hasbro name following a division in the company. Hasbro was primarily a toy manufacturer until entering the doll world by introducing the extremely popular G.I. Joe®—called an "action figure" by manufacturer, consumers, and collectors.

Prices listed are for dolls in near mint, original condition.

Sequence of development and changes in G.I. Joe:

1st Series: 1964; 11-1/2"; identified by letters "TM" in mark; marked on lower back: G.I. Joe TM • Copyright 1964 • By Hasbro® • Patent Pending • Made in U.S.A. ....**$800-$1,000**
2nd Series: 1965; 11-1/2"; "TM" replaced by "®"; First black G.I. Joe introduced; marked on lower back: G.I. Joe® • Copyright 1964 • By Hasbro® • Patent Pending • Made in U.S.A. .**$800-$1,000**
3rd Series: 1966; 11-1/2"; identified by the lack of scar; same mark as 2nd Series. ....**$700-$800**
    Black Action Soldier **$1,900**
    British Commando or Japanese Imperial Soldier **$2,400**
    French Resistance...................**$1,100**
    German Soldier or Russian Infantryman or Australian Jungle Fighter **$1,700**
    Nurse Jane: only female member of series; green eyes; short blond wig; marked "Patent Pend. 1967 Hasbro Made in Hong Kong." **$5,000**
4th Series: 1967; 11-1/2"; identified by lack of scar and addition of patent number; marked: G.I. Joe® Copyright 1964 • By Hasbro® • Pat. No. 3,277,602 • Made in U.S.A. ....**$800-$1,000**

5th Series: 1968; 11-1/2"; identified by return of scar with same patent number marking; mark remains the same as 4th Series.......................................**$300-$350**
    Talking Commander **$900**
6th Series: 1970; 11-1/2"; peacetime adventures in response to anti-war feelings; flocked hair introduced; same mark as 4th and 5th Series. ....**$400-$450**
    Astronaut or Adventure Talking Commander (white or black) ....**$850-$900**
    Talking commander with no beard **$1,250**
7th Series: 1974; 11-3/4"; new "Kung Fu Grip" allows G.I. Joe to grasp objects; same mark as 4th, 5th, and 6th series. ....**$400-$500**
8th Series: 1975; 11-1/2"; Mike Power model only, identified by see-through right arm and leg and mark on back of head: "Hasbro Inc. 1975/Made in Hong Kong." Mark on lower back same as 4th, 5th, 6th, and 7th series. ....**$700-$800**
9th Series: 1975; 11-1/4"; more muscular body with molded-on swimming trunks; new mark introduced: 1975 Hasbro® • Pat. Pend. Pawt. R.I. ....**$300-$400**
10th Series: 1976; 11-1/2" same mark as 9th Series, or "Hasbro Ind. Inc. 1975 Made in Hong Kong."..........................**$100-$300**
11th Series: 1977; 8" action figures...**$75-$100**

G.I. Joes: 11-1/2" Air Force Cadet, Nurse Jane, West Point Cadet, Action Pilot, Sea Adventurer, Action Marine, Action Pilot, Sea Adventurer, and Deep Sea Diver. Values of these action figures range from **$350-$5,000.**

Courtesy of Jordan Miller

Other Hasbro Dolls

Dolly Darling Series: 4-1/2"; plastic and vinyl; molded hair; painted eyes; closed mouth; molded-on shoes; typically marked "1963/Hasbro/Japan." **$65**

Little Miss No Name: 15"; vinyl and jointed hard plastic; rooted hair; big plastic eyes; real tears; closed mouth; burlap dress; typically marked "1965 Hasbro." **$400**

Sweet Cookie: 18"; plastic and vinyl rooted hair; painted eyes; freckles; open/closed mouth; molded and painted teeth; pinafore printed "Sweet Cookie"; typically marked "Hasbro, Inc./Pat. Pend. 1972" on head and "Hasbro/Made in USA" on back. **$100**

Aimee: vinyl head; plastic jointed body; rooted hair; sleep eyes; long lashes; closed, smiling mouth; original gown, gold sandals, and "designer original" jewelry; typically marked "Hasbro Inc. 1972."

16" **$150**
18" **$250**

World of Love Dolls: 9"; portraying a classic "flower child"; vinyl head; plastic body; bendable knees; jointed waist; rooted hair; painted, heavily made-up eyes; closed, smiling mouth; typically marked "Hasbro/US Pat.Pend/1968," "Made in Hong Kong/Hasbro US Pat. Pend/1971" or "Hong Kong/Hasbro/US Patented." ....**$200-$250**

Leggy Series: 10"; vinyl head; plastic body; extremely long, very thin arms and legs; rooted hair; painted eyes; closed, smiling mouth; original "mod" outfits; typically marked "1972 Hasbro/Hong Kong." .... **$125-$150**

Charlie's Angels: 8-1/2"; vinyl head; plastic body; rooted hair; painted facial features; original jump-suit and boots; typically marked "1977/Spelling Goldberg/Productions/All rights/Reserved/Made in Hong Kong//Hasbro Pat. 3740894" and model number; clothing tag "1977 Hasbro/Made in Hong Kong." ....**$150-$175**

Jem Series: 12-1/2"; all vinyl; rooted hair; painted facial features; original fashion and stage costume; typically marked "Hasbro/Hong Kong//Pat. Pend. 1986." .**$150-$200**

The Mamas and The Papas: 4"; realistic characterization; all vinyl; wire armatures; rooted hair; nicely detailed, painted eyes; open/closed mouth; 1960s costumes; typically marked "Hasbro®/Hong Kong." ....**$750-$800/set**

The Monkees: 4"; realistic characterization; all vinyl; wire armatures; rooted hair; nicely detailed, painted eyes; open/closed mouth; original brown corduroy jackets, yellow and brown striped pants; typically marked "1967/Hasbro ®//Hong Kong." .... **$650-$700/set**

Mint boxes of Jem and Rio, **$150** each, considered among the best and most interesting of the dolls of the 1980s.
Courtesy of McMasters-Harris Auction

Hertel, Schwab & Company

Hertel, Schwab & Company operated a porcelain factory in Stutzhaus, near Ohrdruf, Thüringia, Germany, from 1910 until at least 1930. The company was founded by August Hertel and Heinrich Schwab, sculptors who designed the dolls, and a minor partner, porcelain painter Hugo Rosenbush.

Prices listed are for appropriately costumed dolls in good condition.

Character Baby: bisque socket head; composition, bent-limb body; molded and painted hair or good wig; painted or glass eyes; winged brows; open/closed mouth with tongue and upper teeth; typically marked "130," "142," "150," "151," or "152."

10"	$600
14"-18"	$850-$950
20"-24"	$1,000-$1,400
26"	$1,700

Character Child*: bisque socket head; from the Art Character Series; jointed composition body; painted or glass eyes; open or closed mouth; appropriately dressed; typically marked "148," "143," "111," "125," "126," "127," "134," "141," "169," "154," "140," or "157."

148 Glass eyes:
14"-18"	$12,000-$15,000

148 Painted eyes:
14"	$6,200

143 Closed mouth:
16"	$4,500

140 Closed mouth:
16"	$9,000

154/125/126/127 Open mouth:
16"-20"	$3,200-$3,900

134/141/149 Closed mouth:
16"-18"	$8,000-$9,000
24"	$12,000

111 Closed, pouty mouth:
18"	23,000

169 Closed mouth:
18"	$4,000

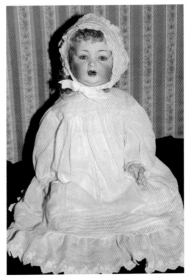

Lovely Hertel, Schwab & Company 24" character baby, **$1,400.**
Courtesy of Susan Miller

Open mouth:

18 " $1,200

154 Closed mouth:

18 " $2,800

Add $500 for jointed toddler body.

Dolly Face: bisque socket head; jointed composition body; good wig; glass eyes; feathered brows; open mouth with teeth; appropriately dressed; typically marked "Made in Germany 136" or "132."

16 "-20 " ....$700-$800

24 "-26 " ....$1,000-$1,200

Hertel, Schwab & Company 20" #136 dolly face, **$800.**
Courtesy of McMasters-Harris Auction

Ernst Heubach

In 1887, Ernst Heubach began manufacturing bisque dolls in his porcelain factory in Köppelsdorf, near Sonneberg, Germany.

In 1919, Heubach and Marseilles merged to become "Vereinigte Köppelsdorfer Porzellanfabrik vorm Armand Marseilles and Ernst Heubach" (United Porcelain Factory of Koppelsdorf). The new company split into two separate entities once again in 1932.

Heubach-Köppelsdorf 9" #320 character baby on jointed toddler body, **$850.**
Courtesy of McMasters-Harris Auction

Prices listed are for appropriately costumed dolls in good condition.

Character Baby*: bisque socket head; bent-limb baby body; some with pierced nostrils; good wig; glass eyes; open mouth; typically marked "Heubach Köppelsdorf," a horseshoe, "300," "320," "342," and possibly others.

6"-10"	$325-$375
12"-16"	$500-$600
20"-24"	$750-$1,000
26"	$1,200

*Add $500 for jointed toddler body

Infant: bisque flange neck; cloth body; composition or celluloid hands, painted hair; glass eyes; closed mouth; typically marked "Heubach/Köppelsdorf/Germany," horseshoe, "338," "339," "340," "349," "350," "399," and possibly others.

10"-12"	$600-$900
14"-16"	$1,000-$1,200

Dolly Face: bisque socket or shoulder head; kid or composition body; good wig; glass eyes; open mouth; typically marked "Heubach/ Köppelsdorf," "Germany," "H/K," horseshoe, "1900," "1901," "1902," "1906," "1909," "250," "251," "275," "302," "312," and possibly others.

Shoulder head:

12"-18"	$300-$375
20"-22"	$450
24"	$600

Group of Heubach black character dolls including 8" #418, **$950**; 7-1/2" #463, **$900**; and 7" #399, **$600**.
Courtesy of David Cobb

Socket head:
12"-18" ....$350-$500
22"-26" ....$600-$800
28"-30" .... **$900-$1,000**
Mold 312*:
10" **$450**
18"-26" ....$700-$900
30" $1,500
36" $2,700
42"-46" ....$3,800-$4,100
Add $300 for high knee flapper body.

Character Child: bisque socket head; jointed, composition body; ethnic and charming character dolls; molded and painted hair or good wig; painted or glass eyes; open or closed mouth; typically marked "Heubach/Köppelsdorf/ Germany," a horseshoe, "261," "262," "269," "399," "414," "463," "452," "445," "SUR 312," and possibly others.
261/262/269:
6" $900
14" $2,000
452:
16" $1,700
445:
18" $2,400
Character clown:
30" $3,200
Black 444:
8"-12" ....$750-$850
16" $1,000
399/414/452*:
8"-12" ....$650-$750
18" $1,000
316/418/463:
8"-13" .... $950-$1,300
18" $2,300
Add $500 for jointed toddler body.

Greif Puppenkunst: ebony-black bisque character head flange neck; cloth body; fantastic modeling; made for Erich Reiser's Fily-Plüshpuppen; solid dome; glass eyes; wide, smiling, open/closed mouth; molded upper and lower teeth; typically marked "Greif Puppenkunst/Germany."
24" $7,500
28" $9,000

Gebrüder Heubach

The Heubach family bought an established porcelain factory in Lichte, Thüringia, Germany, in 1840 and began producing porcelain figurines shortly thereafter. Heubach is not known to have made doll heads until around 1910.

Many heads never had mold numbers; they were simply marked "S" (for sun) or "Q" (for square). No logical numbering system has been deciphered.

The socket or shoulder heads had either molded hair or wigs, and sleeping eyes or the famous painted intaglio eyes. Mold numbers appear to be from 5,625 to 12,386.

Prices listed are for appropriately costumed dolls in good condition.

The following listing should enable you to evaluate mold numbers and sizes not listed by using comparables. With the thousands of dolls made by Gebrüder Heubach, it is impossible to list each.

For Heubach characters, 12"-18" were used as a comparison base, but please remember the dolls actually came in a wide range of sizes from at least 7"-28", and you should use your good judgment and common sense to interpose the value of additional sizes:

Heubach 14" #6692, **$1,200**.
From the collection of Julia Burke.
Courtesy of Julia Burke,
www.juliaburke.com

5626 O/CM, glass eyes, laughing:
   12"-14" .... **$2,000-$2,200**
5636 O/CM, intaglio eyes, two teeth:
   12"-14" .... **$1,600-$1800**
5636/7663 O/CM, glass eyes, laughing:
   12"-14" .... **$2,400-$2,600**
5689 OM, glass eyes, smiling:
   12"-14" .... **$2,700-$3,000**
5730 OM, glass eyes, smiling:
   12"-14" .... **$1,700-$2,000**
5777 OM, glass eyes, socket head, smiling:
   12"-14" .... **$3,100-$3,300**
Shoulder head:
   12"-14" .... **$900-$1,000**

Heubach 17" #6971 character, **$4,500**, with a vintage Ideal teddy bear.

Courtesy of McMasters-Harris Auction

Heubach 15" #7345, **$3,000**; 11" #7604 smiling character, **$1,500**; and 11" #6984 molded hair character, **$1,500**.

Courtesy of David Cobb Auction

6692 CM, intaglio eyes, shoulder head, pouty:
12"-14" ....**$900-$1,000**
6736 Intaglio eyes, laughing:
12"-14" .... **$1,600-$1,800**
6774 Intaglio eyes, whistling:
12"-14" .... **$1,400-$1,500**
6894/6898/7602/7315 CM, intaglio eyes, socket head, pouty:
12"-14" .... **$1,200-$1,400**
6969/6970/7246/7374/7407/8018 CM, glass eyes, pouty:
12"-14" .... **$3,200-$3,400**
6969/6970/7246/7374/7407/8018 CM, intaglio eyes, pouty:
12"-14" .... **$2,000-$2,200**
7054 CM, intaglio eyes, shoulder head, smiling:
12"-14" .... **$1,000-$1,100**
7109 O/CM, intaglio eyes:
12"-14" .... **$1,100-$1,200**
7247 CM, glass eyes:
12"-14" .... **$3,000-$3,400**
7307 O/CM, smiling, teeth, dimples:
12"-14" .... **$3,600-$3,900**
7407 CM, intaglio eyes, full lips:
12"-14" .... **$2,700-$3,000**
7550 O/CM, glass eyes, molded tongue:
12"-14" .... **$2,500-$2,800**
7603 CM, fleece hair:
12"-14" .... **$2,300-$2,500**
7604/7820 O/CM, intaglio eyes, laughing:
12"-14" .... **$1,200-$1,400**
7616 O/CM, glass eyes, molded tongue:
12"-14" .... **$2,500-$2,700**
7620 O/CM, intaglio eyes, protruding ears:
12"-14" .... **$1,500-$1,700**
7622 CM, intaglio eyes, wide lipped, pouty:
12"-14" .... **$1,500-$1,700**
7623 O/CM, intaglio eyes, molded tongue:
12"-14" .... **$1,200-$1,300**
7631 CM, intaglio eyes:
12"-14" .... **$1,050-$1,100**
7644 O/CM, intaglio eyes:
12"-14" .... **$1,100-$1,200**
7646 O/CM, intaglio eyes, wide grin:
12"-14" .... **$2,500-$2,700**
7658 Happy, smiling, molded curly hair:
12"-14" .... **$7,200-$7,400**
7661 O/CM, squinting eyes, crooked mouth:
12"-14" .... **$6,000-$6,200**
7665 O/CM, glass eyes, smiling:
12"-14" .... **$2,300-$2,500**

7669 O/CM, glass eyes, molded tongue:
12"-14" .... **$2,800-$3,000**
7679 O/CM, intaglio eyes, whistler:
12"-14" .... **$1,700-$1,900**
7681 C/M, wide-awake, painted eyes:
12"-14" .... **$2,000-$2,300**
7684 O/CM, intaglio eyes, screaming:
12"-14" .... **$3,200-$3,500**
7686 O/CM, glass eyes, wide mouth:
12"-14" .... **$3,200-$3,500**
7701 CM, intaglio eyes, pouty:
12"-14" .... **$2,400-$2,600**
7711 OM, glass eyes:
12"-14" .... **$2,700-$2,800**
7743 OC/M, glass eyes, protruding ears:
12"-14" .... **$6,100-$6,500**
7745 O/CM, intaglio eyes, molded teeth:
12"-14" .... **$1,700-$1,800**
7746 O/CM, intaglio eyes, lower teeth:
12"-14" .... **$1,600-$1,800**
7748 O/CM, tiny intaglio eyes, fatty neck:
12"-14" .... **$6,800-$7,300**
7749 O/CM, nearly closed, painted eyes:
12"-14" .... **$3,800-$4,200**
7751 O/CM, squinting glass eyes:
12"-14" .... **$4,000-$4,300**
7759 CM, intaglio eyes, pouty:
12"-14" ....**$700-$800**
7761 O/CM, squinting, painted eyes:
12"-14" .... **$5,000-$6,000**
7764 Intaglio eyes, singing:
12"-14" .... **$10,000-$12,000**
7768 CM, intaglio eyes, molded hair in bun:
12"-14" .... **$1,400-$1,600**
7781 O/CM, painted eyes, yawning:
12"-14" .... **$2,200-$2,400**
7788/7850 Coquette, CM, intaglio eyes, socket head:
12"-14" .... **$1,500-$1,700**
7788/7850 Coquette, shoulder head:
12"-14" ....**$900-$1,000**
7802 CM, intaglio eyes, pouty:
12"-14" .... **$1,900-$2,200**
7843 O/CM, squinting, yawning:
12"-14" .... **$1,700-$2,000**
7847 O/CM, intaglio eyes, oversized ears:
12"-14" ....**$3,600-$4000**
7849 CM, intaglio eyes:
12"-14" .... **$1,000-$1,150**
7851 CM, intaglio eyes, molded hair bow:
12"-14" .... **$1,800-$1,950**

Heubach 12" Coquette character, **$900.**
Courtesy of Susan Miller

Gebrüder Heubach characters dolls: 20" #7246 with closed pouty mouth and glass eyes, **$3,200**, and 17" #7603 solid dome with fleece hair, closed mouth, and intaglio eyes, **$2,700.**
Courtesy of David Cobb Auction

7852 CM, intaglio eyes, coiled braids:
  12"-14" .... $2,500-$2,800
7853 CM, painted eyes, downcast:
  12"-14" .... $2,300-$2,600
7862 CM, intaglio eyes, coiled braided hair:
  12"-14" .... $2,000-$2,100
7865 CM, glass eyes:
  12"-14" .... $3,800-$3,950
7877 CM, intaglio eyes, molded bonnet:
  12"-14" .... $1,700-$1,900
7877/7977 Baby Stewart, CM, glass eyes:
  12"-14" .... $2,900-$3,300
7911 O/CM, intaglio eyes, grinning:
  12"-14" .... $1,400-$1,600
7920 CM, glass eyes:
  12"-14" .... $2,700-$3,000
7925 OM, glass eyes, smiling lady:
  12"-14" .... $2,200-$2,700
7925 OM, painted eyes, smiling lady:
  12"-14" .... $1,500-$1,700
7959 O/CM, intaglio eyes, molded bonnet:
  12"-14" .... $2,200-$2,700
7975 CM, glass eyes, removable bonnet:
  12"-14" .... $3,500-$3,700
7977 Baby Stewart, CM, intaglio eyes:
  12"-14" .... $1,900-$2,300
8035 CM, intaglio eyes, full lips:
  18"-20" .... $14,000-$16,000
8050 O/CM, intaglio eyes:
  14"-18" .... $10,000-$15,000
8053 CM, intaglio eyes, glancing:
  14"-18" .... $7,500-$9,500
8058 O/CM, intaglio eyes, teeth:
  14"-18" .... $14,500-$15,500
8107 CM, intaglio eyes, pouty:
  12"-14" .... $1,200-$1,300
8145 CM, intaglio eyes side-glancing:
  12"-14" .... $1,600-$1,900
8191 O/CM, intaglio eyes, laughing boy:
  12"-14" .... $1,200-$1,400
8192 OM, glass eyes, child:
  12"-14" .... $700-$850
8197 CM, glass eyes, molded hair loop:
  12"-14" .... $7,500-$8,500
8306 O/CM, intaglio eyes, molded teeth:
  12"-14" .... $1,500-$1,600
8316 O/CM, glass eyes, molded teeth:
  12"-14" .... $3,700-$4,000

8381 CM, intaglio eyes, exposed ears:
16"-18" .... $15,000-$16,000
8413 O/CM glass eyes, socket head:
12"-14" .... $4,500-$4,800
With tongue, shoulder head:
12"-14" .... $1,500-$1,800
8420 CM, glass eyes, pouty:
12"-14" .... $2,400-$2,600
8459 O/CM, glass eyes, laughing:
12"-14" .... $2,900-$3,200
8467 CM, character, American Indian:
12"-14" .... $4,300-$4,500
8469 O/CM, glass eyes, laughing:
12"-14" .... $2,900-$3,100
8548 C/M, unhappy, grumpy:
12"-14" .... $1,100-$1,300
8550 CM, intaglio eyes, protruding tongue:
12"-14" .... $1,500-$1,700
8555 CM bulging painted eyes:
12"-14" .... $3,300-$3,500
8556 O/CM molded hair ribbon and teeth:
12"-14" .... 11,000-$14,000
8578 CM, intaglio eyes, molded tongue:
12"-14" .... $1,500-$1,800
8590 CM, intaglio eyes, puckered mouth:
12"-14" .... $1,400-$1,600
8596 CM, intaglio eyes, smiling:
12"-14" .... $800-$1,000
8648 CM, intaglio eyes, very pouty:
12"-14" .... $2,300-$2,500
8649 Painted eyes, baby quilted:
12"-14" .... $2,600-$2,800
8724 CM, intaglio eyes, smiling:
12"-14" .... $1,500-$1,700
8774 O/M, intaglio eyes, whistling:
12"-14" .... $1,500-$1,600
8793 CM, intaglio eyes, slight dimple:
12"-14" .... $2,200-$2,400
8868 CM, glass eyes, short chin:
12"-14" .... $2,500-$2,700
8991 O/CM, intaglio eyes, molded tongue:
12"-14" .... $3,400-$3,700
9027 CM, intaglio eyes, tentative smile:
12"-14" .... $4,000-$4,500
9102 Cat, upward-glancing intaglio eyes:
12"-14" .... $4,200-$4,600
9114 Intaglio eyes:
12"-14" .... $1,600-$1,700

9114 Glass eyes:
  12"-14" .... **$2,000-$2,100**

9189 O/CM, intaglio eyes, hair bow:
  12"-14" .... **$1,900-$2,100**

9355 OM, glass eyes, shoulder head:
  12"-14" .... **$1,000-$1,200**

9457 CM, wrinkled character:
  12"-14" .... **$3,200-$3,500**

9496 Character, American Indian:
  12"-14" .... **$3,100-$3,300**

9591 CM, intaglio eyes, fretful frown:
  12"-14" .... **$2,900-$3,200**

9891 CM, intaglio eyes, Aviator:
  12"-14" .... **$2,400-$2,500**

9891 Farmer:
  12"-14" .... **$2,000-$2,400**

9891 Sailor:
  12"-14" .... **$2,200-$2,300**

10511 CM, intaglio eyes, smiling:
  12"-14" .... **$2,100-$2,200**

10532 OM, glass eyes, character:
  12"-14" .... **$1,600-$1,800**

10586/10633 OM glass eyes, shoulder head:
  12"-14" .... **$900-$1000**

10617 OM, small squinting eyes, baby:
  12"-14" .... **$1,000-$1,200**

11173 Tiss Me, glass eyes, indented cheeks:
  12"-14" .... **$2,700-$2,900**

11173 Intaglio eyes:
  12"-14" .... **$2,200-$2,400**

12886 OM, glass eyes, laughing dimples:
  12"-14" .... **$2,700-$2,800**

No mold # CM, intaglio eyes, similar K(star)R 114:
  12"-14" .... **$4,800-$5,100**

No mold # O/CM, teeth resting on tongue:
  12"-14" .... **$5,000-$5,100**

No mold # O/CM, intaglio side-glancing eyes:
  12"-14" .... **$4,000-$4,300**

No mold # Animals with bisque body:
  12"-14" .... **$6,700-$6,800**

No mold # Animals with composition body:
  12"-14" .... **$4,200-$4,400**

No mold # Black character, intaglio eyes:
  12"-14" .... **$3,700-$3,900**

O/CM = Open/Closed Mouth

OM = Open Mouth

CM = Closed Mouth

E. I. Horsman & Company

E. I. Horsman & Company was founded in New York City by Edward Imeson Horsman in 1865. In 1859, at the age of 16, Horsman worked as an office boy for $2 a week; just six years later, he opened a company that was to become a leader in the doll industry.

Bisque

Prices listed are for appropriately costumed dolls in good condition.

Tynie Baby (designed by Bernard Lipfert): bisque flange neck; cloth body; composition hands; molded and painted hair; glass eyes; closed mouth; slightly frowning; typically marked "1924/E.I. Horsman Co./Made in Germany/U."

9" $750
12"-13" .... **$1,100-$1,300**

Composition

Prices listed are for appropriately costumed dolls in good condition.

All composition: (Jo-Jo, Jeanie, Naughty Sue, Roberta, Bright Eyes, Sweetheart) jointed; molded and painted hair or mohair wig; sleep eyes; closed or open mouth with teeth; typically marked "Horsman" hangtag "Gold Medal Doll."

12"-16" ....**$500-$600**
20"-24" ....**$700-$800**

Gene Carr Kids: see Composition Dolls

Baby Bumps: composition flange neck; cloth body; sateen limbs; painted hair and eyes; open/closed mouth; labeled "Genuine/Baby Bumps/Trademark."

White:
9"-12" ....**$400-$500**
18" **$700**

Black:
9"-12" ....**$450-$600**
18" **$750**

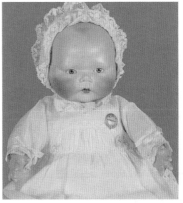

Horsman 14" bisque head Tynie Baby in original condition with "Tynie Baby Horsman's Trade Mark" on button, **$1,400.**

Courtesy of McMasters-Harris Auction

Horsman 19" composition Bright Eyes, made to resemble Shirley Temple's Little Colonel, **$700**.
Courtesy of David Cobb Auction

Baby Butterfly: composition shoulder head and hands; cloth body; painted, black hair; painted Oriental facial features; typically marked "E. I. H."

13" **$1,100**

Baby Chubby: composition shoulder head and limbs; cloth body; molded and painted hair; glassine sleep eyes; real lashes; closed mouth; typically marked "A/Horsman."

14"-16" .... **$350-$400**
24" **$500**

Baby Dimples: composition limbs and flange neck; cloth body; molded and painted hair; tin sleep eyes; open, dimpled mouth with two teeth and molded tongue; typically marked "E.I.H. Co., Inc."

16"-18" .... **$475-$525**
20" **$650**
24" **$725**

Billiken: composition head; beige jointed plush body; stitched claw hands and feet; molded and painted top knot hair; slanted, slit eyes and brows; pug nose; closed, impish watermelon grin mouth; labeled "Licensed Stamp Copyright 1909 by The Billiken Company."

12" **$550**
16" **$700**

Character Baby: composition shoulder head and hands; jointed cloth body; molded and painted hair; painted eyes; nicely molded, closed mouth; typically marked "1910 by E. I. Horsman Co."

11" **$500**
16" **$700**

Child Doll: all jointed composition or composition socket head, shoulder plate, and limbs; cloth body; good wig; tin sleep eyes; open mouth; typically marked "Horsman, Rosebud."

12" **$400**
14"-18" .... **$475-$575**
20"-22" .... **$650-$700**

Ella Cinders: composition character shoulder head and limbs; cloth body; molded and painted black hair with center part; painted wide eyes; freckles; closed mouth; typically marked "©/1925/M. N.S."

18" **$1,800**

HeBee and SheBee: all composition oversized head; painted hair; painted eyes; rosy cheeks and nose; closed mouth; molded chemise and booties; holes in booties for ribbon ties; paper label on foot "Trademark Charles Twelvetrees/Copyrighted 1925."

11" **$1,100**

Jackie Coogan: composition shoulder head and limbs; cloth body; molded and painted brown hair; side-glancing eyes; closed mouth; typically marked "E.I.H. Co./19©21."

13"	$800
16"	$1,100

Mama Doll: composition shoulder head and limbs; cloth body; good wig; tin sleep eyes; open mouth with upper teeth and felt tongue; typically marked "E. I. Horsman."

10"	$350
12"	$425
14"-18"	$500-$600
20"	$675

Peterkins: all composition; molded and painted hair with forehead curl on left side; painted eyes with large pupils; tiny, arched eyebrows; tiny, closed, watermelon mouth; typically marked "E. I. Horsman Inc." or unmarked

11"	$650

Raggedy Man Character Doll: composition, well-molded shoulder head; cloth body; shaped hands; molded and painted hair; painted brown eyes; closed mouth; original patched pants, shirt, jacket, and floppy hat; marked "The Raggedy Man/Trademark/Under License From L. P. Tucks/Mfgd by E. I. Horsman."

16"	$1,400

Tynie Baby: composition flange neck and hands; cloth body; molded and painted hair; sleep eyes; closed, slightly frowning mouth; typically marked "c 1924 E. I. Horsman Inc. Made in Germany."

14"	$600
20"	$700

Whatsit Doll: all jointed composition; molded and painted hair; side-glancing eyes; open/closed mouth with molded tongue; typically marked "Naughty Sue/©1937, Roberta/1938 Horsman."

14"-16"	$700-$800

Horsman 10" Babyland Rag, **$700.**
Courtesy of McMasters-Harris Auction

Hard Plastic and Vinyl

Prices listed are for dolls in near mint, original condition.

BiLo: 14"; vinyl head and swivel limbs; cloth body; molded and painted hair; painted eyes; open/closed mouth; original gown and matching cap; typically marked "Horsman Doll/1972." **$200**

Black Character: vinyl head; one-piece vinyl body; molded hair; painted, squinting eyes; open/closed mouth; typically marked "Horsman."

12"	$500
16"	$750

Child: all hard jointed plastic; saran wig; sleep eyes; open mouth with upper teeth; typically marked "170," "170 Made in USA," "Bright Star," or "Horsman/All Plastic."

15"-17"	$500-$650

Cindy: vinyl head; swivel waist; vinyl, jointed body; high heeled feet; rooted, red hair; painted nails; sleep eyes; pierced ears; closed mouth; original stylish costumes; typically marked "Horsman/83," "Horsman," "88//Horsman," or "818 Pat. 2736135."

10"	$250
19"-20"	$350

Couturier: all vinyl; poseable vinyl body; unusual ball joints at neck, shoulder, and elbows; individual fingers; long neck; high heeled feet; rooted, unusual-color hair; sleep eyes; real lashes; closed mouth; costume of satin and lace; typically marked "82/Horsman."

10"	$250
19"-20"	$350

Disney's Cinderella Gift Set: 11-1/2"; vinyl heads and arms; hard plastic body; rooted hair; painted, side-glancing eyes; pierced ears; closed mouth; included in the set, satin gown and poor version with accessories; typically marked "H."...**$300**

Hansel & Gretel: 15"; all vinyl; unique character face; sleep eyes; typically marked "Michael Meyerberg Inc." **$300/set**

Jackie Kennedy: 25"; soft vinyl head; rigid jointed vinyl body; rooted black hair; sleep eyes; pronounced, arched eyebrows; pierced ears; closed mouth; original, white Schiffli dress, shawl; pearl accessories; typically marked "Horsman, 19©61/JK/25/4."....................................**$300**

Jane: 7"; all vinyl; rooted hair; painted eyes; closed mouth; typically marked "Horsman Doll Inc. 6681." **$200**

Mary Poppins: vinyl head; plastic body; rooted hair; painted, side-glancing eyes; slightly open/closed mouth; typically marked "H."

12"	$125
16"	$200
26"	$400

Michael: 9"; all vinyl; rooted hair; painted eyes; closed mouth; typically marked "9/Horsman Doll/6682." **$200**

Patty Duke/Flying Nun: 11"; vinyl head; plastic body; rooted, blond hair with bangs; painted eyes; closed mouth; typically marked "Horsman Doll/6211."**$300**

Pippi Longstocking: 18"; vinyl head and limbs; cloth body; rooted, braided orange hair; painted eyes; freckles; open/closed mouth; typically marked "25-3/Horsman Dolls Inc./1972." **$175**

Poor Pitiful Pearl: vinyl head; vinyl body; rooted, long straight hair; sleep eyes; closed, thin line mouth; protruding ears; original, patched cotton dress and scarf; typically marked "©1963/Wm. Steig/Horsman."

12"-16"	$300-$400

Ruth's Sister/Ruthie: 27"; vinyl head and arms; plastic body; rooted hair; sleep eyes with lashes; open/closed mouth; typically marked "Horsman/T-27." **$350**

Squalling Baby: 19"; vinyl head and limbs; cloth body; molded hair; painted, squinting eyes; wide, open/closed, yawning mouth; typically marked "Corp. Lastic Plastic 49."...............................**$200**

Tweedie: 14"; vinyl head; rigid vinyl body; rooted hair; sleep eyes; closed mouth; designer costumes; typically marked "38/Horsman" or "Horsman." **$110**

Zodiac Baby: 6"; all jointed vinyl; long, rooted, pink hair; black eyes; open/closed mouth; with charm bracelet with signs of the zodiac; and "Your Individual Horoscope" booklet; typically marked "Horsman Dolls Inc./1968." **$70**

Mary Hoyer Doll Manufacturing Company

The Mary Hoyer Doll Manufacturing Company, named for its founder, was located in Reading, Pennsylvania, from 1925 until the 1970s. Hoyer wanted a small, slim doll that could be sold along with a pattern book of instructions for a knitted and crocheted wardrobe. Recently, the Hoyer family reintroduced a beautiful vinyl Mary Hoyer doll. The doll was warmly embraced by contemporary doll collectors and caused a renewed interest and demand for the original Mary Hoyer dolls.

Composition

Prices listed are for original factory-tagged or authentic "Mary Hoyer Make-At-Home" costumed dolls in good condition.

Mary Hoyer: all composition; jointed at neck, shoulder, and hip; slim body; mohair wig; sleep eyes; real lashes; painted lower lashes; closed mouth; typically marked "The/Mary Hoyer/Doll." 14" **$650**

Hard Plastic

Prices listed are for near mint dolls in original factory-tagged or authentic "Mary Hoyer Make-At-Home" costumes.

Mary Hoyer: all hard plastic; jointed at neck, shoulder, and hip; synthetic wig; sleep eyes; real lashes; lower painted lashes; closed mouth; typically marked "Original/Mary Hoyer/Doll."
    14" **$750**
    Boy with fur or ragged styled wig:
    14" **$800**
    Gigi:
    18" **$2,100**

Mary Hoyer 18" hard plastic Gigi, **$2,100**, holding a first edition of *200 Years of Dolls*.
Courtesy of David Cobb Auction

Vinyl

Prices are for mint dolls with accessories and original box.

Mary Hoyer: all vinyl; jointed at neck, shoulder and hip; synthetic wig; painted eyes; closed mouth; typically marked "Mary Hoyer."
    14" ....**$100-$110**

Ideal® Novelty and Toy Company

In 1902, Morris Mitchom and A. Cohn founded the Ideal Novelty and Toy Company for the express purpose of producing Mitchom's teddy bears. The 1930s were prime years for Ideal. The popularity of the Shirley Temple, Judy Garland, and Deanna Durbin dolls placed the company firmly in the forefront of the industry. Ideal was one of the few large companies that made its own composition dolls. The company was a pioneer in making "unbreakable" dolls in America. It was so proficient, it supplied other manufacturers in addition to meeting its own needs. American Character, Arranbee, Eugenia, and Mary Hoyer were among Ideal's customers. Ideal began experimenting with hard plastic in 1936 and was the first to market a hard plastic doll. Soon the wonderful Toni dolls and the Play Pal Family of dolls brought as much recognition to Ideal as its earlier attempts at perfection. Play Pal children were sculpted according to measurements issued by the U.S. Bureau of Standards of Specifications. They could wear actual clothing of a child at the age of three months, one year, two years, three years, and an older child of 10 or 11 years.

Cloth

Prices listed are for appropriately costumed dolls with good color.

Cloth Character: (Seven Dwarfs, Queen of Hearts, Snow White, Bo Peep, or Oz's Scarecrow) pressed oilcloth mask; cloth body; wool hair; painted facial features; typically marked with character's name printed on clothing.

12"	$450
16"	$800

Composition

Prices listed are for appropriately costumed dolls in good condition.

Deanna Durbin: all jointed composition; brown human hair wig; brown sleep eyes; gray eye shadow; dimples; open mouth with five teeth; marked "Deanna Durbin/Ideal Toy Co."

14"-15"	$950-$1,100
17"-19"	$1,200-$1,300
21"-24"	$1,500-$1,900

Judy Garland/Miss Liberty*: all jointed composition; brown human hair wig; brown sleep eyes; open mouth with six teeth; typically marked "Ideal Doll," "18/Ideal Doll/Made in USA" on back, "11/18" ("21"/"12") on upper left arm, "10" on upper right arm, and "18" on inside of both legs.

16"	$1,900
18"	$3,400

*Deduct $200 for Judy Garland doll dressed as Miss Liberty.

Snow White: all jointed composition; black mohair wig; brown, flirty eyes; open mouth with four teeth; typically marked "Shirley Temple."

12"	$750
18"	$1,000

Teen/Child: (Rosy, Betty Jean, Miss Curity, Teen Star, Little Princess, Pigtail Sally, or Ginger) all jointed composition walker or non-walker body; good wig; sleep eyes; open or closed mouth; typically marked "IDEAL DOLL," "MADE IN USA/IDEAL DOLL."

14"	$550
18"	$750

Ideal 16" Snow White and 12" Seven Dwarfs. If found in good condition, a complete set like this would be valued at **$4,000-$5,000**. This set, showing considerable wear, is valued in the **$1,200-$1,800** range.

Courtesy of McMasters-Harris Auction

Ideal 9" Jiminy Cricket showing the original Ideal label on his foot, **$650.**
Courtesy of McMasters-Harris Auction

Baby Mine: all jointed composition body; wig; sleep eyes; open mouth with teeth; typically marked "Ideal" within a diamond/"U.S.A."; wrist tag "Baby Mine/USA IDEAL."

16"	**$600**
22"	**$750**

Snow White: composition shoulder head and limbs; cloth body; molded and painted black hair with molded blue or red bow; painted, side-glancing eyes; closed, smiling mouth; typically marked "IDEAL DOLL."

13"-15"	**$650-$750**

Mama Baby (Prize Baby, Tickletoes, Baby Smiles): composition head and limbs; cloth body; molded and painted hair or good wig; painted or tin sleep eyes; closed or open mouth with teeth; typically marked "USA," "Ideal," "Ideal Doll Made in USA" within a diamond.

15"	**$400**
17"	**$500**
19"	**$600**

Character Child Doll: Bronco Bill (rodeo costume), Buster (sailor suit), Dolly Varden (low-waisted dress), Jenny Wren (dress and matching hair bow), Sanitary Baby ("can-wash" oilcloth body), Columbia Kids (red, white, and blue stars and stripes), Flossie Flirt (squared-off crier body), Pretty Peggy (smiling and flirty eyes); composition head and limbs; cloth body; good wig; tin sleep eyes; closed mouth; typically marked "Ideal" within a diamond/"U.S.A." or "Ideal Doll/Made in USA."

14"-16"	**$500-$550**
18"	**$600**
21"-22"	**$700-$800**

Uneeda Biscuit Boy: composition head and limbs; cloth body; molded and painted hair; painted eyes; closed mouth; original yellow sateen rain slicker and hat; molded and painted black rain boots; marked with label on raincoat "Uneeda Biscuit/Pat'd Dec 8, 1914/Mfd by Ideal Novelty & Toy Co."

16"	**$700**
24"	**$1,200**

Babies: Hush-a-baby (orange hair and gray eyes), Ticklette (crier in each leg); composition head; cloth body; rubberized limbs; molded and painted hair; sleep eyes; open mouth with teeth; marked "Ideal" within a diamond/"U.S.A.," "USA Patents 1621434," and other patents, "By B. Lipfert."

16"	**$550**
22"	**$700**

Baby Bi-Face (Soozie Smiles): composition hands and two-sided head; cloth body; character tearful and crying or happy and smiling; molded and painted hair and facial features; typically marked "Ideal" within a diamond/"U.S.A."

14"-16"	**$600-$700**

Characters: Mr. Hooligan (plush body), Dandy Kid, Ty Cobb* (baseball uniform), Naughty Marietta (molded hair bow), The Country Cousins (farm costumes,), Russian Boy, Arctic Boy (knit snowsuit), Admiral Dot (sailor clad), Jack Horner, Captain Jinks (khaki suit), ZuZu Kid (clown)*; composition head and hands; cloth body; molded and painted hair and facial features; typically marked "IDEAL" within a diamond and "US of A" at each point.

11"	$350
14"-16"	$600-$650
21"	$750

Add $300 for original Ty Cobb doll.

Betsy Wetsy: composition (Idonite) head; rubber drink-and-wet body; molded and painted hair; sleep eyes; open nurser mouth; typically marked "Ideal."

11"	$350
14"-16"	$400-$450

Wood Segmented Character: composition character heads; wooden spool or segmented body, painted to represent the character's costume; occasionally, felt ornamentation was added; typically marked "Ideal."

Ferdinand the Bull or Jiminy Cricket	$600-$700
Pinocchio, Little King, or Gabby	$700-$800
Superman	$1,500

Flexy Character: Mortimer Snerd, Sunny Sam, Sunny Sue, Fannie Brice, Baby Snooks, or Soldier; 12"; composition hands, feet, and head; wooden, flexible, spring-jointed body; molded and painted hair; painted eyes; closed, mouth; typically marked "Ideal Doll/Made in USA"; hangtag "The Doll of a Thousand Poses/Made in USA/A Flexy Doll (character name)." $600

Magic Skin

Magic Skin was an early synthetic material that looked and felt like human skin. Over time, Magic Skin becomes unstable and deteriorates, becoming badly discolored.

The process may be slowed by regularly rubbing cornstarch into the doll.

Sparkle Plenty, Plassie, Joan Palooka, Babies, Baby Brother and Sister, Coos, Pete and RePete: Magic Skin or hard plastic head; Magic Skin body; yarn or molded and painted hair; insert or sleep eyes; closed mouth; typically marked "Made in U.S.A./Pat.No.2252077."

14"	$200
18"-22"	$275-$350
25"	$400

Hard Plastic & Vinyl

Ideal's patent number for hard plastic was #2252077, and many different dolls can be found marked with this number.

Prices listed are for dolls in near mint, original condition.

Toni Dolls: Miss Curity Nurse, Sara Ann, Mary Hartline, Harriet Hubbard Ayer, and Betsy McCall*; all jointed hard plastic; synthetic wig; sleep eyes with real upper lashes; painted lower lashes; typi-

Ideal 18" all original Miss Revlon with box, **$400.**
Courtesy of McMasters-Harris Auction

cally marked "P90-14," "P91-16," "P92-16," "P93-21," or "P94-22 1/2."

14"-16" ....$650-$700
19" $900
21"-22-1/2" .... $1,100-$1,200

Deduct $100 for 14" Betsy McCall or Harriett Hubbard Ayer.

Saucy Walker: all hard plastic jointed walker body; synthetic wig; flirty, sleep eyes; open mouth with two upper teeth; typically marked "Ideal Doll."

16" $300
22" $400
32" $600

Miss Revlon: vinyl head; solid vinyl jointed body; rooted hair; sleep eyes; pierced ears; closed mouth; polished fingernails and toenails; marked "Ideal Doll/VT" and size number.

10" $300
18"-22" ....$400-$450
36" $500

Thumbelina: vinyl head and hands; cloth body; rooted hair; painted eyes; open/closed mouth; mechanism in center back makes her wiggle; marked "Ideal Toy Corp/©TT-19."

10"-15" ....$300-$350
20" $450

Play Pal Family: vinyl head; plastic body; rooted hair; sleep eyes; smiling mouth; typically marked "Ideal Doll O.E.B-24-3-/Ideal" or "Ideal Toy Corp./SP-#" (# = height of doll).

24" Bonnie, Johnny, or Susy:..... $450
25" Miss Ideal............................ $600
32" Penny $650
36" Pattie................................. 1,200
38" Peter...............................$1,800
42" Daddy's Girl $2,300

Growing Hair Crissy: vinyl head; plastic body; rooted, auburn hair with center ponytail, lengthen by pulling; dark brown eyes; smiling, open/closed mouth with molded teeth; typically marked "1968/Ideal Toy Corp/GH-17-H 129," "1969/Ideal Toy Corp/GH-18 US Pat Pend. # 3,162,976."

17-1/2" Crissy $135
Black Crissy................................ $185
11-1/2" Cinnamon $100
15-1/2" Black Velvet.................. $150
15-1/2" Cricket or Tara.............. $350
15-1/2" Mia, Dina, Velvet $135
17-1/2" Kerry,Brandi or Tessy.... $150
24" Baby Crissy $250

Sara Lee: 17-1/2"; black vinyl head and limbs; cloth body; lifelike features; molded and painted hair; brown sleep eyes; open/closed mouth; typically marked "Ideal Doll." Doll was named after designer Sara Lee Creech. $600

Judy Splinters: vinyl head and limbs; cloth body; yarn hair; large, painted eyes; wide, open/closed, smiling mouth; appropriately dressed; typically marked "Ideal Doll."

18" $350
36" $700

Tiffany Taylor: 14"; vinyl head; shapely plastic jointed body; swivel cap wig (changes hair from blond to brunette); painted eyes; closed mouth; typically marked "1974/Ideal" in an oval, "Hollis, NY 11423/2M 5854-1/2," "1973/CG-19-H-230." $125

Kissy: 22"; vinyl head; plastic body; rooted hair; sleep eyes; open/closed mouth; typically marked "® IDEAL/IDEAL CORP./K-21-L//IDEAL TOY CORP. K-22 PAT. PEND." $275

Kissin Cousins: 11-1/2" $125
Tiny Kissy Baby: 16" $200

Pebbles/Bamm-Bamm: all vinyl; painted facial features; rooted hair; typically marked "Hanna-Barbera Pro. Inc. Ideal Toy Corp. BB12" ("16", "P12", P16"), hangtag "Ideal Bamm-Bamm from the Flintstone's Series."

12" $150
16" $250

Jumeau

Pierre Francois Jumeau began manufacturing dolls in Paris and Montreuil-sous-Bois, France, about 1842, in a partnership called Belton & Jumeau. Although the death of Belton brought the partnership to an end, Jumeau continued creating exquisite bisque bébés. When Pierre retired in 1877-1878, his son, Emile, assumed the responsibilities. Emile resolved to make France the world leader in the doll industry. Today's sophisticated collector has more accurately defined the distinction between spectacular and mediocre quality dolls. Hence, prices for seemingly identical dolls can vary a great deal. When evaluating a Jumeau bébé or Poupée de Modes, remember the ever-important "visual appeal factor."

Rare laughing 22" Jumeau #208 character with glass eyes and wide open-closed mouth with molded tongue and teeth, **$600.**
Photo courtesy of Sotheby's of New York.

Jumeau 19" Poupée de Modes
Portrait kid body, **$7,800.**
Courtesy of McMasters-Harris Auction

Prices listed are for beautifully dressed dolls in good condition.

Poupée de Modes (Fashion-Type Dolls)*: bisque socket head; kid-lined shoulder plate; kid body; slender waist; stitched fingers; good wig; paperweight eyes, black accented under-cut; finely feathered brows; pierced ears; closed mouth; pronounced lip bow; body stamped "Jumeau/Medaille D'Or Paris"; head marked with a size number only, or a red artist check mark.

10"	**$2,600**
17"-19"	**$4,600-$4,900**
22"-24"	**$5,300-$6,000**

Portrait-face Poupée de Modes with extremely delicate and individualized modeled face:

14"	**$6,500**
17"-19"	**$7,000-$7,900**
26"	**$14,000**

*Add $1,500 for Jumeau Poupée de Modes with stamped wooden bodies.

Portrait Jumeau Bébé: pressed bisque socket head; straight-wrist, wood-and-composition body; good wig; large, almond-shaped, beautiful, spiral, threaded enamel, paperweight eyes, may have tri-color irises, finely black lined undercut; feathered brows; pierced ears; closed mouth; body stamped "Jumeau/Medaille D'Or/ Paris"; head marked "Déposé" and a size number, or a size number only (do not confuse with Déposé Jumeau, Déposé Tete, or Déposé E. J.—this particular bébé was marked only "Déposé," along with a size number). The Portrait Bébé has several distinct classifications:

17" First Series, almond-eyes
Jumeau bébé, **$25,000.**
Courtesy of James Julia Auctions, Inc.

First of Premiere Series: Delicately blushed bisque; very almond shaped, wraparound, spiral threaded enamel paperweight eyes; wide spaced, shaped, and feathered brows. Size numbers: #2/0-9", #1-16-1/2", #3-20", #4-23", #5-25".

12"	**$19,000**
17"	**$25,000**
20-1/2"	**$39,000**
23"	**$55,000**
26"	**$67,000**

Second or Encore Series: Delicately blushed bisque; defined eyelid, slightly rounded cut eyes; wide spaced, finely feathered brows. Size numbers: #3-11", #4-12", #6-14-1/2", #8-18"-19", #10-21-1/2", #12-25".

11"	**$7,500**
13"-17"	**$9,200-$10,200**
20-1/2"	**$13,500**
24"	**$22,300**

13" Encore or Second Series
Jumeau bébé, **$9,200.**
Courtesy of James Julia Auctions, Inc.

Standard or Ultimate Series: Pale bisque, may be peppered; round face; deep cut paperweight eyes; wide spaced, thin feathered brows. Size numbers: #1-9", #3-16" (may have variations in size numbers).

10"-11"	**$6,800-$7,400**
14"-19"	**$8,200-$9,700**
23"	**$13,000**

Marked Déposé:

15"	**$8,500**
19"-20-1/2"	**$10,500-$11,600**

Incised Jumeau (Framed of Cartouche): (1878 only) pressed bisque socket head; straight-wrist, wood and composition body; good wig; enamel paperweight eyes; feathered brows; pierced ears; closed mouth; typically marked incised "Jumeau" within a winged frame or box (cartouche); body stamped "Jumeau/ Medaille D'Or/Paris." Size numbers: #1-12".

13"	**$7,600**
17"	**$8,900**

Long Face Triste: pressed bisque socket head; straight-wrist, wood-and-composition body; good wig; oval paperweight eyes; feathered brows; applied pierced ears; closed mouth; typically marked with size number (#9-#16) only; stamped in blue ink "Jumeau/Medaille D'OR/Paris." Size numbers: #9-21"; #13-28-1/2"; #16-33-1/2".

21"	**$28,000**
24"	**$31,000**
30"-33-1/2"	**$35,000-$39,500**

E. J. Jumeau Bébé: bisque head; jointed wood-and-composition body; good wig; paperweight eyes; feathered brows; pierced ears, applied on larger sizes; closed mouth.

Early: pressed bisque; substantial, almost chubby; straight wrist body; marked with size number above "E.J."; body stamped in blue "Jumeau/Medaille D'Or/Paris." Size numbers: #6-17-1/2"; #9-23-1/2"; #12-26".

12"-16"	**$10,000-$14,000**
20-1/2"	**$16,000**
23"	**$21,000**

Mid: poured or pressed bisque; trimmer French bodies with jointed wrists and attached ball joints; marked with size number between "E" and "J"; body stamped in blue "Jumeau/Medaille D'Or/Paris," or with oval paper label "Bébé Jumeau/Diplome d'Honneur." Size numbers: #6-15"; #9-20".

10"	**$8,500**
14"	**$9,200**
19"-22"	**$11,000-$13,500**
24"-26"	**$17,000-$19,500**

Late: poured bisque; trimmer French bodies; straight or jointed wrists; attached ball joints; marked with size

12" Ultimate Series Jumeau bébé, **$7,900.**
Courtesy of David Cobb Auction

29" Long Face Triste Jumeau bébé, **$33,000.**
Courtesy of James Julia Auctions, Inc.

18" Jumeau E.J. Bébé, **$15,000.**
Courtesy of David Cobb Auction

15" Mid E6J Jumeau bébé, **$9,500.**
Courtesy of Susan Miller

22" Déposé Jumeau bébé,
$9,500.

Courtesy of James Julia Auctions, Inc.

25" closed mouth Tete
Jumeau bébé, **$7,300.**

*From the collection of Diana
Alexander.*

number between "E" and "J" and "DÉPOSÉ" above;
body stamped in blue "Jumeau/Medaille D'Or/Paris,"
or with oval paper label "Bébé Jumeau/Diplome
d'Honneur." Size numbers: #7-16"; #11-24"; #12-27".

10"-17"	**$7,500-$8,500**
19"-20-1/2"	**$8,800-$9,400**
24"-25"	**$12,000-$13,100**
28"-30"	**$15,000-$17,000**

E. J. A. Bébé: 26"; bisque socket head; composition-
and-wood chubby bodies with straight wrists; narrow,
almond-shaped eyes; closely resembles the portrait
Jumeau; 25"-26"; closed mouth; beautifully dressed;
marked "E.J.A."; body stamped "Jumeau/Medaille
D'Or/Paris." Size number: #10-26"...................... **$37,500**

Déposé Jumeau Bébé: bisque socket head; straight- or
jointed-wrist; wood-and-composition body; good wig;
paperweight eyes; feathered brows; pierced ears; closed
mouth with slight space between lips; marked "DÉPO-
SÉ/JUMEAU"; body stamped in blue "Jumeau/Medaille
D'Or/Paris." Size numbers: #5-14-1/2"; #9-20"; #11-24".

14"-17"	**$6,700-$7,200**
19"-22"	**$8,500-$9,500**
24"	**$10,000**
25"-28"	**$11,500-$12,500**

10X*: 22"; pressed bisque socket head; straight wrist;
wood-and-composition body; good wig; paperweight
eyes, finely lined in black; feathered brows; applied
pierced ears; closed mouth; typically marked incised
10X; body stamped "Jumeau/Medaille D'Or/Paris."

22"	**$21,000**

*Add 1,000 for fine bisque lower arms.

Tete Jumeau Bébé: bisque socket head; straight- or
jointed-wrist, wood-and-composition, ball-jointed body;
good wig; paperweight eyes, finely lined in black; heavy,
feathered brows; pierced ears; closed mouth; marked
with red stamp "Déposé Tete Jumeau Bte SGDG"; body
stamped in blue "Jumeau/Medaille D'Or/Paris," or with
oval paper label "Bébé Jumeau/Diplome d'Honneur."

11"	**$7,100**
13"-15"	**$4,900-$5,400**
12"-25"	**$6,600-$7,300**
28"-30"	**$8,100-$8,700**
34"	**$9,600**

Black Tete:

17"	**$9,000**
22"	**$12,000**

Adult Tete: bisque socket head, adult face; jointed
composition, shapely woman's body; marked with red
stamp "Déposé Tete Jumeau Bte SGDG"; stamped in
red "Tete Jumeau."

14"	**$5,700**
20"-21"	**$7,300**

ED Bébé: (1892-1899); bisque socket head; wood-and-composition jointed body; good wig; paperweight eyes, finely lined in black; feathered brows; pierced ears; closed mouth; marked "ED" and a size number only. (If the word "Déposé" is included in the marking, see Etienne Denamur).

17" $5,900
19" $6,500

Paris Bébé/Français: (after the 1892 judgment) bisque socket head; wood-and-composition, jointed body; distinct aquiline nose; good wig; paperweight eyes; pierced ears; closed mouth. Marked "B F" or "Paris Bébé"; body may be stamped or have a paper label.

16"-18" .... $6,500-$6,800
22" $7,600
25" $8,400

Open Mouth Bébé: bisque socket head; wood-and-composition, jointed body; good wig; paperweight eyes; feathered brows; molded, pierced ears; open mouth with molded upper teeth; marked with red stamps "Tete Jumeau," "Déposé Tete Jumeau Bte SGDG," and/or incised "1907"; body may have paper label "Bébé Jumeau Diplome d'Honneur."

14"-17" .... $3,200-$3,700
19"-21" .... $3,900-$4,100
24" $4,600
28"-34" .... $4,900-$5,300

25" open mouth Tete Jumeau with pale bisque and delicate coloring in her original costume with Bébé pin and matching bonnet. Not shown: doll's original box, which adds to her value of **$8,200.**
From the collection of Mr. & Mrs. Adam Condo.

S.F.B.J. Dolls: dolls marked with both known S.F.B.J. molds numbers such as 221, 230, or 301, in addition to "Jumeau."

221:
    Great Ladies: 9"-11" .... $850-$900
230:
    18"-21" .... $2,400-$2,800
    16" $3,200
301:
    14" $950
    24" $1,400

Jumeau Character Doll: expressive character face; glass eyes; French, jointed-composition body; most are marked with the red Tete stamp. Dolls numbering from 201 to 225 were released as Jumeau character dolls; character dolls with mold numbers higher than 226 are typically marked "S.F.B.J."; Jumeau characters are rare and desirable.

208 Open/closed wide, laughing mouth, squinting eyes:
    22" $60,000
203/211 Two-Face character:
    24" $115,000
200 Series (rare, very expressive characters):
    9"-25" .... $75,000-$150,000

Stunning 24" Jumeau "1907" French bébé, **$4,600.**
From the collection of Sandra and Summer Ann Czossek.

Kämmer & Reinhardt

Kämmer & Reinhardt was founded by Ernst Kämmer and Franz Reinhardt in 1886 in Waltershausen, Thüringia, Germany. Kämmer was the designer and modeler. In 1902, the company bought the Henrich Handwerck factory and began, by association, an important collaboration with Simon & Halbig. Simon & Halbig made most of the bisque heads and was a part of the company by 1920.

From 1886 to 1909, Kämmer & Reinhardt made only dolly face dolls, but caused quite a stir when it introduced its K ★ R character doll on a bent-limb baby body at the 1909 Munich Exhibit.

Cloth

Prices listed are for appropriately costumed dolls in good condition.

Cloth covered wire-armature bodies; wooden feet; painted needle-sculpted, facial features; authentically dressed in perfect miniature felt costumes, representing various professions and stations in life; value is dependent upon visual appeal and condition.

12" ....**$400-$600**

Composition

Prices listed are for appropriately costumed dolls in good condition.

Baby/Puz: composition head and limbs; cloth or composition body; molded and painted hair; flirty or sleep glass eyes; open mouth; typically marked "K ★ R 929", "926," or unmarked except for hangtag "K ★ R PUZ Germany."

28"-24" .... **$950-$1,050**

15" Kämmer & Reinhardt composition Puz, **$700.**

Courtesy of Sandra Haroldson, Sandra Lee Products, www.sandralee.com

Bisque

Prices listed are for appropriately costumed dolls in good condition.

Closed Mouth Child*: bisque socket head; jointed wood-and-composition body; good wig; glass eyes; feathered brows; pierced ears; closed mouth; typically marked "K & R 191," "K & R 192," "192G," or "191G."

6"-8"	$900-$1,000
9"	$2,200
14"-18"	$3,400-$3,800
22"-24"	$4,200-$4,500

Add $200 for flirty eyes; $300 for flapper or walker body; $300 for black version.

Lovely 24" Kämmer & Reinhardt/Simon & Halbig child with peaches and cream bisque and beautiful brown eyes, **$1,600.**

From the collection of Sommer Ann Czossek.

Dolly Face Socket-Head*: bisque socket head; jointed wood-and-composition body; good wig; glass eyes; feathered brows; pierced ears; open mouth; typically marked "K ★ R Simon & Halbig 403," "Halbig/ K ★ R," "K ★ R 191," "192," "290," or "402."

5"	$750
8"	$1,100
12"-14"	$950-$1,000
18"-22"	$1,175-$1,500
28"-30"	$1,800-$2,200
34"-36"	$2,900-$3,400
40"-42"	$4,500-$4,900

Open Mouth 192:

14"-18"	$1,150-$1,500
22"	$1,800
22"-28"	$2,100-$2,800

Deduct $300 for five-piece body with painted shoes.

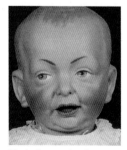

Nicely decorated and presented, unusually large 24" #100 painted eye Kaiser Baby, **$1,800.**

Courtesy of McMasters-Harris Auction

Kämmer & Reinhardt 20" #101 Peter with closed mouth and painted eyes, **$6,900.**
Courtesy of David Cobb Auction

Rare 12" #102 Walter, **$32,000.**
Courtesy of Sotheby's Auctions

Dolly Face Shoulder Head: bisque shoulder head; kid body; bisque arms; good wig; glass eyes; open mouth; typically marked "SH/ K ★ R." or "377 K ★ R."

16"-18"	**$650-$800**
20"-24"	$900-$1,050

Characters*: bisque socket or shoulder head; kid, composition, jointed or bent-limb baby body; molded and painted hair or good wig; sleep or painted eyes; closed or open/closed mouth; typically marked "K ★ R" and a mold number.

*Add $300 to any 7"-12" in character with jointed "chubby toddler" body with starfish hands.

For Kämmer & Reinhardt characters, 13"-15" dolls were used as a comparison base, but please remember the dolls actually came in a wide range of sizes from at least 8"-40", and you should use your good judgment and common sense to interpose the value of additional sizes:

100 O/CM, glass eyes, Kaiser Baby:
  13"-15" .... **$2,000-$2,500**
100 O/CM, painted eyes, Kaiser Baby:
  13"-15" .... $900-$1,200
101 CM, painted eyes, Peter or Marie:
  13"-15" .... **$4,600-$5,500**
101 C/M, glass eyes, Peter or Marie:
  13"-15" ....**$17,000-$23,000**
102 CM, painted eyes, Walter or Elsa:
  13"-15" ....**$36,000-$46,000**
103 CM, painted eyes:
  13"-15" ....**$100,000-$115,000**
104 CM, painted eyes, laughing:
  13"-15" ....**$110,000-$125,000**

Kämmer & Reinhardt character children: 20" glass eyes, #101 Peter, **$20,000**; 20" glass eyes, #101 Marie, **$20,000**; and 16" painted eyes, #114 Hans, **$6,500.**
Courtesy of David Cobb Auction

Fine group of Kämmer & Reinhardt character babies: 15" #100, **$1,200**; 22" #116A, **$5,700**; 20" #121 with flirty eyes, **$2,100**; 20" #122, **$2,000**; 18" #127, **$2,900**; and 20" #128, **$2,100.**
Courtesy of David Cobb Auction

105 O/CM, painted eyes:
13"-15" ....$150,000-$180,000
106 CM, painted eyes:
13"-15" ....$135,00-$150,000
107 CM, painted eyes, Carl:
13"-15" ....$50,000-$65,000
108 CM, painted eyes:
25" $290,000
109 CM, painted eyes, Elisa:
13"-15" ....$14,000-$18,000
109 CM, glass eyes:
13"-15" ....$22,000-$25,000
112 or 112X O/CM, painted eyes:
13"-15" ....$20,000-$24,000
112A O/CM, glass eyes:
13"-15" ....$22,000-$25,000
114 CM, painted eyes, Gretchen or Hans:
13"-15" .... $5,500-$6,000
114 CM, glass eyes, Gretchen or Hans:
13"-15" ....$12,500-$15,000
115 CM, glass eyes, solid dome:
13"-15" .... $7,000-$7,700
115A CM, glass eyes:
13"-15" .... $5,200-$5,500
116 O/CM, glass eyes:
13"-15" .... $5,800-$6,200
116A O/CM, glass eyes:
13"-15" .... $3,700-$4,000
117 or 117A CM, glass eyes, Mein Liebling:
13"-15" .... $5,000-$5,900
20"-23" .... $6,900-$7,700
117 OM, glass eyes, (no "N" in marking):
13"-15" .... $2,500-$2,800
20"-23" .... $4,300-$4,750
117N OM, glass eyes, Mein Neuer Liebling:
13"-15" .... $1,600-$1,900
118 or 118A OM, glass eyes:
13"-15" .... $2,700-$3,000
119 O/CM, glass eyes:
13"-15" ....$13,500-$15,000
121 OM, glass eyes:
13"-15" .... $1,250-$1,350
122 OM, glass eyes:
13"-15" .... $1,400-$1,500
123 or 124 CM, glass eyes, laughing Max or Moritz:
17" $32,000
126 or 22 OM, glass eyes:
13"-15" ....$750-$900
127 or 135 OM, glass eyes:
13"-15" .... $2,200-$2,400

Extremely rare Kammer & Reinhardt 21" #107 with closed pouty mouth and painted eyes, **$67,000**.
Courtesy of David Cobb Auction

Perfectly charming Kämmer & Reinhardt 14" painted eyes, #109 character toddler, **$16,000**.
Courtesy of James Julia Auctions, Inc.

Wonderful Kammer & Reinhardt 13" #114 Hans, **$5,000**, and 11" #114 Gretchen, **$4,000**.
Courtesy of David Cobb Auction

Kämmer & Reinhardt character babies—26" #127, **$3,900**, and 15" #122, **$1,500**—with an early mohair dog.

Kammer & Reinhardt 16" #126 bisque character, **$950**, and 21" #920 composition character, **$750**.

Courtesy of David Cobb Auction

Mischievous Kämmer & Reinhardt 17" #124 Moritz and #123 Max character toddlers with replaced bodies. Max and Moritz must have appropriate body with molded and painted shoes with slightly turned-up toes to command a value of **$60,000-$70,000.**

Courtesy of James Julia Auctions, Inc.

128 OM, glass eyes:
  13"-15" .... **$1,700-$1,900**
171 or 172 O/CM, glass eyes, infant:
  13"-15" .... **$3,800-$4,200**
173 or 175 Cloth body infant:
  13"-15" .... **$1,800-$2,000**
175 Painted bisque, glass eyes:
  13"-15" .... **$1,600-$1,750**
200 OM, painted eyes, shoulder head:
  13"-15" ....**$800-$900**
201 CM, painted eyes, shoulder head:
  13"-15" .... **$2,300-$2,500**
214 Painted eyes, shoulder head:
  13"-15" .... **$3,700-$3,800**

Add $500 for jointed toddler body; $300 for black version; $200 for flirty eyes to any character.
O/CM = Open/Closed Mouth
OM = Open Mouth
CM = Closed Mouth

Kenner Parker Toys, Inc.

In 1985, Kenner became an independent company with two divisions, Parker Brothers and Kenner products. Kenner, once a subsidiary of General Mills, produced many dolls as well as popular figures.

Prices listed are for dolls in near mint, original condition.

Dolls

Boy Scout Bob (white), Steve (black): 9"; vinyl and plastic; molded and painted hair; painted eyes; closed, smiling mouth; typically marked "1974 G.M.F.G./Kenner Prod/Cinti. Ohio/NO 7000/Made in Hong Kong." **$200**
Blythe: 12"; oversized, hard plastic head; tiny, fully jointed body; rooted hair; eyes change color as ring is pulled; green, blue, brown, purple (some Blythe dolls have amber in place of purple); closed mouth; original "mod"-type dress and high plastic boots; typically marked "Blythe TM/Kenner Products/Cincinnati, Ohio/1972 General Mills/Fun Group Inc./Patents Pending/Made in Hong Kong." **$2,800**
There has been an irrational demand and escalation in the value assigned to Blythe. In the last few years Blythe has gone from $175 for a mint doll to $2,800!
Baby Alive: 16"; all jointed vinyl; rooted hair; painted eyes; open, feeding mouth; with food, bottle, dish, and spoon, which activates chewing motion; doll smacks her lips after spoon or bottle is removed; bubbles and fills her diaper like a real baby; requires two batteries; typically marked "1973 G.M.F.G. Inc./KENNER PRODUCTS DIV/Cinti,O/Made in Hong Kong." **$185**
Gabbigale: 18"; vinyl head; jointed, plastic body; rooted, blond hair; painted blue eyes; open/closed, smiling mouth; pull string battery operated recorder to repeat; typically marked "1972 Kenner Products Co/99" on head and "Gabbi-

This well-loved Blythe doll with worn clothing and discolored legs is having a really bad hair day. Nevertheless, Blythe is so much in demand that even in this condition, expect a value of **$500.**

gale/1972 Kenner Products/General Mills Fun Group Inc./Patents Pending." ... **$160**
Baby Won't Let Go: 17"; vinyl head; vinyl and hard plastic body; hand grips; rooted hair; painted eyes; open/closed mouth; typically marked "4046 Taiwan K002 GMFGI 1977 93//1977 Kenner Prod. Div. Cin't/Ohio 45202 26150," "45202/28100," or "26150//1977/96." **$125**
Stretch Armstrong: 13"; all heavy, stretch vinyl; jointed at neck; will stretch to over four feet and return to original shape; molded and painted hair and

expressive facial features; typically un-marked. **$225**

Shawn Cassidy: 12"; all solid jointed vinyl; realistic characterization; typically marked "1978 USCI//GMFGI 1978 Kenner Prod./Cincinnati Ohio 45202//Made in Hong Kong." **$125**

Parker Stevenson: 12"; all solid jointed vinyl; typically marked "GMFGI 1978 Kenner Prod./CINCINNATI Ohio 45202//Made in Hong Kong." **$115**

International Velvet: 11-1/2"; vinyl head; plastic jointed body; rooted, long hair; painted eyes; open/closed, wide, smiling mouth; typically marked "43/Hong Kong/1976 USCI//1978 GMFGI Kenner Prod./Cincinnati Ohio 45202/Made in Hong Kong//Metro-Goldwyn-Mayer." **$125**

Cover Girl Darci: 12-1/2"; all poseable vinyl; rooted hair; painted features; typically marked "140 Hong Kong/GMFGI 1978." **$135**

Cover Girl Erica: 12-1/4"; typically marked "CRG PRODUCTS CORP./1978 Kenner Cincinnati 47400 Made In Hong Kong." **$250**

Black Cover Girl Dana: 12-1/2"; typically marked "56 Hong Kong/GMFGI 1978." **$175**

Dusty: 11-1/2"; all vinyl; spring-loaded arms and body; plays golf or tennis; rooted platinum "shag-style" hair; painted eyes; freckles; open/closed, smiling mouth with molded upper teeth; typically marked "Kenner" "GMFGI/1974." ... **$175**

Figures

Most Star Wars figures were reissued during the 1990s. Prices given are for original 1970s figures in mint condition.

Star Wars: large size; typically marked "GMFGI 1978" and "GMFGI 1978 Kenner Prod/Cincinnati, Ohio 45202/Made in Hong Kong," "GMIFGI 1974//1974 GMGI KENNER PROD. 33, 862, 512."

    13" Boba Fett **$375**
    12" C3PO **$185**
    15" Chewbacca **$220**
    15" Darth Vader........................ **$250**

    12" Han Solo **$650**
    15" IG 88 .... **$875**
    8 -1/2" Jawa **$175**
    11-1/2" Leia **$350**
    13" Suke Skywalker **$375**
    12" Obi Wan Kenobi **$225**
    7-1/2" R2D2............................. **$225**
    12" Stormtrooper **$300**
    9" Yoda **$175**
    3" small figures .... **$75-$200**

Strawberry Shortcake Collection: vinyl head; rigid vinyl or hard plastic body; bendable limbs; rooted hair; originally had fragrance of "fruit-character-name" (Lemon, Grape, Strawberry, Green Apple, etc.); painted features; typically marked "AMERICAN GREETING CORP. 1982//AGC/1982."

    15" Sour Grapes, Purple
    Pieman...............................**$300-$350**
    5" Strawberry Shortcake and other
    characters ....**$175-$200**

Allow extra for Peash Blush or Plum Pudding.

Lovely Kenner 18" vinyl Lauren teen doll in mint condition with original box, **$125**.
Photograph courtesy of Julia Burke, www.juliaburke.com

J. D. Kestner

Johann Danie Kestner, the charismatic founder of the Kestner empire, opened the Kestner factory in 1816. By 1820, Kestner was manufacturing a complete line of toys and dolls made from both wood and papier-mâché. Kestner dolls, as we think of them today, were introduced following Kestner's acquisition of the Ohrdug porcelain factory in 1860.

Kestner 24" Bru-type closed mouth with molded teeth, **$17,000.**
Courtesy of McMaster-Harris Auction

Kestner 19" closed mouth XII, **$7,000.**
Courtesy of David Cobb Auction

Prices listed are for appropriately costumed dolls in good condition.

Closed Mouth, Turn Shoulder Head: bisque shoulder head, slightly turned; kid body; bisque forearms; plaster dome; good wig; glass eyes; long eyelashes; heavy brows; closed mouth, with slightly parted lips; typically marked "Germany," letter, or size number only.

10"-14"	**$900-$1,200**
18"-22"	**$1,500-$1,800**
24"-26"	**$2,000-$2,200**

Closed Mouth, Socket Head: bisque socket head; wood-and-composition jointed body; straight wrists; plaster dome; good wig; glass eyes; closed mouth; typically marked "103," "111," "128," "169," or no mold number but a letter or size number only.

8"	**$2,900**
12"-16"	**$2,500-$2,900**
18"-20"	**$3,250-$3,500**
24"-26"	**$4,200-$4,900**
32"	**$5,500**

Closed, Pouty Mouth: bisque socket head; wood-and-composition jointed body; straight wrists; plaster dome; good wig; glass eyes; heavy, feathered brows; closed, pouty mouth; typically marked "X," "XI," "XII," "103," or no mold number but a letter or size number.

10"-14"	**$3,500-$4,000**
18"-20"	**$4,500-$5,000**
24"	**$5,400**
28"	**$6,700**
X: 15"	**$4,500**
XI: 16"	**$5,700**
XII: 17"-19"	**$5,800-$7,000**

Closed Mouth, French-Look*: bisque socket head; jointed body, may have additional ankle joints or kid body with matched bisque shoulder plate; plaster dome;

7" all bisque Kestner 150, **$475.**

Photo courtesy of James D. Julia Inc.

Closed mouth Kestner sisters, a 15" XII with slightly parted lips and a hint of a molded tongue, **$5,400,** and a 12" little sister marked "7," **$3,400.**

Courtesy of David Cobb Auction

good wig; large, oval or almond-shaped glass eyes; long lashes; finely feathered brows; closed mouth; full, slightly parted lips with a hint of a molded tongue or teeth; typically marked with letter or size number only.

16"-18"	**$10,000-$12,000+**
20"	**$15,000+**
28"	**$25,000+**

Deduct $1,000 for kid body.

A.T. Type: finest bisque socket head; straight wrist jointed composition body; glass eyes finely lined in black; multi-stroke feathered, somewhat heavy brows; accent nostril and eye corners; closed mouth with deeper hued defined space between slightly parted lips; typically marked with size number only (#7-12", #15-23").

12"	**$9,800**
16"	**$11,800**

Kestner 26" #171 child, **$1,600**, and 24" #257 character baby, **$2,700**, with a 1900s Comical Animal Five Pins game by Parker Brothers.
Courtesy of David Cobb Auction

Kestner 26" #171, **$1,600**.
From the collection of Barbara Szwajkowski.

Beautiful 26" Kestner #164 child, **$1,600**.
From the collection of Debbie Recksiek.

Open Mouth, Carved Square-Teeth: bisque socket or shoulder head and forearms; kid or wood and composition body; plaster dome; good wig; glass eyes; feathered brows; open mouth with carved square-teeth (cut or carved into the lip–not separate teeth); typically marked "Made in Germany" and/or letter or size number only.

Shoulder head:

12"-14"	$1,450-$1,650
20"-22"	$2,100-$2,200
24"	$2,500

Socket head:

18"	$2,300
22"	$2,500

Open Mouth, Turned Head: bisque, slightly turned shoulder head and forearms; kid body; plaster dome; good wig; glass eyes; featured brows; open mouth with teeth; typically marked "Made in Germany" and/or letter or size number.

12"-16"	$650-$850
18"	$950
20"-22"	$1,000-$1,100

Tiny Doll*: bisque socket head; five-piece composition or papier-mâché body; molded and painted shoes; plaster dome; good wig; glass eyes; open mouth with tiny teeth; typically marked "155," "170," or "133."

7"-8"	$1,100-$1,200

*Add $300 for fully jointed body.

Dolly Face*: bisque socket head; jointed wood-and-composition body; plaster dome; good wig; glass eyes;

Kestner 33" #196, rare large size dolly face girl with fur brows, **$2,500**.
Courtesy of David Cobb Auction

Irresistible Kestner 24" flirty-eye #260 character on jointed toddler body, **$3,200.**

From the collection of Sandra Czossek

31" Kestner #211 character boy and 32" #260 character girl. Although both dolls have been redressed and have replaced human hair wigs, they are nevertheless appropriate and charming, **$3,500** and **$3,600,** respectively.

Courtesy of David Cobb Auction

23" Kestner #211 character baby and a 16" #226 character baby, **$1,450.**

Courtesy of David Cobb Auction

feathered brows; open mouth with teeth; typically marked "Made in Germany"/"141," "142," "144," "146," "164," "167," "168," "171," or "196."

10"	**$850**
12"-18"	**$1,050-$1,250**
24"-28"	**$1,500-$1,750**
32"	**$3,200**
40"-42"	**$4,500-$4,900**

*Add $500 to 18" mold 171 with blond mohair wig, known as Daisy.

Unique Dolly Face: bisque socket head; unique, almost character face; jointed wood-and-composition body; plaster dome; good wig; glass eyes; feathered or fur brows; open mouth; chubby cheeks; typically marked "Made in Germany JDK/," "128," "129," "149," "152," "160," "161," "173," "174," "214," "215," "249."

10"	**$950**
12"-16"	**$1,450-$1,650**
22"-26"	**$1,800-$2,000**
28"-32"	**$2,200-$2,700**
36"	**$3,600**
40"-42"	**$4,900-$5,400**

Dolly Face Shoulder Head: bisque shoulder head and forearms; kid body; plaster dome; good wig; glass eyes; feathered or fur brows; open mouth; typically marked "Made in Germany"/"145," "147," "148," "154," "159," "166," or "195."

10"-14"	**$450-$550**
18"-24"	**$700-$1,100**
28"-30"	**$1,250-$1,500**
36"	**$2,300**

Solid Dome Character Baby*: (often called Baby Jean, Sally, or Sammy) bisque socket head; fat-cheeked face; composition bent-limb baby body; painted hair; glass eyes; feathered brows; open or open/closed mouth; typically marked "J.D.K." size number only.

12"-14"	**$1,500-$1,600**
18"-20"	**$2,000-$2,200**
24"	**$2,700**

*Add $500 for jointed toddler body or $600 for black version.

Character Baby Shoulder Head: bisque shoulder head; rivet-jointed, kid body; composition limbs; solid dome; glass eyes; open/closed mouth; typically marked "Made in Germany/J.D.K./" "210," "234," "235," or "238."

12"-14"	**$1,200-$1,500**
18"	**$1,900**
22"	**$2,500**

Character Baby Socket Head: bisque socket head; composition, bent-limb baby body; plaster dome; good wig; glass eyes; winged, feathered brows; open mouth

This lovely, ever-popular 18" Kestner #245 Hilda is in wonderful, pristine condition with original box, which adds to her value of **$9,000.**
Courtesy of David Cobb Auction

with teeth; appropriately dressed; typically marked "Made in Germany J.D.K./" "211," "226," "236," "262," "257," "260," or "263."

10"	$850
12"-16"	$1,000-$1,450
18"-20"	$1,600-$1,700
24"	$2,700

Hilda Character Baby*: bisque socket head; composition, bent-limb baby body; molded and painted hair or good wig; glass eyes; open mouth with two upper teeth; typically marked "J.D.K./ ges.gesch K 14 1070/Made in Germany," "237," "245," and possibly "Hilda."

12"-16"	$3,700-$4,600
18"	$5,000
20"-24"	$5,300-$6,700
26"	$7,500
28"-30"	$8,700-$9,500

*Add $500 for jointed toddler body or $600 for black version.

Cunning Character*: exceptional character face; bisque socket head; composition, jointed, or bent limb baby body;

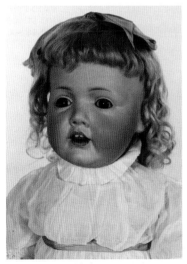

24" Kestner #245 Hilda, **$6,700.**
Courtesy of David Cobb Auction

Kestner 24" closed mouth pouty child marked "K/14" on a jointed Kestner body, **$4,200.**
Courtesy of David Cobb Auction

Kestner 10" Siegfried #272 character baby, **$1,800.**
Courtesy of David Cobb Auction

18" gorgeous Kestner #172 Gibson Girl, **$4,200.**
Courtesy of David Cobb Auction

molded hair or good wig; glass eyes; open mouth with teeth, appears to have a slight overbite or molded tongue; typically marked "Made in Germany/J.D.K.," "247," "JDK," or "267."

10"-12"	**$1,500-$1,800**
14"	**$2,300**
18"	**$3,200**

Add $500 for jointed toddler body or $600 for black version.

Flange Neck Character Baby: bisque character face; cloth body; solid dome; painted hair; glass eyes; typically marked "255/O.I.C." or "Siegfried 272."

10"-14"	**$1,800-$2,400**
16"	**$2,700**

Lady Character Face: bisque socket head; composition woman's body; cinched waist; molded bosom; good wig; glass eyes; open mouth; typically marked "162."

10"-12"	**$1,600-$1,800**
16"-18"	**$2,500-$2,900**
20"	**$3,200**

Gibson Girl: bisque shoulder head and forearms; kid body; good wig in Gibson style; glass eyes; closed mouth; regal bearing and upward-glancing eyes; typically marked "172."

10"-12"	**$1,500-$1,800**
16"	**$3,100**
22"	**$4,800**

Character Child: bisque socket head; memorable character modeling; jointed wood-and-composition body; good wig; glass or painted eyes; typically marked with size number and/or mold number.

For characters, the 18" doll was used as a comparison base, but please remember the dolls actually came in a wide range of sizes, from 8" up to 42" or more, and you should use your good judgment and common sense to interpose the value of additional sizes.

JDK O/CM; glass eyes; expressive:

18"	**$8,700**

143 OM; glass eyes; pug nose:

18"	**$2,300**

178 O/C mouth; painted eyes; overbite:

18" $6,500

178 O/CM; glass eyes; overbite:

18" $7,500

179 O/CM; painted eyes; tongue:

18" $7,200

179 O/CM; glass eyes; tongue:

18" $7,600

180 O/CM; painted eyes; teeth:

18" $6,400

181 O/CM; painted eyes; teeth:

18" $6,950

182 CM; painted eyes:

18" $7,200

183 O/CM; glass eyes; smiling:

18" $6,500

184 CM; glass eyes; flyaway brows:

18" $7,000

185 O/CM; painted eyes; fully molded teeth:

18" $7,200

186 O/CM; grinning; upper and lower teeth:

18" $7,600

187 CM; painted eyes; slight grin:

18" $7,300

189 CM; glass eyes; pensive:

18" $6,900

190 O/CM; painted eyes; hint of a tongue:

18" $6,400

190 O/CM; glass eyes; hint of a tongue:

18" $7,500

203 CM; glass eyes; molded tongue:

18" $6,300

206 CM; tiny glass eyes; chin dimple:

18" $29,000

208 CM; painted eyes; character:

18" $28,000

212 CM; small glass eyes; pouty:

18" 12,000

220 OM; glass eyes; broad smile:

18" $9,200

239 OM; glass eyes; double chin:

18" $7,900

241 OM; glass eyes; overbite:

18" $8,200

O/CM = Open/Closed Mouth

OM = Open Mouth

CM = Closed Mouth

Boxed Set Interchangeable Character Heads: 15"; four bisque socket heads; jointed composition and wood body..**$15,000**

11-1/2" Kestner #185 character, **$5,700.**
Courtesy of David Cobb Auction

Kestner 26" #143 charming, open mouth child on a marked Kestner body, **$2,800.**
Courtesy of David Cobb Auction

Kestner 15" boxed character set, including a painted eye #178 on doll, painted eye #186, painted eye #190, and a glass eye #174, **$15,000,** holding an early Kestner socket head on an early papier-mâché body.
Courtesy of Bertoia Auctions

Kewpies

Kewpies, those sweet, little elfin-like creatures, made their debut in the December 1909 issue of Ladies Home Journal. Famous illustrator Rose O'Neill designed the Kewpies and held the design patents for them until her death in 1944.

George Borgfeldt held the manufacturing rights for many years, eventually passing them to Joseph Kallus, who retained them until 1984, when Jesco took possession of the rights to the Kewpie trademark and copyright. It is reported that at the peak of the Kewpie craze, 30 German factories were producing bisque Kewpies in order to meet demand. The Cameo Doll Company of Port Allegheny, Pennsylvania manufactured composition plastic and vinyl Kewpies.

12" Cameo composition Kewpie with original box. In mint condition with original box and hangtag, expect a value of **$1,000.**
Courtesy of McMasters-Harris Auction

10" rare large-size all bisque Kewpie couple in their original crepe paper costumes, **$2,000.**

Courtesy of McMasters-Harris Auction

13" Kestner bisque head Kewpie on a jointed composition body, **$7,000.**

Courtesy of McMasters-Harris Auction

Krueger 18" cloth Kewpie, **$700.**

Courtesy of McMasters-Harris Auction

Prices listed are for dolls and figurines in good condition.

Dolls

All Bisque: jointed at shoulder only; typically signed "O'Neill" on sole of foot; may also have German manufacturer marking.

2"-4"	$225-$275
6"-7"	$475-$575
8"-9"	$725-$875
12"	$1,750

Bisque Head: composition jointed body; starfish hands; long torso with rounded tummy; wings on sides of neck; typically marked "Ges.gesch/O'Neill J.D.K."

10"-12"	$6,100-$6,900
14"	$7,900
20"	$18,000

Bisque Head: flange neck; cloth body; painted or glass eyes; typically marked "A.B. & G 1377/O'Neill."

Painted eye:

12"	$2,600

Glass eye:

	$3,500

Celluloid: jointed arms; typically marked "JUNO," paper label "Germany," or unmarked.

2"-4"	$75-$125
8"	$275
10"-12"	$400-$450
15"	$600

Composition: jointed at shoulder and occasionally the hip; starfish hands; blue-tipped wings on back; typically marked with red, heart-shaped paper label "Kewpie/Des & Copyright/by/Rose O'Neill."

8"	$375
12"	$650

Composition Head: flange neck; cloth body; composition starfish hands; typically marked "O'Neill," "Cameo," or unmarked.

12"	$400

Cloth Kuddle Kewpies: all cloth; satin or plush body; mask-type Kewpie face; typically marked with cloth label "Krueger" or "King Pat. number 1785800."

10"-12"	$375-$450
18"-20"	$700-$800

Hard Plastic Kewpies: all plastic; jointed at shoulder only; painted features; typically marked "Cameo."

8"-10"	$250-$275
12"	$325
16"	$500

Hard Plastic Kewpies: fully jointed at neck, shoulder, and hip; sleep eyes; typically marked "Cameo."

12"-16"	$650-$750

Vinyl Jesco: made using Cameo's original molds; molded and painted top-knot hair; side-glancing eyes; original clothing; typically marked "Jesco."

9"	**$80**
14"-18"	**$200-$250**
22"-24"	**$300-$325**
27"	**$400**

Vinyl Pin-Hinged Limbs: painted features; original, one-piece pajama outfit; typically marked "Cameo" on head and body, and "S1/61C2/63" on doll's bottom.

16"-18"	**$350-$450**

Vinyl Ragsy Kewpie: blue vinyl; molded to resemble stitching; painted features; typically marked "Cameo 65 JLK" on head and "Cameo 6S" on back.

8"	**$100**
10"	**$150**

Red Plush Kewpie: plush body; vinyl face; painted features; typically marked with cloth label "Knickerbocker Toy Co. Inc./N.Y. U.S.A./Kewpie/Designed and Copyrighted/by Rose O'Neill/Licensed by Cameo Doll Co. 1964."

6"-12"	**$75-$100**

Bisque Action Kewpie Figurines: Typically marked with a paper label; incised "O'Neill" on the bottom of the foot, "©," or unmarked.

Blunderboo*: 4"	**$900**
Bride and Groom: 4"	**$950**
Driving a Chariot or Riding an Animal: 5"	**$6,000**
Farmer: 4"	**$1,250**
Fireman: 4"	**$1,400**
Gardener: 4"	**$1,250**
Governor: 4"	**$1,500**
Guitar Player: 3-1/2"	**$700**
Holding Cat: 4"	**$800**
Holding Pen: 3"	**$650**
Hottentot (Black Kewpie): 3-1/2"	**$650**
Hottentot (Black Kewpie): 5"	**$1,000**
In a Basket with Flowers: 4"	**$1,750**
In a Drawstring Bag or Egg: 4-1/2"	**$3,500**
Kewpie Doodle Dog: 1-1/2"	**$1,500**
Kewpie Doodle Dog: 3"	**$3,000**
On Bench with Doodle Dog: 4"	**$5,200**
On Stomach: 3-1/2"	**$700**
Reading a Book: 3-1/2"	**$1,250**
Sitting in High Back Chair: 4"	**$900**
Soldier: 4-1/2"	**$1,500**
Buttonhole Kewpies: 1-3/4"	**$250**
Soldier and Nurse: 6"	**$8,600**
Thinker: 6"	**$800**
Traveler with Suitcase: 3-1/2"	**$600**
Two Kewpies Hugging: 3-1/2"	**$500**
Two Kewpies Reading Book: 5-1/2"	**$2,600**
Wearing Helmet: 6"	**$1,500**
With Broom or Mop: 4"	**$900**
With Butterfly: 4"	**$1,250**
With Dog Doodle: 3-1/2"	**$2,000**

With Ink Well: 3-1/2" $900
With Ladybug: 4" $750
With Outhouse: 3" $1,700
With Pumpkin: 4" $800
With Rabbit: 2-1/2" $750
With Rose: 2" $600
With Tea Table: 4" $3,600
With Teddy Bear: 4" $1,200
With Turkey: 2" $800
With Umbrella: 3-1/2" $800
With Umbrella and Doodle Dog: 3-1/2" $1,500
In a Bisque Swing: 3" $4,500
Kewpie Mountain or Tree (25 or more figures): $28,000
*Tumbling

Rare Kewpie Mountain, **$28,000.**
Photo courtesy of Christie's of London.

Kley & Hahn

Albert Kley and Paul Hahn began business in Ohrdruf, Thüringia, Germany in 1902, with just 15 employees.

Mold numbers indicate that several porcelain factories contributed to the Kley & Hahn inventory. Molds in the 200 series and 680 series and the Walküre dolls were made by J. D. Kestner; the 100 series by Hertel, Schwab & Company; and the 500 series by Bahr & Pröschild.

Large and lovely 32" Kley & Hahn Walküre, **$1,700.**
Courtesy of Susan Miller

Prices listed are for appropriately costumed dolls in good condition.

Dolly Face: bisque socket head; jointed wood-and-composition body; good wig; glass eyes; feathered brows; open mouth; typically marked "Special 65 Germany," "Dollar Princess," "Majestie," or "Princess."

20"-22"	$600-$700
26"-28"	$900-$950

Walküre: bisque socket head; jointed wood-and-composition body; good wig; glass eyes; molded, feathered brows; open mouth; typically marked "Walküre Germany," "250," or "282."

16"-20"	$750-$850
24"-28"	$1,100-$1,400
34"-36"	$1,800-$2,000

Character Baby*: bisque head; composition, bent-limb baby body; solid dome with molded and painted hair or

28" Kley & Hahn Walküre, **$1,400.**
Courtesy of David Cobb Auction

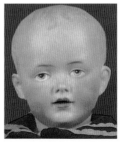

Kley & Hahn 14" #531 character toddler, **$850.**
Courtesy of McMasters-Harris Auction

Kley & Hahn 24" #680 flirty eye character on toddler body, which adds about **$500** to the total value of **$1,900.**
Courtesy of David Cobb Auction

good wig; painted or glass eyes; open or open/closed mouth; typically marked "Germany K & H" within a ribbon "133," "135," "138," "158," "160," "167," "176," "292," "525," "531," "571," "680," and possible others.

12"-16"	$800-$900
20"-24"	$1,000-$1,400
26"-28"	$1,700-$1,900
42"	$4,700

(known as Giant Baby with 27" head circumference and 32" waist)

Add $500 for jointed toddler body.

Character Child*: bisque socket head; jointed, composition body; molded and painted hair or good wig; painted or glass eyes; typically marked with mold number.

154 or 166 CM, glass eyes:

16"	$3,100
20"	$4,000

OM, glass eyes:

16"	$1,900
24"	$2,500

159 or 567 Multiface, glass or painted eyes:

12"	$2,300
16"	$2,700

162 or 554 Crying expression:

18"	$2,900
25"	$4,000

169 CM, glass eyes:

14"	$2,900
18"	$3,900

OM, glass eyes:

22"	$2,000

520 or 526 CM, painted eyes:

14"	$5,700
18"	$6,400
22"	$7,300

536 or 546 CM, glass eyes:

18"	$7,500

536 or 546 CM, painted eyes:

18"	$7,200

547 CM, glass eyes:

18"	$7,400

549 CM, painted eyes:

14"	$5,400
22"	$7,800

568 O/CM, glass eyes:

22"	$2,900

Add $500 for jointed toddler body.
O/CM = Open/Closed Mouth
OM = Open Mouth
CM = Closed Mouth

Kley & Hahn character babies: 12" #169, 13" #554, and 10" #535, **$1,200**, **$2,000**, and **$1,200**, respectively.
Courtesy of David Cobb Auction

Kley & Hahn 16" closed mouth #536 character with intaglio eyes, **$6,900**, and 17" Kestner #143 open mouth child, **$2,200**.
Courtesy of David Cobb Auction

Knickerbocker Doll & Toy Company

The Knickerbocker Doll & Toy Company was established in New York City in 1925. Disney characters were among its premium products.

In 2000, Knickerbocker was acquired by celebrity Marie Osmond, a familiar and well-loved leader in the collectible doll market.

Cloth Dolls

Prices listed are for appropriately costumed dolls with good color.

Dwarf: pressed mask face; velveteen body; clothing body structure; cardboard in bottom of feet; cotton gauntlet hands; mohair wig and beard; painted, expressive face; slightly pointed, velveteen feet curved upwards; cap with name in all capital letters, some on a slant; typically marked with wrist tag only, "Walt Disney's/Snow White and/The Seven Dwarves//America's/Premier Line of Stuffed Toys/Walt Disney's/Mickey Mouse/and/Donald Duck/Manufacturers/Knickerbocker Toy Co. Inc./New York City."

14" **$400**

Disney Characters: all cloth; typically marked on foot "Walt Disney's (character name) Knickerbocker Toy Co./Design Patent No. 82862"; hangtag "(Character Name) Mfg. Knickerbocker."

Mickey Mouse:
13" .... **$2,000-$2,200**
Mickey Mouse in cowboy outfit complete with guns, lasso, and hat.......... **$4,000**
Pinocchio or Minnie Mouse:
13" .... **$1,000-$1,100**
Donald Duck or Jiminy Cricket:
13" .... **$900-$1,000**

All characters are comparable in quality. Value is based on the popularity of the character.

Katzenjammer Kids: (Hans, Mama, Captain, or Inspector): all cloth; applied and painted hair; glass bug-eyes; bulbous, stuffed nose; painted facial features; closed mouth; typically marked with wrist tag only "Katzenjammer/Kids/Fritz/Knickerbocker/Toy Co. Inc./New York Toy Co. Inc./New York/Licensed by King Features Syndicate Inc."

13" **$700**
14"-16" .... **$900-$1,000**

Holly Hobbie: all cloth; yellow yarn hair; printed facial features; typically marked with tag sewn into dress "Holly Hobbie/Knickerbocker Toy Co. Inc"; tags may vary.

10" **$75**
16"-24" .... **$100-$145**

Knickerbocker 11" composition Snow White and 9" composition Seven Dwarfs. An entire set in this condition has a value of **$3,500-$3,800.**

Courtesy of Alderfer Auction Company

Composition

Prices listed are for appropriately costumed dolls in good condition.

Dwarf: all jointed composition; painted or mohair hair, beard; painted eyes and expressive facial features; name on cap in all capital letters, some slanted; typically marked "Walt Disney Knickerbocker Toy Co."

9" **$400**

Snow White: all jointed composition; mohair wig or molded and painted black hair with molded and painted blue ribbon; painted side-glancing eyes; closed mouth; typically marked "Snow White Walt Disney//Knickerbocker Toy Co./New York" on body.

14" **$650**
20" **$900**

Girl: all jointed composition; mohair wig; sleep eyes; light gray eye shadow; open mouth; typically marked "Knickerbocker Toy Co./New York" on back.

15" **$600**

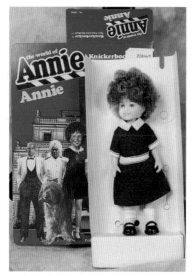

Knickerbocker 7" vinyl Annie character doll in mint condition with original box, **$90**.

Courtesy of Julia Burke, www.juliaburke.com

Character: all jointed composition; realistic character face and body modeling; painted facial features; typically marked "(character name) W. D. PR. KN. T. Co. USA," "Knickerbocker Toy," "Walt Disney//Knickerbocker," "(character name) King Syndicated/Knickerbocker," hangtag "Columbia Pictures Corp. Blondie with Baby Dumplin Dagwood and Daisy," "King Syndicate," and perhaps others.

13" Dagwood	**$1,400**
11" Blondie	**$2,000**
10" Alexander or Cookie	**$900**
10" Jiminy Cricket	**$900**
10" Donald Duck	**$1,500**
10" Pinocchio	**$1,200**
14" Pinocchio	**$1,900**

Vinyl

Prices listed are for dolls in near mint, original condition.

Annie: 7"; vinyl character head; plastic body; rooted hair; painted eyes; marked "1982 CPI Inc. 1982 CTNYNS, Inc/1982 Knickerbocker Toy Co. Inc. H-15." **$90**

Daddy Warbucks: 7"; vinyl character head; plastic body; solid dome; painted eyes; closed mouth; typically marked "1982 CPI Inc. 1982 CTNYNS Inc./1982 Knickerbocker Toy Co. Inc H-22." **$75**

Miss Hannigan: 7"; vinyl character head; plastic body; rooted hair; painted eyes; closed mouth; typically marked "1982 CPI Inc. 1982 CTNYNS Inc./1982 Knickerbocker Toy Co. Inc H-22." **$125**

Punjab: 7"; dark vinyl character head; dark plastic body; molded and painted hair and facial features; closed mouth; typically marked "1982 CPI Inc. 1982 CTNYNS Inc./1982 Knickerbocker Toy Co. Inc H-22." **$90**

Molly: 5-3/4"; vinyl character head; plastic body; rooted dark hair; painted eyes; open/closed, wide, smiling mouth; typically marked "1982 CPI Inc. 1982 CTNYNS Inc./1982 Knickerbocker Toy Co. Inc H-17." **$65**

Little House on the Prairie Child: vinyl head, hands, and legs; cloth body; rooted hair; painted eyes; smiling mouth; typically marked "1978 ED FRIENDLY PRODUCTIONS INC/LIC JLM/Made in Taiwan T-2" on back of head; dress tagged "Little House on the Prairie Made by Knickerbocker Toy Co." **$125**

Soupy Sales: vinyl head; cloth body; molded and painted hair; character face; painted eyes; heavy brows; closed mouth; non-removable clothes; typically marked "1965 Knickerbocker" on back of head, tagged "Soupy Sales/1966 Soupy Sales W.M.C." **$300**

Holly Hobbie: 10-1/2"; all jointed vinyl; rooted, long hair; round, freckled character face; painted features; closed mouth; typically marked "KTD/GAC/1974." ... **$85**

Käthe Kruse

Käthe Kruse dolls have been in production from 1910 to the present. The company was formerly located in Bad Kosen, Silesia, Charlottenburg, Prussia, and eventually Donauworth, Bavaria.

Artist Käthe Kruse founded the company and spent years developing a soft, lifelike cloth doll that could withstand a child's loving. Daughter Hannah took over the doll manufacturing business after her mother's death in 1968.

Käthe Kruse dolls were made of waterproof treated muslin, cotton, wool, and stockinette. The earliest dolls were marked in black, red, or purple ink on the bottom of the foot with the name "Käthe Kruse" and a three- to five-digit number.

Prices listed are for originally costumed dolls with no damage.

17" original later #I, signed Käthe Kruse child, **$4,800.**
Courtesy of James Julia Auctions, Inc.

I, Early 16" Wide hips	**$5,900**
I, Later 17" More slender hips	**$4,800**
I, 1H 17-1/2" Wigged	**$4,200**
I, Bambino 8-1/2" Special doll	**$2,800**
II 13" Schlenkerchen, smiling	**$12,500**
V 17-1/2 to 19-1/2" Du Mein, open eyes	**$8,100**
V 17-1/2 to 19-1/2" Traumerchen, closed eyes	**$7,800**
VI 21-1/2 to 23-1/2" Du Mein, open eyes	**$8,500**
VI 21-1/2 to 23-1/2" Traumerchen, closed eyes	**$8,200**
VII 14" Pensive or pouty, wide hips	**$3,100**
VIII 21" Deutsches Kind, swivel head, wig	**$3,700**
IX 14" Klein Deutsches Kind, swivel head, wig	**$2,350**
X 14" Swivel head, painted hair	**$2,700**
Celluloid 16" All celluloid	**$750**
US Zone/Germany 14" Very heavily painted	**$1,900**

Käthe Kruse 14" hard
plastic child, **$850.**
Courtesy of McMasters-Harris Auction

Hard Plastic 14" Human hair wig, pink muslin
body.. **$850**
Hard Plastic 20" Human hair wig, pink muslin
body.. **$1,100**
Contemporary 10" Däumlinchen, Doggi, stuffed
body.. **$500**
Contemporary 14" Rumpumpel baby and toddler,
stuffed body **$700**
Contemporary 14" All hard plastic................. **$350**
Manniken 40" to 60" Used in store display .. **$3,000**
Quality Käthe Kruse Look-A-Like or Type: (Heine &
Schneider) 18"; beautifully painted, pressed or mask
socket head; stuffed cloth body; neck, shoulder, hip
joints; mitt stitched or composition hands; typically
marked "Schneider Kunst Puppen Atelier Karl Schneider Bad-Kosen." **$2,300**

18" quality Käthe Kruse Look-
A-Like or Type by Heine &
Schneider, **$2,300.**
Courtesy of McMasters-Harris Auction

Gebrüder Kuhnlenz

The firm of Gebrüder Kuhnlenz was founded by brothers Julius, Cuno, and Bruno Kuhnlenz in 1884. The Porzellanfabric (porcelain factory) was located in Kronach, Bavaria. The bisque was quite pale; brows were heavy and close together; and dolls were frequently found with very good quality paperweight eyes, finely lined in black, with long lashes. The open-mouth dolls have square, unglazed teeth with lips more orange than red.

Prices listed are for appropriately costumed dolls in good condition.

Closed Mouth Shoulder Head: pale bisque shoulder head; kid, often ladytype body; bisque arms; good wig; glass or paperweight eyes; softly feathered brows; closed mouth; typically marked "G K 38."

14"16"	$1,300-$1,900
20"-22"	$2,700-$2,900
24"	$3,100

Closed Mouth Socket Head: pale bisque socket head, jointed wood-and-composition body or kid lined shoulder plate and kid body; good wig; glass or paperweight eyes; heavy feathered brows; closed mouth; typically marked "28," "31," "32," "50," or "51."

Socket head:

7-1/2"	$1,700
16"-18"	$2,900-$3,200
20"	$3,800

Swivel head/kid body:

14"	$1,500
20"	$2,900

French Look*: pale bisque socket head; jointed wood-and-composition body; good wig; glass or paperweight eyes; feathered brows; closed mouth; typically marked "34."

14"	$4,700
18"-20"	$6,200-$6,800
22"	$7,300

Add $500 for black version.

20" #51 closed mouth Kuhnlenz, **$3,800.**
Courtesy of James Julia Auctions, Inc.

Gebrüder Kuhnlenz 18" #41 open mouth with two upper square cut teeth, **$1,600.**

Courtesy of McMasters-Harris Auction

Unique Look: bisque socket head; jointed wood-and-composition body; good wig; glass or paperweight eyes, finely lined in black; long lashes; heavy brows; open mouth; typically marked "GK," "41," "44," "54," or "56."

16"-20" .... **$1,500-$1,700**
24"-28" .... **$2,000-$2,500**

Dolly Face Shoulder Head: bisque shoulder head and lower arms; kid body; good wig; glass eyes, finely lined in black; heavy brows; open mouth; typically marked "13," "47," or "61."

16"-18" ....**$800-$900**
22" **$1,100**

Dolly Face Socket Head: bisque socket head; jointed wood-and-composition body; good wig; glass eyes; feathered brows; open mouth; typically marked "G.K." or "165."

16"-20" ....**$550-$650**
28"-30" .... **$1,000-$1,200**
32"-34" .... **$1,400-$1,600**

Tiny Doll: bisque socket head; five-piece composition or papier-mâché body with molded and painted shoes; mohair wig; glass eyes; open mouth; typically marked "44" and a sunburst.

7-1/2" **$400**

16" #51 open mouth Kuhnlenz, **$1,500.**

From the collection of Carol Wagner of Forever Yours.

Lenci

In 1918, Elana Konig Scavini and her brother, Bubine Konig, made their first felt doll in the Scavini's apartment. Bubine steam-pressed the faces and Elana did the artistic work. This was the beginning of the world-famous Lenci doll.

The Lenci trademark was registered in 1919 as a child's spinning top with the words "Ludus Est Nobis Constanter Industria (taken from the Latin motto, freely translated to mean "To Play Is Our Constant Work"), forming the acronym "LENCI."

By the 1920s, the dolls produced by the Lenci factory had achieved worldwide recognition for their artistic beauty.

Left: Rare 16" Lenci Bambino in original condition, **$2,800.**
Courtesy of Christies of London

Lenci 19" hard face in original-labeled "Lenci/Made in Italy" dress, **$950.**

Courtesy of McMasters-Harris Auction

Prices listed are for originally costumed dolls with no damage.

Adult, Teenager, or Child: all jointed felt; pressed face; mohair wig; painted eyes; closed mouth; typically marked with hangtag, clothing label, and/or "Lenci" stamped on foot, or unmarked.

9"-12"	**$750-$1,100**
15"-18"	**$1,500-$1,700**
21"-26-1/2"	**$2,300-$2,750**
29"-35"	**$3,300-$3,900**
38"-40"	**$4,400-$4,750**

Bambino: all felt; bent-limb body; pressed face; hand in fist position; mohair wig; painted eyes; closed mouth; typically marked with "Bambino" hangtag or "Bambino" clothing label.

13"-16"	**$2,500-$2,800**
17"-20-1/2"	**$3,000-$3,200**

Floppy Limb Felt Dolls: all felt; swivel neck; long arms and legs; mohair wig; felt eyes and lips; painted rosy cheeks; typically marked with hangtag attached to clothing.

23"-37"	**$1,200-$1,400**

Mascotte: loop at top for hanging; all felt; mohair wig; painted eyes; closed mouth; surprised expression; original tagged costume.

8"-8-1/2"	**$700**

Miniature: all felt; mohair wig; painted, round eyes; mouth with surprised "oh" expression; original tagged costume; heart-shaped wrist tag.

9"-9-1/2"	**$600**

Hard Face: flocked hard plastic head; cloth body; felt limbs; mohair wig; painted eyes; small mouth; typically marked with hangtag, clothing label, and "Lenci/Made in Italy."

11"-12"	**$350**
19"-20-1/2"	**$950**

Chubby Cheeked: all felt; pressed felt character face; full, round cheeks; tiny nose; smile line under eyes; mohair wig; painted eyes; small, closed mouth; typically marked with hangtag, clothing label, and "Lenci" stamped on foot or unmarked. 17"-18" **$3,800**

Contemporary*: 1980-on; beautifully made, all jointed felt; mohair wig; painted eyes; closed mouth; typically marked with hangtag, clothing label, and "Lenci" along with production number stamped on foot; original blue fabric-covered box and brightly colored, lithograph numbered and signed certificate.

13"-22" ....$300-$400
27"-28-1/2" $650
Add $200 for wide-awake or surprise eyes.

Special Lenci Dolls:

Sports Characters:
15"-18" .... $4,500-$4,700
21"-24" .... $5,200-$5,400
Brown or Black Island Character:
15"-21" .... $3,000-$3,700
31" $5,200
Aviator (Amelia Earhart):
18"-19" $4,900
Tom Mix:
18"-19" $5,000
Oriental Character:
16" $4,500
18"-21" .... $5,000-$5,600
Rudolph Valenetino:
30" $15,000

Quality Lenci Look-A-Like or Type: So popular and successful were the Lenci dolls that many companies, such as Alpha, Anili, American Stuffed Novelty, Fiori, Raynal, and countless others could not resist the temptation to copy them.

Child or Adult: Made in the Lenci style; typically marked with cloth label, hangtag, wrist tag or unmarked.

14"-16" ....$775-$875
20" $1,000

R. John Wright Dolls: All felt dolls by this gifted America artist are of superb quality; typically marked "Wright Little People," character name, and production number; clothing tagged "RJ Wright," brass RJW button on clothing or doll.

16"-18" .... $1,500-$1,700
20" $2,300

Nicely executed 16" Lenci-type doll by Venus, made in Paris, **$875.**
Courtesy of McMasters-Harris Auction

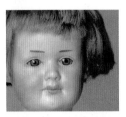

Armand Marseille

Armand Marseille founded his famous doll company in 1885 in Sonneberg and Köppelsdorf, Thüringia, Germany.

From 1900 until 1930, Marseille was one of the largest suppliers of bisque doll heads in the world, reportedly producing a thousand heads a day.

25" Armand Marseille #370, one of the most frequently found antique bisque dolls, **$625.**
Photo courtesy of James D. Julia Inc.

Prices listed are for appropriately costumed dolls in good condition.

Standard Dolly Face, Shoulder Head: bisque shoulder head; kid, cloth, or imitation leather body; good wig; glass eyes; may have fur brows; open mouth; typically marked "Made in Germany," "A. M.," "Armand Marseille," "270," "370," "376," "920," "957," "2015," "3200," "Alma," "Darling," "Duchess," "Floradora," "Lily," "Lissy," "Mabel," "My Dearie," "My Playmate," or "Rosebud."

10"-14"	$350-$400
20"-24"	$500-$600
28"-30"	$700-$750

Better Dolly Face, Shoulder Head: bisque shoulder head; kid body; good wig; glass eyes; open mouth; typically marked "AM/DEP/Made in Germany," "Armand Marseille," "1374," "1890," "1892," "1894," "1895," "1896," "1897," "1899," "1900," "1901," "1902," "1903," "1905," "1909," "2000," "3091," "3093," "3095," "3200," "3300," "3500," "3700," "4008," "Baby Betty," "Beauty," "Jubilee," "Majestic," "Princess," or "Queen Louise."

10"-14"	$450-$500
20"-24"	$600-$700
28"-30"	$825-$900

Dolly Face Socket Head*: bisque socket head; jointed wood-and-composition body; good wig; glass eyes; open mouth; typically marked "Made in Germany/Armand Marseille," "384," "390," 390n," "391," "395," "1894," "1897," "2010," "3600," "Baby Betty," "Floradora," "Queen Louise," or "Rosebud." (Several share a name with shoulder heads.)

10"-14"	$500-$550
20"-24"	$650-$750
28"-30"	$1,000-$1,400
40"-42"	$3,000-$3,500

Add $200-$400 for nice, soft coloring or an exceptionally pretty doll.

Character Baby: bisque, character socket head; composition bent-limb baby body; typically marked "Germany A. M. DRGM," "259," "326," "327," "329," "347," "352," "360a," "750," "760," "790," "900," "927," "970," "971," "980," "984," "985," "990," "991," "996," "1330," or "1333."

8"-12"	$500-$650
16"-20"	$900-$975
26"	$1,500

Infant: (Dream Baby, Kiddie Joy, Our Pet) bisque socket head or flange neck; composition bent-limb baby or cloth body; typically marked "AM Germany," "341," "351," "342," or "Our Pet." A "K" at the end of the marking designates a composition body.

Armand Marseille 24" Queen Louise, **$750.**
Courtesy of Susan Miller

Armand Marseille 16" #326 character baby, **$900.**
Courtesy of Susan Miller

15" #329 George Borgfeldt & Co. character baby by Armand Marseille, **$775.**
Photo courtesy of James D. Julia Inc.

Collectible DOLLS **187**

Armand Marseille 23" #980 character toddler, **$1,350**, and 25" #351 solid dome character baby, **$1,200**.
Courtesy of David Cobb Auction

13" Armand Marseille #231 Fanny, **$7,200.**
Photo courtesy of James D. Julia Inc.

OM, cloth body:
10"-12" ....$475-$500
16"-18" ....$700-$800
22" $1,000
OM, composition body:
10"-12" ....$525-$550
16"-18" ....$800-$875
22" $1,100
CM, cloth body:
10"-12" ....$550-$575
16"-18" ....$850-$900
22" $1,200
CM, composition body:
10"-12" ....$625-$650
16"-18" ....$925-$975
22" $1,200

Named Character Baby: bisque socket head or flange neck; kid or cloth body or composition body; painted hair or good wig; sleep eyes; soft brows; open or closed mouth; dimples; may have pierced nostrils; typically marked "Baby Gloria/A Germany M," "Melitta," "Ellar," "Phyllis," or "Gloria."

Flange neck, kid or cloth body:
12"-14" ....$900-$950
18" $1,000
Socket head, composition body:
12"-14" ....$1,200-$1,300
18" $1,500
Add $300 for black version of any doll.

Character Doll: expressive bisque character face; various body types; molded and painted hair or good wig; glass or painted eyes; open, closed, or open/closed mouth; typically marked with mold number or "AM" only.

For characters, 16"-18" was used as a comparison base, but please remember the dolls actually came in a wide range of sizes from at least 9"to 24", and you should use your good judgment and common sense to interpose the value to additional sizes.

230 CM, glass eyes, solid dome Fanny:
16"-18" ....$8,500-$9,700
231 CM, glass eyes, wigged Fanny:
16"-18" ....$7,900-$9,500

233 OM, glass eyes:
  16"-18" ....$800-$900
250 OM, painted eyes (248 GB):
  16"-18" .... $2,300-$2,500
251 CM, glass eyes, tongue (248 GB):
  16"-18" .... $4,200-$4,600
255 OM, glass eyes, two rows teeth:
  16"-18" .... $4,300-$4,550
300 CM, glass eyes, molded:
  16"-18" .... $2,600-$2,800
310 CM, glass eyes:
  16"-18" .... $3,200-$3,300
328 OM, glass eyes:
  16"-18" .... $1,000-$1,200
340 OM, glass eyes:
  16"-18" .... $4,000-$4,500
345 CM, intaglio eyes:
  16"-18" .... $4,300-$4,700
350 CM, glass eyes:
  16"-18" .... $2,950-$3,100
362 Black character:
  16"-18" .... $1,300-$1,600
372 or 375 OM, glass eyes:
  16"-18" .... $1,300-$1,400
400 or 401 OM, glass eyes, lady:
  16"-18" .... $1,700-$1,900
CM, glass eyes, lady:
  16"-18" .... $3,750-$4,000
410 OM, glass eyes, two rows of teeth:
  16"-18" .... $2,700-$2,900
451 OM, glass eyes:
  16"-18" .... $1,300-$1,400
520 CM, glass eyes (232 GB):
  16"-18" .... $2,100-$2,300
530 OC/M intaglio eye molded teeth:
  16"-18" .... $5,500-$5,800
550 CM, glass eyes:
  16"-18" .... $4,500-$4,700
560 O/CM, painted eyes (232 GB):
  16"-18" .... $5,750-$6,200
560a OM, glass eyes:
  16"-18" .... $1,000-$1,300
570 O/CM, glass eyes (232 GB):
  16"-18" .... $1,900-$2,200
580 or 590 O/CM, glass eyes:
  16"-18" .... $2,100-$2,450
590 OM, glass eyes:
  16"-18" .... $1,200-$1,300
600 CM, painted eyes (234 GB):
  16"-18" .... $1,200-$1,400

Armand Marseille 21" #372 Kiddie Joy
with molded hair, **$1,600.**
Courtesy of McMasters-Harris Auction

14" Armand Marseille #401 Flapper Lady, **$1,600.**
Photo courtesy of James D. Julia Inc.

Darling 13" AM #550 character girl, **$3,200.**
Courtesy of James Julia Auctions, Inc.

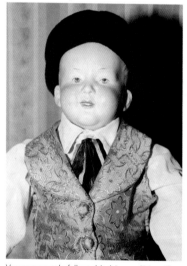

Very rare, wonderfully molded Armand Marseille 16" #530 character boy with intaglio eyes, **$5,500.**
Courtesy of Susan Miller

620 O/CM, glass eyes (234 GB):
   16"-18" .... **$1,750-$1,900**
640a CM, painted eyes (234 GB):
   16"-18" .... **$1,900-$2,200**
700 CM, glass eyes:
   16"-18" .... **$8,300-$8,700**
 CM, painted eyes:
   16"-18" .... **$6,900-$7,600**
710 CM, glass eyes:
   16"-18" .... **$4,000-$4,500**
711 CM, glass eyes:
   16"-18" .... **$4,700-$5,100**
800 O/CM, glass eyes (234 GB):
   16"-18" .... **$2,750-$2,900**
810 O/CM, glass eyes:
   16"-18" .... **$3,500-$3,800**
820 O/CM, glass eyes:
   16"-18" .... **$3,200-$3,600**
920 OM, glass eyes:
   16"-18" ....**$800-$900**
950 CM, painted eyes:
   16"-18" .... **$2,800-$3,200**
AM CM, intaglio eyes, expressive
(marked only AM):
   16"-18" ....**$7,500 or more**

Add $500 for jointed toddler or $300 for high knee, flapper body on any doll.
OM = Open Mouth
CM = Closed Mouth
O/CM = Open/Closed Mouth
AM = Armand Marseille
GB = George Borgfeldt

Mattel® Inc.

In 1945, Mattel's founders, Harold Matson and Elliot Handler, established the company's headquarters in Hawthorne, California.

Mattel, the world's largest toy manufacturer, produced quality dolls that have quickly attained collectible status. The high quality and imaginative concepts have no doubt contributed to this phenomenon. All Mattel dolls are well marked. (Also see Barbie & Friends.)

Prices listed are for dolls in near mint, original condition.

Tiny Cheerful Tearful: 6-1/2"; all vinyl; marked "1966 Mattel Inc. Hong Kong." **$85**

The Sunshine Family: (9-1/2" Steve, 9" Stephie, and 3" Sweets) vinyl and plastic; marked "1973 Mattel Inc." on heads; "1973/Mattel Inc./Taiwan" on back; wrist tag "The Sunshine Family." **$175/set**

Buffie: 10"; vinyl and plastic; holding 3-1/2" Mrs. Beasley doll; marked "1967/Mattel Inc./U.S. & For/Pats. Pend Mexico." **$400**

      6" Buffie; holding 2" Mrs. Beasley **$450**

Bouncy Baby: 11"; vinyl and plastic; spring action limbs; giggles; marked "1968 Mattel Inc./Mexico/U. S. Patent Pending" on the back; dress tag reads "Bouncy Baby/1968 Mattel Inc./Hong Kong." **$85**

Guardian Goddesses: 12"; adult figure; test market dolls only; Moonmystic and Sunspell; arms go up and down; when limbs are pulled, gowns fly off and reveal "Super Girl" outfit, 1979-1980. .... **$500**

      Guardian Goddess Outfits: (Fire, Ice, Lion,

      Eagle) .... **$250 each**

Shrinking Violet: 15"; cloth; pull-string talker and facial movements; cloth label sewn into seam marked "Mattel Shrinking Violet" and "63 The Funny Company All Rights Reserved Through Out The World" on reverse side. **$200**

Saucy: 16"; vinyl and plastic; eyes and mouth form eight different expressions; marked "1972 Mattel Inc. Mexico" on head; "1972 Mattel Inc. Mexico/US Patent Pend." on back... **$135**

Talking Baby Tenderlove: 16"; vinyl; open nurser mouth; pull-string talker in plastic hair ribbon on back of head; marked "677K 1969 Mattel Inc./Mexico." . **$100**

Mint condition Mattel 16" Talking Mrs. Beasley in original box, **$600**.

Courtesy of McMasters-Harris Auction

25" Charmin' Chatty in mint condition. In this extraordinary condition with original box and added accessories, expect a value of **$500 or more.**
Courtesy of McMasters-Harris Auction

Talking Mrs. Beasley: 16"; vinyl head; blue and white polka-dot cloth body; black plastic glasses; pull-string talker; cloth tag "Mattel Mrs. Beasley" sewn into seam. **$450**

Sister Bell: 17"; hard plastic head; cloth body; pull-string talker, marked "Mattel Inc./Hawthorne Calif." on head; "Mattel Inc. 1961" on tag sewn into seam. ... **$135**

Chatty Cathy: 20"; vinyl and plastic; marked "Chatty Cathy 1960/Chatty Baby 1961 By Mattel Inc./U.S. Pat. 301718/Other U.S. and Foreign Pats. Pend./Pat'd in Canada 1962"; dress tag reads "Chatty Cathy Mattel." **$450**

    Chatty Cathy black version **$1,100**

Living Baby Tenderlove: 20"; vinyl; rooted skull cap; marked "140/1970 Mattel Inc. Mexico/US and Foreign Patented." **$125**

Doctor Dolittle: 22"; vinyl head; cloth body; pull-string talker; marked "Dr. Dolittle/MCMLXVII Twentieth Century Fox/Film Corp. Inc." on tag sewn into seam... **$135**

Charmin' Chatty: 25"; vinyl and plastic; record fits into slot on side of doll; pull-string operates talker; marked "Charmin Chatty 1961 Mattel, Inc." **$250**

    Chatty Baby: 18" **$175**
    Tiny Chatty Baby: 15" **$125**
    Tiny Chatty Baby Brother: 15" **$135**
    Singing Chatty: 17" **$225**

Collector Doll Series

Classic Beauty: 1977-1978; vinyl and plastic; very pretty facial modeling; with wrist tag. .... **$400-$600**

La Cheri Collection: also known as "French Country Garden Collection"; tagged with serial number and date... **$500-$600**

Mariko Collection: ivory complexion; limited to 1,800 .... **$300-$350**

Sekiguchi of Japan: Mattel owned exclusive distribution rights in the United States. .... **$300-$350**

Kiddles

Liddle Kiddles: 2"-4"; all vinyl; rooted hair; painted features; original costumes and accessories; typically marked "1965 (1966 or 1967) Mattel Inc./Japan." .... **$100-$300**

Mego

Mego marketed dolls during the 1970s and 1980s until going bankrupt in 1983. Mego is best known for its well-made and accurately costumed action figures.

Prices listed are for dolls in near mint, original condition.

Action Jackson: 8".............................$40
Dinah-mite: 8" $75
Superman: 8"..................................$100
Batman (1st; removable cowl-mask):
   8"..$250
Batman or Robin: 8".......................$175
Aquaman or Captain America: 8" ...$100
Tarzan: 8"..$40
Spider-Man: 8" $100
Shazam: 8".....................................$100
Penguin, Joker, or Riddler: 8" $125
Mr. Mxyzptlk: 8" $75
Waltons Mom & Pop, pair: 8" $85
Waltons Grandma & Grandpa, pair: 8".$85
Waltons, John Boy & Mary Ellen, pair:
   8" $85
Fighting Batman or Robin: 8" $100
Fighting Riddler or Joker: 8"...........$100
C.H.I.P.S. Jon or Ponch: 8" $75
Captain Patch or Jean Lafitte: 8" $125
Long John Silver or Blackbeard: 8".. $125
Mighty Thor: 8" $150
Conan: 8" $200
The Thing: 8".....................................$30
Wonder Woman: 8"..........................$100
Super Girl: 8"..................................$150
Bat Girl: 8" $100
Cat Woman: 8" $125
Frankenstein or Dracula: 8"..............$50
Wolfman: 8".......................................$45
Mummy: 8" $100
Wyatt Earp or Cochise: 8" $65
Davy Crockett or Wild Bill Hickok: 8" .. $65
Buffalo Bill Cody or Sitting Bull: 8" ...$85
Cornelius, Planet of the Apes: 8"....$150
Dr. Zaius, Zira, or Soldier Ape: 8" ...$150
Romulan: 8" $1,200
Captain Kirk: 8" $150
Mr. Spock: 8" $125

Mego 12" Cher in mint condition with original box, **$175.**

Photograph courtesy of Julia Burke, www.juliaburke.com

Dr. "Bones" McCoy: 8" **$175**
Lt. Uhura: 8" **$150**
Mr. "Scottie" Scott: 8" **$200**
Klingon: 8" **$75**
Andorian: 8" **$750**
The Keeper: 8" **$275**
Dorothy & Toto: 8" **$75**
Cowardly Lion, Tin Man, or Scarecrow:
   8" **$75**
Munchkins: 8" **$150**
Glinda the Good Witch: 8" **$95**
Wicked Witch: 8" **$100**
King Arthur, Sir Galahad, Lancelot,
Ivanhoe, Black Knight: 8" **$125**
Robin Hood or Will Scarlet: 8" **$150**
Little John or Friar Tuck: 8" **$125**
Green Arrow: 8" **$60**
Green Goblin: 8" **$75**
The Lizard: 8" **$100**
The Falcon: 8" **$75**
The Invincible Iron Man: 8" **$50**
The Incredible Hulk: 8" **$100**
The Human Torch: 8" **$30**
Mr. Fantastic: 8" **$30**
Invisible Girl: 8" **$30**
Neprunain: 8" **$70**
The Gorn or The Cheron: 8" **$100**
Zon, 1 Million BC: 8" **$100**

Trag, Grok, or Orm: 8" **$50**
Alfalfa, Spanky, or Darla: 8" **$85**
Buckwheat: 8" **$100**
Mickey or Porky: 8" **$40**
Galen: 8" **$45**
General Ursus: 8" **$45**
Peter Burke or Alan Verdono: 8" **$60**
Fonzie: 8" **$100**
Richie or Potsy: 8" **$75**
Kojack: 8" **$100**
Captain or Tenille: 12" **$100**
Sonny: 12" **$150**
Cher: 12" **$175**
Diana Ross: 12" **$150**
Jaclyn Smith: 12" **$95**
Joe Namath: 12" **$225**
Laverne, Shirley, Lenny, or Squiggy:
   12" **$125**
Suzanne Somers: 12" **$75**
Wonder Woman: 12" **$200**
Star Treck Captain Kirk , Llia, or Mr.
Spock: 12" **$150**
Arcturian: 12" **$175**
Maddie Mod: 12" **$100**
Farrah Fawcett: 12" **$75**
KISS, set: 12" **$800**
Kriss, Gene, Ace, or Peter: 12" **$200**
Peter: 12" **$200**

Modern Collectible Dolls

"Modern doll" is the term applied to any doll made after World War II. This section includes various dolls from numerous manufacturers. To simplify your search, the modern collectible dolls category has been subdivided into hard plastic/vinyl and contemporary porcelain.

The hard plastic and vinyl dolls described within this section are among collectors' favorites. Contemporary porcelain dolls, from well-known and gifted artists, have been successful in recruiting new doll collectors.

Add a "contemporary" doll to your collection because you adore it, but avoid buying one as an investment.

Prices listed are for original dolls in mint condition.

Hard Plastic/Vinyl

Annette Himstedt Children: 19"-31"; vinyl head and arms; cloth body; typically marked "Annette Himstedt/ Puppen Kind," signature on neck, wrist tag with character name and clothing tag (designed by Annette Himstedt for Mattel).

Timi, Toni, Panchita, Pancho, or Melvin	**$650**
Baby, Leischen, Tara, Annchen, Lona, or Kima	**$850**
Fiene, Kai, Janka, Liliane, Adriene, or Ayoka	**$900**
Neblina, Taki, Freeke, Bibbi, or Makimura	**$1,300**
Michiko, Malin, Frederike, or Tinka	**$1,500**
Kasimir, Annika	**$1,800**

Barefoot Children: 26"; vinyl head and limbs with detailed bare feet; cloth body; marked "Annette Himstedt AH 1985/26.8.86" (designed by Annette Himstedt for Mattel).

Fatou (black)	**$1,100**
Paula (pensive)	**$650**
Bastian (boy)	**$850**
Kathe (full pouty face)	**$850**
Ellen (innocent and peaceful)	**$900**
Lisa (happy)	**$850**

16" Twiggy vinyl portrait doll, a really cool and groovy doll by the Franklin Mint, **$400.**
Courtesy of the Franklin Mint

13" modern collectible hard plastic Buddy Lee dolls in wonderful original condition, **$700 each.**
Photo courtesy of James D. Julia Inc.

Beatles: 5"; oversized vinyl heads; miniature plastic body; plastic guitars with names; marked "Remco Ind. Inc. 1964 (Seltael, Inc, NEMS)." .... **$800-$1,000**

Buddy Lee: 13"; hard plastic; typically marked "Buddy Lee." .... **$700-$900**

Cabbage Patch: 15"-17"; vinyl head; cloth body; typically marked "Corp R 1978-1982 Original Appalachian Art Works Inc. Manufactured by Coleco Ind. Inc. Made in Hong Kong." Coleco foreign affiliates' marks may appear; they were: "Jesmar S. A." Spain; "Triang Pedigree" South Africa; "Lili Ledy" Mexico; and "Tsukuda Original" Japan. Any of these may appear in the marking (for a listing of special dolls and production numbers, see the second edition of 200 Years of Dolls).

Prior to 1989	$50-$100
After 1989	$5- $45
Early 1978-1982	$100-$500
Boxed Porcelain	$100-$200

Daisy May: 12"-20"; vinyl; shapely body; cloth label "Exclusive License/Baby Barry/Toy NYC/Al Capp/Dog Patch Family"

(by Baby Barry Toy Company).

12"-20" .... **$450-$575**

Dawn Model Agency:(Dawn, Angie, Glori, Dale (black version), April, Dinah, Melanie, Daphne): 6"; marked production year (1969-1972) "Topper Corp/Hong Kong" and "H11A," "11C," "A11A," "K10," "H-7/110," "11-7," "878/K11A," "2/H-11," "A8-10," "H-17," "4/H 72," "543/H11a," "92/H-17," "154/S11," "51/D10," "4/H86," "K10/A," "AK11/H-7," and possibly others (by Deluxe Reading)................ **$150-$200**

Dick Clark: 26"; vinyl head and hands; cloth "to-autograph" body; smiling with molded teeth; original suede saddle shoes; marked "JURO" (by Juro Novelty Company).

Mint... **$750**
With signatures...................... **$400**

Elmer Fudd: 8"; vinyl; carries shotgun; marked "© WARNER BROS-SEVEN ARTS INC 1968//MADE IN HONG KONG" (by R. Dakin & Company). **$200**

FayZah Spanos Babies and Children: 25"; vinyl head and limbs; cloth body; marked "FAYZAH SPANOS." **$300**

Gerber Baby: 17"; vinyl head and hands; cloth gingham body; rolling eyes; marked "Gerber Products"//production year (by Atlanta Novelty, earlier dolls also by Sun Rubber and possibly others; markings and values may vary)..............**$150-$200**

Ginny Type/Look-a-Like: 8"; hard plastic; very similar in appearance to the popular Ginny doll; with or without a walker body.

Julie or Gigi (A&H Doll Mfg.) . **$125**
Mary Lu (Doll Bodies Inc.)....... **$125**
Lolly-Pop with pastel fantasy hair colors (Virga).......................... **$250**
Pam (Fortune Doll Company) . **$175**
Ginger (Cosmopolitan) **$350**

Heidi Ott Children: 8"-16"; vinyl head and lower limbs; cloth body; marked "Swiss design/Heidi Ott."

8"-12" .... **$150-$175**
16" **$200**

Hildegarde Günzel Children: 21"-30"; vinyl head and limbs; cloth body; marked "H. Günzel/China" (designed by Hildegarde Günzel for Alexander).

    Megan, Marissa, Monica, Tricia, Chipie Baby, Lamponi, or Matthias .... **$200-$300**

    Marie or Binella....................... **$700**

Hummel Dolls Peterle & Rose: 11"; vinyl; exact replica of the famous Hummel figurines; marked "original M T Hummel V GOEBEL," wrist tag "AUS DENHAUSE GOEBEL." .... **$100-$200**

Julie Good-Kruger Children: 20"; all vinyl or vinyl head and limbs and cloth body; marked "Julie Good-Kruger© (production date)." .... **$200-$300**

Lee Middleton Babies or Toddlers: 11"-22"; vinyl head and limbs; cloth body; tiny Bible tied to wrist; marked character name and production number "Lee Middleton (date) fish (a Christian symbol) The Middleton Doll Co" and signature.

    11" **$125**

    20"-22" .... **$225-$275**

Lilli: 11-1/2"; vinyl; curvaceous body; ponytail; heavily lined black and white painted eyes; closed mouth; fashionably dressed; marked "Germany" (by Bild Lilli); very similar in appearance to Barbie®.

    In original plastic tube with metal rod stand............................. **$8,000**

    Without tube **$5,000**

Lissi Dolls: 19-3/4"; vinyl head and limbs; cloth body; marked "Anneliese S. Bätes" signature (may be any one of many names released by Lissi Dolls of West Germany)................................... **$100-$125**

Little Iodine: 13"-21"; vinyl head; one-piece latex body; molded loop for ribbon (by Juro Novelty Company).

    13"-18" .... **$100-$125**

    21" **$175**

8" Ginger, a Ginny Look-a-Like in Mousketeer costume, **$350**, ready to go trick-or-treating with an early German papier-mâché pumpkin.
Courtesy of Bertoia Auctions

Littlechap Family: 10"-14"; vinyl; tagged clothes; marked "Remco Ind. Inc./1963// US & Foreign Pat/Pend. Hong Kong."

    10"-14" .... **$140-$165**

LuAnn Simms: 14"; jointed hard plastic; saran wig; marked "Made in USA," "170," or "180" (made by Roberta, Horsman, and Valentine for Belle Toys)............ **$450**

18" hard plastic Wanda the Walking Wonder Doll in original costume, **$200**.

Photo courtesy of James D. Julia Inc.

Miss Seventeen: 15"; shapely body; insert skull cap hair pulled back tightly; long red cape; marked "US Patent 2925784/British Patent 804566/Made in Hong Kong" (by Marx). ....**$500-$700**

Old Cottage: 8"-9"; vinyl or plastic head; cloth body; fanciful or historical costumes; marked with hangtag "Old Cottage Toys" or "Old Cottage Industries/Great Britain." ....**$200-$600, depending on appeal**

Tweedledee & Tweedeldum: ....**$1,500-$1,600**

Penny Brite: 8"; vinyl; slender body; smiling; molded teeth; typically marked "Topp Corp.," may have registration number (by Deluxe Reading)...............**$75-$100**

Robin Woods Child: 8"-17"; vinyl; multi-layered costumes; typically marked "Robin Woods," year. (In 1992 Robin Woods joined Alexander Doll Company. Prices listed are for dolls produced before that date.)

  8" **$125**
  14"-17" ....**$200-$300**

Sandra Sue: 8"; hard plastic; slender jointed body; stitched wig; sleep eyes; painted, orangish-brown brows and lashes; closed mouth; unmarked, except for incised number inside arm or leg (by Richwood Toys Inc.). ....**$225-$400, depending on appeal**

Cindy Lou: 14"; hard plastic; dressed to match Sandra Sue..**$550-$600**

Teenage or Bride Dolls: 15"-24"; jointed hard plastic; good wig; sleep eyes; open or closed mouth; typically marked "Made in the U. S. A.," unmarked or letter or number only.

  15"-17" ....**$400-$450**
  18"-20" ....**$500-$650**
  22"-24" ....**$700-$750**

Tina Cassini: 12"; vinyl; teen body; heart-shaped plastic stand ™ "Tina"; "Cassini" fashions; marked "Tina Cassini Made in British Hong Kong," gold wrist tag "Oleg Cassini Tina Cassini by Ross Products, Inc."; fashion booklet with photos of original designed Oleg Cassini Fashions (by Ross Products). ....**$700-$900**

Trolls: 1"-15"; comical characters; bushy hair; round, acrylic, insert eyes; wide, smiling, closed mouth; original felt costume; marked "Dam Thing."

  1"-3" **$45**
  4"-10" ....**$100-$150**
  11"-14" ....**$200-$300**
  15" **$375**

Wanda the Walking Wonder: 17-19"; hard plastic; walker body; marked "19" (by Advanced Doll Company).

  17"-19" ....**$175-$225**

Molly-'es

Molly-'es is the trade name used by the International Doll Company, founded in 1929 by Marysia (Mollye) Goldman of Philadelphia, Pennsylvania.

The International Doll Company was originally a cottage-type industry, with neighborhood women sewing doll dresses in their homes. Eventually, Mollye opened a factory, which reportedly employed as many as 500 people.

Mollye purchased good quality dolls of composition, hard plastic, and vinyl from various manufacturers, dressed them in her original costumes, and sold them under her name. Except for hangtags, earlier Molly-'es dolls are unmarked; later vinyl dolls were marked "Mollye" on the head.

Cloth
Prices listed are for appropriately costumed dolls with good color.

Child Mask-Type Face: all cloth; mask-type face; yarn hair; painted eyes, long lashes; small, closed mouth; typically unmarked or hangtag only.

13"-18"	$200-$250
24"-29"	$300-$350

International Children Series: all cloth; mask-type face; mohair wig; painted facial features; regional costume; typically unmarked or hangtag only.

13"-15"	$135-$170
27"	$325

Character: all cloth; mask-type face; yarn hair; painted, big, round, side-glancing eyes; smiling, watermelon mouth; typically unmarked or hangtag only.

15"-18"	$250-$300
24"	$350

Composition
Prices listed are for appropriately costumed dolls in good condition.

Baby: all jointed composition; molded and painted hair; sleep eyes; closed mouth; typically unmarked or hangtag only.

14"-15"	$275-$325
18"-21"	$375-$475

Lady/Teen: all jointed composition; good wig; sleep eyes; real lashes; closed mouth; typically unmarked or hangtag only.

15"-18"	$575-$625
21"	$750
27"	$950

Thief of Baghdad Series: (Sultan, Thief, or Princess) all jointed composition; good wig, may have mohair beard and brows; detailed, painted eyes; closed mouth; typically unmarked or hangtag only.

15"	$850
19"	$1,100

Hard Plastic & Vinyl

Prices listed are for dolls in near mint, original condition.

Lady/Teen: jointed hard plastic; good wig; sleep eyes; closed mouth; typically marked "X," "200," unmarked, or hangtag only.

14"-17"	$500-$600
20"	$700
25"-28"	$800-$900

Child/Baby: jointed vinyl; rooted hair; sleep eyes; closed mouth; typically marked "Mollye," "15," or "450."

9"-12"	$100-$125
16"	$145

Beautiful 15" Molly-'es composition teen in mint condition with hangtag, **$700.**

Courtesy of Julia Burke, www. juliaburke.com

Morimura Brothers

Morimura Brothers, an 1870s Japanese import house, began producing dolls in 1915. With the onset of World War I, the flow of bisque dolls from Europe had virtually ceased. Morimura Brothers stepped in to supply Japanese-made bisque-head dolls to American customers.

Morimura Brothers set out to imitate the much-loved German doll and achieved a certain degree of success. There are many fine examples available, and they continue to escalate in price.

Prices listed are for appropriately costumed dolls in good condition.

Character Baby: bisque socket head; composition bent-limb baby body; good wig; glass eyes; open mouth; typically marked "M B" (within a circle), "Japan," "Nippon," "Yamato," "FY," "MB," or "JW."

10"-12"	$150-$300
18"-22"	$550-$650

Hilda Look-a-like, Heubach type, and 300 Series:

14"-15"	$800-$1,000
20"-22"	$1,250-$1,300

Dolly Face*: bisque shoulder or socket head; jointed composition or kid body; good wig; glass eyes; open mouth; typically marked "MB" within a circle, "NIPPON," "JW," "Yamato," "FY," or "MB."

10"-15"	$350-$450
18"-22"	$500-$600
24"	$700

Deduct 20% for lesser-quality examples.

22" and 24" Morimura Brothers twin FY Nippon #504 character babies in an early Hayward-Wakefield coach, **$750** and **$850,** respectively. *Courtesy of David Cobb Auction*

Cute little 14" Morimura Brothers character baby, **$350.** *Courtesy of Julia Burke, www.juliaburke.com*

Nancy Ann Storybook Dolls

Nancy Ann Storybook Dolls were produced by a California-based company founded by Nancy Ann Abbott and her partner, A. L. Rowland, in 1936.

During the 1960s, the company, which at its peak was producing over 8,000 dolls a day, began to experience technical problems. Doll production ceased not long after Abbott's death in 1964.

Prices listed are for all original dolls with no damage.

Little Miss Nancy Ann: 9"; hard plastic or vinyl and hard plastic; saran wig; typically marked "Nancy Ann." **$300**
Miss Nancy Ann/Little Margie Ann: 10"; jointed vinyl teen type; rooted hair; sleep eyes with lashes; closed mouth; pierced ears; typically marked "Nancy Ann." **$350**
Nancy Ann/Style Show: 17"-18"; jointed hard plastic with synthetic wig or vinyl head with rooted hair; sleep eyes with lashes; closed mouth; typically marked "17B" or "18B" or unmarked with hangtag only..**$1,250**
Muffie: 8"; jointed hard plastic; good wig; sleep eyes; closed mouth; typically marked "StoryBook Dolls California/Muffie" or "Muffie."

    Painted lashes, no eyebrows, straight leg, non-walker (1953) **$500**
    Molded lashes, painted eyebrows, straight-leg walker (1954)......................**$400**
    Vinyl head, rooted saran hair, straight-leg or bent-knee walker (1955) **$250**
    Unmarked, molded lashes, wig, reissue straight-leg walker (1968)..............**$150**

Storybook Dolls

Painted Bisque: one-piece head and body; jointed shoulder and hip; mohair wig; painted eyes; tiny closed mouth.
Judy Ann: classic characteristics with molded and painted bangs and white socks.
  Mark I: "Made in Japan," "87 Made in Japan," or "88 Made in Japan"
  Mark II: "Made in Japan," "Japan," "AMERICA," "Made in Japan 1146," or "Made in Japan 1148"
  Mark III: "STORYBOOK USA" or "Story Book USA"
  Mark IV: "StoryBook Doll USA"
  Mark V: "StoryBook Doll USA/Trade Mark Reg." or "Nancy Ann StoryBook Dolls/ USA Trademark Reg."
Hard Plastic: jointed hard plastic or vinyl head with rooted hair; mohair or synthetic wig; painted or sleep eyes; closed mouth.

Painted bisque, Mark I.. $900
Painted bisque, Mark I or II $1,400
Painted bisque, Mark III "AMERICA" or "JUDY ANN USA" * $1,200
Painted bisque, Mark III $1,200
Painted bisque, bangs, molded socks, Mark IV $1,000
Painted bisque, molded socks, Mark IV* $700
Painted bisque, transition dolls, Mark IV* $350
Painted bisque, one-piece head, torso, and legs, Mark IV $250
Plastic, painted eyes, Mark V.. $250
Plastic, black sleep eyes, Mark V $150
Plastic, blue sleep eyes... $125

*Add $500 for molded and painted hair or $300 for "Pudgies" with chubby tummies.

Other Storybook Dolls

Prices listed are for original dolls in perfect, near mint condition with boxes.

Judy Ann in Fairyland in rare, red, book-shaped box $4,200
Roy Rogers and Dale Evans... $4,000
Flower Girl $2,100
Easter Parade.. $1,500
Masquerade... $1,700
Pirate.. $2,000
Margie Ann $2,200
Little Eva $5,000
Around the World.. $1,500
Sports Motif... $2,300
Topsy and Eva $5,300
Oriental.. $2,700
Storybook Literary Set $7,500

Nancy Ann Storybook
Dolls: 5" painted bisque
Little Eva, **$5,000**, and
Margie Ann in school
dress #79 in original
box, **$2,200**.
Courtesy of McMasters-Harris Auction

Peggy Nisbet Limited

The very English Peggy Nisbet began her journey into doll making history with a single doll in 1952. Recently Peggy Nisbet Limited and her subsidiaries have formed The House of Nisbet, under the direction of Nisbet's son-in-law. In addition to the well-known petite fashion doll, bears, toys, and teaching accessories also bear the Nisbet name.

Nisbet 8" Tiny Tim carried by Bob Cratchit character dolls, **$350.**
Courtesy of Diane S. Hartman from "What-A-Doll,"
Adollisborn@hotmail.com

Prices listed are for dolls in mint, original condition with average appeal. Within a classification, any practically desirable doll could be worth much more depending on appeal or notoriety.

Nisbet Collectible Character Dolls: 7"-8"; vinyl; molded and painted lifelike character face; beautifully costumed and accessorized; typically having wrist tag with character identification and history.

Entertainment Personalities . **$150 or more**
Political Personalities . . . . **$250 or more**
Royal Family, Past or Present . **$225 or more**
Historical or Literary . . . . **$200 or more**
Regency Guardsmen . . . . **$125 or more**

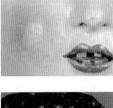

Papier-Mâché Dolls

Various German manufacturers made doll heads from the special type of composition known as papier-mâché. The wood, rag, and paper fibers were responsible for much of papier-mâché's strength. Papier-mâché, carton paté (French), and holz-masse (German) are interchangeable terms for the paper-based composition.

Papier-mâché dolls were individually hand-made as early as the 16th century. The development of the pressure-mold process in the early 1800s allowed papier-mâché dolls to be mass-produced.

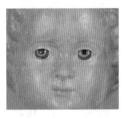

32" French type papier-mâché doll, **$4,500.**
Courtesy of McMasters-Harris Auction

23" early papier-mâché doll with glass eyes and mohair wig, **$2,600.**
From the Jean Campbell collection

Papier-mâché 9" molded hair, known as Milliner's Model with topknot, **$1,300.**

Courtesy of McMasters-Harris Auction

Early black 12" papier-mâché character with squeaker bellows within muslin torso, **$1,600.**

Courtesy of Susan Miller

Later 30" molded hair papier-mâché doll, marked "M & S Superior" shoulder head, **$1,200.**

Courtesy of McMasters-Harris Auction

Prices listed are for appropriately costumed dolls in good condition.

French-Type: (although German in origin) shoulder head; pink kid body; wooden limbs; painted black pate; hair stippled around face; nailed-on human hair wig; glass, almond-shaped eyes; pierced nostrils; closed or open mouth with bamboo teeth; typically unmarked.

10"-12"	$1,600-$1,800
16"-22"	$2,400-$3,300
32"	$4,500

Early Papier-Mâché: shoulder head; kid or cloth body; kid or wooden limbs; molded and painted black or nailed on wig; painted or glass eyes; may have pierced nostrils; closed mouth; typically unmarked.

Glass eye:

14"-18"	$1,900-$2,500
22"-26"	$3,000-$3,600

Painted eye:

14"-18"	$1,150-$1,500
22"-24"	$1,750-$1,950
32"	$3,100

Molded Hair Papier-Mâché/Milliner's Model*: shoulder head; thin, tightly stuffed kid body; wooden limbs; painted, flat shoes; stylishly molded and painted hair; painted eyes; closed mouth; typically unmarked. (Classification is determined primarily by hairstyle. The U.F.D.C. named these demure little ladies "Molded Hair Papier-Mâchés," however, most still refer to them as Milliner's Models.)

Fancy hairstyle:

8"-12"	$1,200-$1,700
18"-20"	$3,100-$3,600
24"	$4,500

Common hairstyle:

8"-12"	$650-$900
18"-20"	$1,400-$1,600
24"	$2,000

*Add $200-$400 for a rare and unusual hairstyle and/or $400-$800 for glass eyes.

L. Moss: black papier-mâché character head; cloth body; molded and painted, tightly curled hair; glass eyes; molded tear on cheek; closed mouth; appropriately dressed; unmarked.

22"-24"	$8,500-$10,000
30"	$12,000

Later Molded Hair: shoulder head; cloth body; leather hands; molded and painted wavy hair; painted eyes; closed mouth; typically marked "M & S Superior" or unmarked.

14"-18"	$450-$600
22"-24"	$800-$850
30"	$1,250

Parian-Type Dolls

Various German porcelain factories produced parian dolls from the late 1850s through the early 1880s. Parian is a generic term for the very pale or untinted bisque dolls of the 19th century. The Dresden porcelain factories were responsible for most of the early fine parian doll heads. The hardness of the paste made it possible to cast intricately detailed molds. Authentic parian dolls are typically unmarked or marked only with a number.

Prices listed are for beautifully dressed dolls in good condition. Slight flakes from a delicate ruffle or petal of a flower would detract from the value in direct relation to the degree of damage.

Plain hairstyle: no decoration in hair or shoulder plate; may or may not have pierced ears; painted eyes:

14"-18" ....$500-$600

Men's hairstyle: molded hat; decorated shirt and tie; painted eyes:

14"-18" .... $900-$1,600

Men's hairstyle: decorated shirt and tie shoulder plate; glass eyes:

18"-22" .... $3,200-$3,600

Molded head band: no decoration on shoulder plate; may or may not have pierced ears; painted eyes:

14"-18" ....$800-$1,000

Solid dome: good wig; plain or modest shoulder plate; may or may not have pierced ears; painted eyes:

14"-18" .... $800-$1,100

Solid dome: good wig; plain or modest shoulder plate; may or may not have pierced ears; glass eyes:

14"-18" .... $1,200-$1,500

Curly hair style: bow; decorated shoulder plate; high neck ruffled blouse; brooch; intaglio eyes; open/closed mouth; molded teeth; marked "8552" (Irish Queen by Limbach):

14"-18" .... $950-$1,300

14" parian doll with plain hairstyle, painted eyes, and little decoration, **$500.**
Courtesy of Susan Miller

20" parian-type doll with glass eyes, pierced ears, hair bow, and necklace, **$2,400**; 16" parian-type with glass eyes, pierced ears, beautifully detailed ruffled bodice, and elaborately styled hair, **$2,700.**

Photo courtesy of Sotheby's Auctions

Moderately fancy hairstyle: decorated shoulder plate; may or may not have pierced ears; painted eyes:

14"-18" .... **$1,000-$1,400**

Moderately fancy hairstyle: decorated shoulder plate; may or may not have pierced ears; glass eyes:

14"-18" .... **$1,100-$1,700**

Moderately fancy hairstyle: decorated shoulder plate; applied flowers or necklace; luster hat, snood, or tiara; may or may not have pierced ears; painted eyes:

14"-18" .... **$1,400-$1,900**

Moderately fancy hairstyle: decorated shoulder plate; applied flowers or necklace; luster hat, snood, or tiara; may or may not have pierced ears; glass eyes:

14"-18" .... **$1,800-$2,300**

Elaborate hairstyle or explicitly detailed and decorated bonnet and shoulder plate; may or may not have pierced ears; painted eyes:

14"-18" .... **$1,600-$2,200**

Elaborate hairstyle or explicitly detailed and decorated bonnet and shoulder plate; may or may not have pierced ears; glass eyes:

14"-18" .... **2,200-$2,900**

Elaborate hairstyle and shoulder plate; swivel neck; may or may not have pierced ears; glass eyes:

18"-22" .... **$3,500-$4,000**

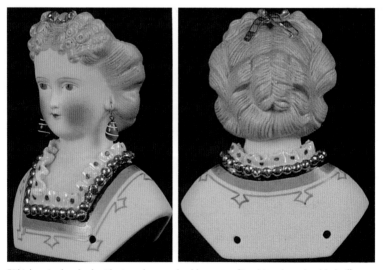

5" high parian head only with pierced ears and gold accent, café au lait curls, and molded ruffles, **$1,500.**

Courtesy of McMasters-Harris Auction

Pleasant Company

Pleasant T. Rowland was a respected educator and author of language arts material in 1985 when she founded the American Girls Series in Middleton, Wisconsin.

Each character doll was offered with an accompanying story, along with an array of furniture and accessories. When asked why she developed the stories, Ms. Rowland said she "wanted to give girls a reminder that growing up in America is, has been, and can always be an experience to treasure."

Pleasant Company was so successful that it gained the attention of the world's largest toy manufacturer, Mattel. In 1998 Mattel purchased the Pleasant Company for $700 million. Pleasant Company continues to operate as an independent subsidiary based in Wisconsin.

Prices listed are for perfect dolls in mint condition.

First dolls from 1985-1997: 18"; vinyl head and limbs; cloth body; full synthetic wig; sleep eyes; open/close smiling mouth with molded teeth.

Kirsten: young girl from the 1854 period $175
Accessories:
    Personal accessories $85
    Kirsten Learns a Lesson book with extras...................................... $250
    Kirsten's Surprise book with extras.. $265
    Happy Birthday Kirsten book with extras $450
    Kirsten Saves the Day book with extras $200
    Changes For Kirsten book with extras $200
    Kirsten's trunk $225
    Kirsten's bed $75
Samantha: young girl from the 1904 period...................................... $175
Accessories:
    Personal accessories $95
    Samantha Learns a Lesson book with extras................................... $200
    Samantha's Surprise book with extras... $175
    Happy Birthday Samantha book with extras $450
    Samantha Saves the Day book with extras...................................... $250
    Changes For Samantha book with extras.. $200
    Samantha's trunk $250
    Samantha's bed $125

Molly: young girl from the 1944 period... $175
Accessories:
    Personal accessories.. **$95**
    Molly Learns a Lesson book with extras.. **$250**
    Molly's Surprise book with extra **$175**
    Happy Birthday Molly book with extras... **$250**
    Molly Saves the Day book with extras.. **$250**
    Changes For Molly book with extras... **$150**
    Molly's trunk **$175**
    Molly's bed **$150**
Felicity: introduced in 1991.. **$150**
Addy: introduced in 1993.. **$175**
Baby Doll: introduced in 1993 .... **$100**

Pleasant Company 18" Felicity, **$150**, with her Felicity Saves the Day book and accessories, **$100**.
Courtesy of David Cobb Auction

Raggedy Ann & Andy®

The story of Raggedy Ann & Andy is a complex and emotional American legend. In 1915, Johnny Gruelle registered the trademark and patented a Raggedy Ann doll pattern. Beginning with *The Raggedy Ann Stories*, published in 1918, Gruelle wrote 25 books about Raggedy Ann and her adventures before his untimely death in 1938. The Chicago firm of P. F. Volland published Gruelle's Raggedy Ann stories and suggested that a rag doll could help promote book sales. The first Raggedy Anns were made by the Gruelle family. It is estimated that about 200 family-crafted Raggedy Anns were produced before the patent rights were given to Volland. In 1934, Volland declared bankruptcy, and the Exposition Doll and Toy Company assumed production of Raggedy Ann & Andy dolls. Exposition had the legal rights to produce Raggedy Ann & Andy dolls, however, they voluntarily withdrew from their contract when the Gruelles became embroiled in a copyright suit. The legal battle was over production of an unauthorized Molly-'es version of Raggedy Ann & Andy. Molly-'es Doll Outfitters produced Raggedy Ann & Andy dolls from 1935 to 1938 without permission from the Gruelle family, which had retained the copyright to the dolls, regardless of the manufacturer. After winning the lawsuit, the Gruelle family entered into an agreement with the Georgene Novelties Company. Georgene continued to produce Raggedy Ann & Andy for the next 25 years. When the contract with Georgene expired, Knickerbocker was awarded the license to manufacture Raggedys and use the Raggedy Ann & Andy names in 1962. Warner Communications sold Knickerbocker Toy Company, and with it the license for Raggedy Ann, to Hasbro Industries in 1982. In 1993 Applause released traditional Raggedy Ann & Andy dolls with embroidered, stitched features, along with Molly-'es reproductions.

18" Volland Andy and 16-1/2" Volland Ann, **$3,600** each, with a collection of 1918 Volland books.

Courtesy of McMasters-Harris Auction

24" Georgene Novelties Raggedy Ann & Andy with black outlined nose, **$2,900 each.**

From the collection of Rusty Herlocher

Prices listed are for originally dressed dolls in very good condition. Early Raggedys are forgiven for showing slight wear; parenthetically, an early Raggedy in excellent condition is so very rare that it would be valued at two or three times the amounts listed.

First Gruelle Family Hand-Crafted Raggedy Ann: 1918; cloth body with loosely jointed limbs; long face with hand-painted features; brown yarn hair; candy heart in body (often sucked on by a child, so look for stains on the chest); homespun calico dress and white apron; typically marked with rubber-stamped date on tummy or back, or unmarked.

16" Ann only **$8,500**

Volland Raggedy Ann or Andy: 1920-1934; cloth; movable arms and legs; brown yarn hair; painted features; button eyes; typically marked "Patented Sept. 7, 1915."

16" Ann or Andy **$3,600**
outlined nose **$4,600**
14" Beloved Belindy **$3,800**
outlined nose **$4,500**

Characters: Wonderfully imaginative rag dolls from Johnny Gruelle's books; hangtags "I am a Volland Doll, my name is (Percy Policeman/Uncle Clem, etc.), you can read about me in a book called (Beloved Belindy) and other Raggedy Ann books. The P. F. Volland Co. Joliet, Illinois."

14"-18" **$3,200**

Exposition Doll and Toy Company: 1935; 18"; brown yarn hair; painted features; these extremely rare dolls were produced for only a few months; about one dozen dolls are known to be in collections **$9,000**

Molly-'es Raggedy Ann or Andy: 1935-1938; all cloth; often patterned materials; auburn yarn hair; printed features; black-outlined nose; heart on chest; typically marked "Raggedy Ann & Andy Dolls Manufactured by Molly-'es Doll Outfitters" or unmarked.

17"-22" Ann or Andy .... **$2,700-$3,000**
14" Baby Ann .... **$3,600-$4,000**

Georgene*: 1938-1962; all cloth; stitched elbow and knee seams; printed heart on chest; silk-screen or printed features; button eyes; orangish-red yarn hair; Ann has a top-knot (few longer strands on top) to which a ribbon can be tied; typically marked with cloth label sewn into side "Johnny Gruelle's Own Raggedy Ann & Andy Dolls.../Georgene Manufacturers/Made in U.S.A."

13" Awake-Asleep Ann **$1,200**
outlined nose **$2,000**
15"-24" Ann or Andy .... **$600-$700**
outlined nose .... **$1,800-$2,900**
31"-36" .... **$1,300-$1,400**

45"-50" .... **$1,600-$2,000**
14"-18" Beloved Belindy..... **$3,600**

*While Georgene manufactured Raggedys, the company rights were renewed in Johnny Gruelle's name, except in 1946. Tagged in part "...1946 by Myrtle Gruelle Silsby..." This tag adds an additional $200 to any doll.

Knickerbocker Toy Company Raggedy Ann or Andy: 1963-1982; silk-screen printed face; red shades of yarn hair; typically marked with cloth label "Raggedy Ann or Andy.../Knickerbocker Toy Co."/country of origin.

Huggers:

7" **$200**
12"-15" .... **$150-$225**
19"-24" .... **$350-$400**
36"-40" .... **$1,000-$1,400**
78" **$2,500**
Musical.................................... **$350**
Beloved Belindy....................... **$1,500**
Camel with Wrinkled Knees **$500**
Raggedy Arthur **$400**

Hasbro/Playskool: currently available.

Applause: 1993; embroidered-type face play doll.

12" **$65**

Other Raggedy Dolls

Prices listed are for original dolls in perfect, near mint condition with boxes.

Porcelain Limited Edition: 1983; 19"; by Ideal.. **$350**

Wendy Lawton's Marcella: 1987; 17"; by Wendy Lawton; porcelain Marcella holding a small Raggedy Ann. **$750**

Anniversary Doll: 1992; 19"; by Applause. Ann or Andy.. **$150**

Molly-E Baby Ann: 1993; 13"; by Applause... **$200**

Mop Top Wendy and Billy: 1993; by Alexander Doll Co. **$200/set**

Stamp Ann Doll: 1997; 17"; copy of the commemorative stamp from the U.S. Postal Service. **$150**

15" Georgene Novelties Beloved Belindy with original box, **$3,600**.
Courtesy of McMasters-Harris Auction

Group of Raggedy Ann and Andy dolls ranging from a 45" Knickerbocker, **$1,700**, to a 15" Georgene, **$600**.

Ravca Dolls

Dolls known as the "Real People Dolls" were artistic creations of Bernard Ravca, originally of Paris, France, and later the United States. The French government had sponsored a trip to United States for Ravca to exhibit his dolls in the French Pavilion at the 1939 New York World's Fair.

While Ravca was representing his country in the United States, France fell under Nazi oppression. He spent years raising money for the Free French War Relief and orphans of the resistance movement. During Hitler's occupation of France, Ravca's entire family was lost, his studio pillaged, and his bank accounts seized. Ravca began life anew, becoming a U.S. citizen in 1947.

The sadness and loss that was so much a part of his life is reflected in his work. All facets of human emotion are conveyed, some unpleasant, but also joy and happiness.

Prices listed are for dolls in good condition.

Ravca Character: cloth; silk stockinette drawn over face and arms; cloth-covered, straw-filled wire armature body; wool wig; painted facial features; original clothing; typically marked with hangtag "Original Ravca Fabrication Française," character name, and perhaps region; "Bernard Ravca" signature, printed clothing label, or unmarked.

10"-15"	$400-$500
20"-30"	$600-$1,000
42"	$4,200

Charming 15" Ravca peddler character doll, **$500.**
Courtesy of Julia Burke, www.juliaburke.com

Theodor Recknagel

Production of dolls by Theodor Recknagel, located in Alexandri-
enthal, near Oeslau, Thüringia, Germany, began about 1893, when
he registered two mulatto doll heads, which were tinted rather
than painted.

Prices listed are for appropriately costumed dolls in good condition.

Dolly Face*: bisque socket head; jointed
wood and composition body; good wig;
glass eyes; open mouth; typically marked
"1909 DEP R/A," "RA 1907," "1914," and
possibly others.

12"-16"	**$250-$375**
20"-24"	**$450-$550**

**Add $150 for black version or exceptionally
pretty face.*

Character Baby: bisque flange or socket
head; cloth, composition bent-limb baby
or jointed body; painted or glass eyes;
open or closed mouth; typically marked
"RA," "AR," "22," "23," "28," "43," "44,"
"55," "86," "121," "126," "127," "128,"
"129," "131," "132," "134," "135," "136,"
"137," "138," "1927," and possibly others.

8"-12"	**$350-$400**
16"-18"	**$500-$600**
20"	**$700**

Characters: bisque socket heads; wood
and composition body; varying characteristics, including molded bonnet, cap,
and/or hair ornaments; painted or glass
eyes; closed or open/closed mouth; typically marked "AR," "RA," and possibly
others.

12"-14"	**$1,200-$1,600**
16"-18"	**$1,900-$2,100**

Max/Moritz: bisque character socket
head; molded and painted hair and facial features; papier-mâché body; molded and painted hair and facial features;
typically marked "31" or "32."

8"-10"	**$800-$1,000**

Incredibly pretty, nicely decorated 16" Recknagel #1907 child, **$525.**
Courtesy of James Julia Auctions, Inc.

10" Recknagel Bonnet Baby Character with
intaglio eyes, **$1,000.**
Courtesy of McMasters-Harris Auction

Santons

Santons (little saints) is a generic term used to identify the detailed clay figures individually made, for over 200 years, by artists working independently in studios within the boundaries of Provence, France.

Prices listed are for dolls in good condition with no damage.

Figurines: 1"-6"; small clay immobile; brightly hand painted; may depict adult, child, or animal; typically marked with initials or name of artist. .... **$50-$100**

Characters: 8"-12"; clay head and limbs; cloth covered wire armature body; authentically costumed, carrying appropriate accessories; typically marked with artist signature (Jouglas, Carbonet, Carbonel, Berger, and possibly others).

      8"-9" .... **$170-$200**

      10"-12" .... **$200-$300**

Wonderful examples of 10" santons signed S. Jouglas, **$250 each.**
Courtesy of Julia Burke, www.juliaburke.com

Sasha Dolls

Sasha dolls were designed by Sasha Morgenthaler. Gotz of Germany produced the first Sasha dolls, according to Morgenthaler's artistic specifications and high standards. The licensing rights were later transferred to Trendon Toy, Ltd., Reddish, Stockport, England, which continued producing Sasha dolls until the company went out of business in 1986. All Sasha dolls are similar in appearance with wistful, serious expressions, slightly darkened skin tone, and realistic body construction. A limited edition doll series was introduced in 1981 and scheduled to continue for several years, however, the closing of Trendon Toy, Ltd. in 1986 makes it highly unlikely that the final series reached the planned production quantities. In 1995, Gotz re-introduced Sashas; although similar in appearance to the earlier dolls, they are easily recognized by the "Gotz" markings.

16" boxed Trendon Toys Sasha doll in gingham dress, **$300.**

Courtesy of Julia Burke, www.juliaburke.com

Prices listed are for dolls in near mint, original condition.

Sasha Serie: 16"; similar in appearance to early Gotz; marked "Sasha Serie."..**$2,400**

Trendon Toys, Ltd.: 16"; straight upper eyelid; marked with wrist tag only. .... **$300-$600**

Dolls with no Philtrum and hand painted eyes.................**$4,000-$5,500**

Bent-limb Baby: 12"; rigid plastic, jointed at neck, shoulder, and hip; cup-like hands; rooted hair; painted eyes; closed mouth; marked with wrist tag only.

White	$250
Black	$300
Sexed	$400

20th Anniversary Sasha: 16"; black hair; copy of first Sasha doll; made by Trendon Toys, Ltd.; wearing blue corduroy dress. **$400**

Limited Edition Series: 16"; with certificate and wrist tag.

Velvet: girl; black hair; gray eyes; blue velvet dress; 1981, limited to 5,000. .... **$500**

Pintuck: girl; light hair; brown eyes; cotton dress with pin tucking; 1982, limited to 6,000. .... **$500**

Kiltie: girl; human hair; gray eyes; black watch tartan dress; amethyst necklace; 1983, limited to 4,000. . **$550**

Harlequin: girl; long hair; straw hat; carrying wooden guitar; 1984, limited to 5,000. .... **$600**

Prince Gregor: boy; dark hair; tunic top; 1985, limited to 4,000. .... **$600**

Princess: girl; long blond hair; blue eyes; pink dress; blue velvet cape; 1986, limited to 3,500. .... **$1,900**

Sasha Sari: 16"; wearing exquisitely made sari from India; marked with wrist tag only. **$1,200**

Early Morgenthaler Original: 20"; original artist doll. .... **$9,000 or more**

20" portrait doll by Sasha Morgenthaler, **$9,000.**
Courtesy of McMasters-Harris Auction

Bruno Schmidt

In 1900, Bruno Schmidt founded his bisque doll factory in Walter-shausen, Germany.

Schmidt's doll company manufactured and distributed several very desirable and highly collectible character dolls, purchased exclusively from Bähr & Pröschild.

Schmidt eventually purchased the Bähr & Pröschild Company. Bruno Schmidt doll heads often bear both firms' trademarks, as well as two sets of mold numbers. The three-digit numbers were Bähr & Pröschild's; the four-digit mold numbers beginning with a "2" were registered by Bruno Schmidt

Prices listed are for appropriately costumed dolls in good condition.

Dolly Face*: bisque socket head; jointed composition body; good wig; glass eyes; open mouth; typically marked "B.S.W." within a heart and/or "2154."

16"-20"	$700-$1,000
24"-28"	$1,400-$1,800
30"-32"	$2,400-$2,900

*Add $200 for flirty eyes.

Character Doll*: bisque socket head; jointed composition body; molded and painted hair or good wig; painted or glass eyes; open, closed, or open/closed mouth; typically marked "BSW" within a heart, and a number "2020," "2023," "2025," "2033," "2048," "2068," "2070," "2072," "2074," "2075," "2081," "2084," "2085," "2092," "2094," "2095," "2096," "2097," or "2099"; may also include a three-digit number, beginning with "5," such as 524, 537, 538, or 539.

2023, 2025, or 2026 CM, glass eyes:
18"-20" .... $6,000-$7,500

Beautiful 20" painted eye character #2023 boy by Bruno Schmidt, **$5,000.**
Courtsey Roberta and Ziggy of Roberta's Doll House, 800-569-9739

Very rare large 24" glass-eyed Wendy, **$40,000**, holding a #426 Bruno Schmidt all bisque, **$425.**

Courtesy of James Julia Auctions, Inc.

2023, 2025, or 2026 CM, painted eyes:
18"-20" .... **$4,700-$5,000**
2033 (Wendy) CM, glass eyes:
18"-20" .... **$30,000-$37,000**
2048, 2094, or 2096 (Tommy Tucker) OM, glass eyes:
18"-20" .... **$2,100-$2,200**
2048 (Tommy Tucker) CM, glass eyes:
18"-20" .... **$3,850-$4,100**
2072 CM, glass eyes:
18"-20" .... **$5,000-$5,300**
2072 OM, glass eyes:
18"-20" .... **$2,000-$2,100**
2092, 2097, or 2099 OM, glass eyes:
18"-20" .... **$1,100-$1,200**

Add $500 for jointed toddler body and/or $200 for flirty eyes to any character doll.

Bruno Schmidt 26" #2097 character baby, **$1,800**, and 23" Franz Schmidt #1272 with a retractable tongue, **$1,500.**

Courtesy of David Cobb Auction

Franz Schmidt

This bisque doll company was founded by Franz Schmidt in 1890 in Georgenthal, Thüringia, Germany. Franz Schmidt dolls are well known for their charming modeling and consistently excellent quality. Simon & Halbig porcelain factory supplied the bisque heads according to designs and specifications set forth by Schmidt.

Prices listed are for appropriately costumed dolls in good condition.

Dolly Face: bisque socket or shoulder head; kid or jointed composition body; good wig; glass eyes; open mouth; typically marked "269," "293," "1180," "1250," "1253," "1370," "S & Co. Simon & Halbig," "FS & C Simon & Halbig," and possibly others.

Shoulder head:
12"-14"	$300-$350
18"-22"	$500-$650
24"-26"	$800-$900

Socket head:
12"-14"	$550-$650
18"-24"	$800-$1,100
28"-30"	$1,300-$1,600
36"	$2,800
42"	$4,200

Character Baby*: bisque socket head; composition bent-limb baby body; good wig or solid dome; glass eyes; open mouth; often with pierced nostrils; typically marked "FS & C," "1271," "1272," "1295," "1296," "1297," "1310," and possibly others.

12"-14"	$800-$850
16"-20"	$900-$1,200
24"-26"	$1,700-$1,900
28"	$2,500

*Add $500 for jointed toddler or key-wound walker body, or $400-$600 for black version.

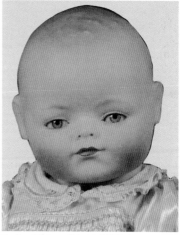

Darling 14" Franz Schmidt #1285 character baby, **$1,200.**
Courtesy of McMasters-Harris Auction

28" Franz Schmidt #1295 open mouth breather with original box, **$2,500.**

Courtesy of David Cobb Auction

Character Doll: bisque socket head; jointed composition body; molded and painted hair or good wig; glass or painted eyes; open, closed, or open/closed mouth; typically marked "1262," "1263," "1266," "1267," "1286," and possibly others.

    1262 O/CM, painted eyes:
        18"-20" ....**$13,000-$15,200**
    1263 CM, painted eyes:
        18"-20" ....**$22,000-$25,000**
    1266 O/CM, painted eyes:
        18"-20" ....**$5,100-$5,400**
    1267 or 1270 CM, painted eyes:
        18"-20" ....**$3,000-$3,200**
    1286 OM, smiling, glass eyes:
        18"-20" ....**$4,900-$5,200**

Schmitt et Fils

Schmitt et Fils, which translates to Schmitt and Sons, was located at Nogent-sur-Marne, Seine and Paris, France. Maurice and Charles Schmitt manufactured bébés from 1863 to 1891.

Prices listed are for appropriately costumed dolls in good condition.

Bébé*: bisque socket head; jointed wood-and-composition, flat bottom body; straight wrists; long , flat feet; good wig; oval-cut paperweight eyes, richly lined in black; blush eye shadow; thick, short lashes; feathered brows; pierced, lightly blushed ears; closed mouth with slight space between lips; typically marked "SCH" with crossed hammers and a shield.

12"-16" ....$18,000-$24,000
18"-22" ....$26,000-$30,000
26" $32,000

OM Bébé with teeth:

22" $28,000

*Add $3,000 for a "cup and saucer" neck (bébés with the neck ending in a dome shape that fits into the socket, eliminating the line at the base of the neck).

Very appealing, beautifully costumed 24" Schmitt et Fils bébé, **$31,000.**
Courtesy of James Julia Auctions, Inc.

20" Schmitt et Fils bébé #9 with matching #9 Schmitt body, **$28,000.**
Courtesy of David Cobb Auction

Schoenau & Hoffmeister

The Schoenau & Hoffmeister porcelain factory was located in Burg-grub, Upper Franconia, Germany. Founded in 1901 by Arthur Schoenau and Carl Hoffmeister of Sonneberg, the factory produced bisque doll heads until 1953.

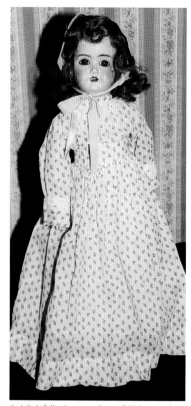

A delightfully charming, beautiful blue-eyed 20" Schoenau & Hoffmeister child, **$700.**

From the collection of the delightfully charming, beautiful blue-eyed Clara MacDonald

Prices listed are for appropriately costumed dolls in good condition.

Dolly Face: bisque shoulder or socket head; jointed composition or kid body; good wig; glass eyes; open mouth; typically marked "SH," a five-pointed star, "PB," "1400," "1800," "1904," "1906," "2500," "4500," "4700," "5300," "5700," or "5800."

14"-18"	$500-$600
22"-24"	$800-$900
28"-32"	$1,200-$1,500
36"-38"	$2,000-$2,500
40"	$3,000

Character Baby: bisque socket head; composition bent-limb baby body; good wig; glass eyes; open mouth; typically marked "S H" with "P.B.H," "Porzellanfabrik Burggrub," "900," "169," "769," "Special," and "Burggrub Baby."

12"-16"	$500-$700
20"-24"	$850-$1,000
26"-28"	$1,200-$1,400

26" Schoenau & Hoffmeister "Porzellanfabrik Burggrub," **$1,700**, and a 24" Armand Marseille (Edmund Edelmann) Melitta character toddler, **$2,700.**

Courtesy of David Cobb Auction

Solid Dome Infant: bisque flange neck; cloth body; painted hair; small glass sleep eyes; closed mouth; appropriately dressed; typically marked "N.K.B.," may also have stamp in German.

10"-14" .... $850-$950

Hanna Character Baby*: bisque socket head; composition bent-limb baby body; good wig; large, rounded glass eyes; no painted upper lashes; winged, feathered brows; open, slightly smiling mouth; typically marked "S (star with PB) H/Hanna."

16"-20" .... $1,000-$1,400
22"-26" .... $1,600-$1,900

*Add $500 for jointed toddler body. Add $300 for black version.

"Künstlerkopf": (Art Doll Head) bisque, slender-face child doll; glass eyes; open mouth; typically marked "Künstlerkopf," and/or "4000," "4600," "5000," or "5500."

16" $900
24" $1,400

Das Lachende Baby: (The Laughing Baby) bisque, full-faced socket head; composition bent-limb body; good wig; glass eyes; open, smiling mouth with two upper teeth; typically marked "Porzellanfabrik/Burggrub/Das Lachende Baby/1930/Made in Germany/D.R.G.M."

14"-16" .... $1,700-$1,900
20"-22" .... $2,500-$2,800
24" $3,000

Princess Elizabeth: bisque socket head; jointed composition body; blond mohair wig; oval blue sleep, slightly squinting eyes; rosy cheeks; open, smiling mouth; pretty expression; typically marked "Porzellanfabrik/Burggrub/Princess Elizabeth/Made in Germany."

14"-18" .... $2,200-$2,500
22"-24" .... $2,900-$3,200

Character Doll: bisque socket head; jointed composition body; good wig; deeply cut, rounded eyes; winged brows; open mouth; wistful expression; typically marked "S (pb) within a star," "H," and "OX."

12" $2,400
18"-20" .... $3,200-$3,600
22" $4,000

24" Schoenhut & Hoffmeister Hanna toddler, **$1,700.**
Courtesy of Susan Miller

23" Schoenau & Hoffmeister Princess Elizabeth character toddler, **$3,000.**
Courtesy of David Cobb Auction

A. Schoenhut & Company

Albert Schoenhut founded A. Schoenhut & Company in Philadelphia, Pennsylvania, in 1872, continuing a family tradition of toy makers. Arriving to the United States at the age of 17, Schoenhut worked at several different jobs before he established his own toy factory at the age of 22.

The famous Humpty Dumpty Circus, introduced in 1903, included Schoenhut's first attempt at doll making. In 1909, Schoenhut filed a patent application for his swivel, spring-jointed dolls, but the patent was not granted until 1911.

Beautifully detailed A. Schoenhut 19" Bonnet Girl, **$8,000.**

Courtesy of McMasters-Harris Auction

Prices listed are for originally costumed dolls in good to very good condition. Slight rubs and chips are somewhat acceptable.

Character: wooden, spring-jointed body; carved, molded (possibly with a ribbon or bow) hair or good wig; intaglio eyes; closed or open/closed mouth; typically marked with paper label "Schoenhut Doll/Pat. Jan 17th 1911/U.S.A.," incised on back "Schoenhut Doll, Pat. Jan 17 '11 U.S.A./& Foreign Countries."

Carved hair, intaglio eyes:
14"-16" .... **$2,800-$2,900**
19"-21" .... **$3,000-$3,300**
Wearing wig, intaglio eyes:
14"-16" .... **$2,000-$2,100**
19"-21" .... **$2,300-$2,500**

Bonnet Girl: molded and painted hair around face; cap molded to head; intaglio eyes; open/closed mouth; typically marked with paper label "Schoenhut Doll/Pat. Jan 17th 1911/U.S.A." on back:
14" **$6,500**
19" **$8,000**

Schnickel-Fritz: molded, wavy hair; squinting, painted eyes; toothy grin:
16" **$4,200**

Five A. Schoenhut wooden characters all re-dressed with replaced shoes including a 19" manikin, **$2,500**; 16" worn sleep-eye child with face-rubs, **$700**; 16" Miss Dolly, **$600**; 7" Jiggs, **$300**; and 9" Maggie, **$350**. If these characters were in original condition, the values would be **$3,100**, **$1,400**, **$1,300**, **$750**, and **$750**, respectively.
Courtesy of David Cobb Auction

A pair of 7-1/2" Barney Google dolls, **$550** each; pair of 8-1/2" Spark Plug dolls, **$700** each; and Maggie and Jiggs, **$750** each, backed by a 1923 lithographed poster.
Courtesy of David Cobb Auction

Tootsie Wootsie: lightly molded, short hair; small eyes; open/closed mouth: 16" **$5,000**

Black Child: molded, curly hair; slightly side-glancing eyes: 16" **$5,200**

Manikin: pensive expression, mature look male:
    19" **$3,100**

Schoenhut Baby: wooden, jointed toddler or bent-limb baby body; painted hair; painted eyes; open or closed mouth; typically marked "©," label reading "C" in center; "H. E. Schoenhut 1913" printed on rim; "Schoenhut Doll/Pat. Jan 17th 1911/U.S.A." inscribed on shoulder; blue stamped "Patent applied for; Schoenhut Doll."
  Toddler body:
    11" **$1,000**
    14"-17" .... **$1,100-$1,300**
  Bent-limb baby body:
    11" **$1,000**
    17"-19" .... **$1,000-$1,100**

Miss Dolly: (Dolly Face) wooden, spring-jointed body; good wig; painted or decal rounded eyes; open/closed mouth with painted teeth; typically marked with "Schoenhut/Doll Pat. Jan 17 '11 U.S.A./& Foreign Countries" incised on back.
    14"-16" .... **$1,100-$1,300**
    19"-21" .... **$1,500-$1,700**

Walker Body: wooden, jointed at shoulder and hip; painted features; typically marked with label reading "C" in center; "H. E. Schoenhut 1913" printed on rim; or "Schoenhut Doll/Pat. Jan 17 '11 U.S.A./& Foreign Countries."
    11" **$900**
    14"-17" .... **$1,100-$1,300**

Sleep-Eye Child: wooden; good wig; sleep eyes; open mouth with teeth; typically marked "Schoenhut Doll/Pat. Jan 17th 1911/USA," "C" in center; "H. E. Schoenhut 1913" printed on rim.
    14"-16" .... **$1,100-$1,200**
    19"-21" .... **$1,300-$1,400**

Group of Schoenhut circus
characters including Animal
Trainer, **$450**; Lady Bareback
Rider, **$500**; Ringmaster (2),
$550; Monkeys (2), **$450**;
Negro Dude (3), $750; Chinese
Acrobat (4), **$450**.
Courtesy of David Cobb Auction

Composition: all jointed composition; molded and
painted hair; painted eyes; small closed mouth; typically marked with paper label reading "Schoenhut
Toys/Made in U.S.A."

13" **$800**

Mama Doll: hollow wooden head and hands; cloth
body; mohair wig; painted features; typically marked
with Schoenhut stamp on head:

14"-16" ....**$800-$900**

**Character Figures (Lion Tamer, Roly-Poly, Clown,
Farmer, Milkmaid, Ringmaster, Acrobat, Maggie,
Jiggs, Barney Google, Spark Plug, and others):** 5"-
9" comical, jointed characters; good modeling; painted
features. ....**$450-$800**

Early Humpty Dumpty Circus: complete with tent, animals, and figures... **$3,900**

Later Humpty Dumpty Circus Parade: #18, complete
with tent, animals, and figures. **$2,600**

Simon & Halbig

The Simon & Halbig porcelain factory was located in Frafenhain and Hidburghausen, near Ohrdruf, Thüringia, Germany. Founded by Wilham Simon and Carl Halbig in 1839, it began producing dolls in the late 1860s or early 1870s. The company's tinted and untinted bisque shoulder heads with molded hair and delicate decoration are typical of the prodigious number of fine-quality dolls it produced. Kid-bodied shoulder heads from the 1880s closely followed the French classic standard of large, often paperweight eyes, pierced ears, and heavy brows. A number of swivel heads on kid-lined shoulder plates were made entirely in the French manner. Virtually any combination of features have been found with the Simon & Halbig mark, including solid dome, open pate or Belton-type; molded and painted hair or wigged; painted, stationary, sleep paperweight or flirty eyes; open, closed, or open/closed mouths; and pierced or unpierced ears. It was not unusual for a particular mold to have been produced with a variety of characteristics. Most Simon & Halbig dolls are fully marked. The ampersand was added to the mark in 1905.

Prices listed are for appropriately costumed dolls in good condition.

Child Dolls

Unique Face: socket head; jointed composition body; good wig; glass eyes; feathered brows; pierced ears; open mouth; typically marked "Simon & Halbig," "S & H," "759," "769," "719," "749," "939," "949," "979."

12"-16"	**$2,000-$2,600**
22"	**$3,400**
30"	**$5,300**

Santa: socket head; jointed composition body; good wig; glass eyes; pierced ears; open mouth; typically marked "Simon & Halbig," "S & H," "1248," or "1249."

14"-20"	**$1,400-$1,800**
24"-28"	**$2,200-$2,600**
32"-34"	**$2,900-$3,300**

Simon & Halbig 22" #1039 nicely costumed, flirty-eyed cutie, **$1,600.**
From the collection of Ginger Sands.

Simon & Halbig dolls: 24"
#570, **$1,200**; 23" 550,
$1,150; and 22" 540 dolly
face, **$1,100.**

Courtesy of David Cobb Auction

Cute little 14" Simon & Halbig
#1079, **$850.**

*From the collection of Pat and
Bill Tyson.*

Dolly Face Socket Head: socket head; jointed composition body; good wig; glass eyes; softly feathered brows; pierced ears; open mouth; typically marked "Simon & Halbig," "S & H," "540," "550," "570," "1079," "1078," and "Baby Blanche."

18"-22"	**$950-$1,100**
24"-26"	**$1,200-$1,400**

Baby Blanche, 540, 550, and 570:

24"	**$950**

Dolly Face Shoulder Head: shoulder head; kid body; bisque arms; good wig; glass eyes; pierced ears; open mouth; typically marked "Simon & Halbig," "S & H," "1040," "1080," "1250," and "1260."

14"-18"	**$950-$1,000**
24"-28"	**$1,400-$1,600**
30"	**$1,900**

Note: Add $300 for an open mouth doll with square teeth, or $500 for black version.

Character Dolls*

Due to the wide variety of Simon & Halbig character dolls, the following information is arranged by mold numbers.

*Add $300 for an open mouth doll with square teeth and/or $500 for a jointed toddler body.

SH Fashion doll; socket head; shoulder plate; kid body; good wig, glass eyes; CM.

12"	**$3,300**
18"	**$4,200**

SH Fashion doll; socket head; wooden lady's body; good wig, glass eyes; CM.

10"	**$5,300**
16"	**$7,000**

Simon & Halbig Socket head; well-defined eyes and nose modeling; OM; tentative smile.

28"	**$36,000**
30"	**$42,500**

SH Shoulder head lady; glass eyes; molded hair with bow; pierced ears; CM.

12"	**$2,400**
16"	**$4,000**

SH Shoulder head lady; painted eyes; molded hair with bow; pierced ears; CM.

12"	**$1,950**
16"	**$3,800**

SH IV Socket head; good wig; glass, stationary eyes; CM.

14"	**$24,000**
18"	**$34,500**

110 Socket head; glass eyes; O/CM smiling mouth; molded tongue and teeth.

14" **$6,750**

120 Character baby face; glass eyes; OM.

12" **$3,200**

21" **$5,700**

150 Socket head; good wig; intaglio eyes; CM.

16" **$22,000**

26" **$59,000**

151 Socket head; good wig; dimples; intaglio eyes; O/CM; smiling with teeth.

14" **$9,000**

23" **$18,000**

152 Socket head; long nose; molded eyelids; painted eyes; CM.

18" **$28,000**

24" **$36,000**

153 Socket head; molded hair; painted eyes; CM (Little Duke).

18" **$49,000**

172 Character baby; molded hair.

14" **$4,400**

411 Fashion lady; shoulder head; cloth and kid body; glass eyes; good wig; O/CM with molded teeth.

18" **$5,600**

600 Baby; good wig; dimples; glass eyes; OM.

16" **$2,000**

601 Socket head; smiling with molded teeth; glass eyes; OM.

31" **$19,500**

616 Baby; good wig; glass eyes; OM.

20" **$1,850**

719 Socket head; round face; glass eyes; CM.

20" **$6,900**

23" **$7,800**

720, 740, 940, or 950 Shoulder head; glass eyes; CM.

12" **$1,500**

739 Dolly face; good wig; glass eyes; OM.

18" **$2,600**

26" **$5,000**

749 Socket head; glass eyes; CM.

20" **$4,400**

24" **$4,950**

905 Socket head; good wig; glass eyes; CM.

16" **$4,750**

905/908 Shoulder head; good wig; glass eyes; OM.

16" **$3,800**

919 Child, glass eyes; CM.

17" **$10,000**

20" **$15,000**

Beautiful 20" Simon & Halbig #152 character lady, **$30,000.**
Courtesy of McMasters-Harris Auction

20" closed mouth Simon & Halbig #950 character doll, **$2,200.**
Courtesy of David Cobb Auction

19" Simon & Halbig #1159 lady doll, **$2,700**.
Courtesy of McMasters-Harris Auction

920 Shoulder head; glass eyes; solid dome with wig; CM.
  18" **$3,400**
929 Child; glass eyes; CM.
  20" **$5,400**
939 Socket head; glass eyes; OM.
  18" **$4,100**
  27" **$6,000**
941 Shoulder head; good wig; glass eyes; OM.
  22" **$1,850**
949 Socket head; glass eyes; CM.
  16" **$3,700**
  24" **$4,600**
949 Shoulder head; glass eye OM.
  18" **$1,700**
969 Shoulder head; glass eyes; smiling OM.
  20" **$3,650**
979 Socket head; glass eyes; OM.
  18" **$4,100**
989 Socket head; glass eyes; CM.
  22" **$4,750**
  24" **$6,100**

1009, 1010, or 1109 Shoulder head; good wig; glass eyes; OM.
  16" **$1,450**
  20" **$1,700**
1039 Pull-string walker body; good wig; glass eyes; OM.
  22" **$2,000**
1039 Key-wind walker body; good wig; sleep eyes; OM.
  22" **$2,400**
1039 Socket head; good wig; flirty eyes; OM.
  16" **$1,300**
  24" **$2,000**
1139 Socket head; good wig; glass eyes; OM.
  24" **$3,400**
1159 Lady's body; good wig; glass eyes; OM.
  12" **$1,900**
  24" **$3,600**
1160 Shoulder head; fancy mohair wig; glass eyes; CM (Little Women).
  6"-7" ....**$550-$600**
  10"-14" ....**$700-$950**
1269 Socket head; good wig; sleep eyes; OM.
  18" **$1,600**
1279 Socket head; good wig; glass eyes; OM w/pursed lips, upper teeth.
  12" **$2,600**
  24" **$5,500**
1294 Baby socket head; good wig; flirty eyes; OM.
  18" **$1,200**
  24" **$2,000**
1299 Socket head; good wig; glass eyes; OM.
  12" **$1,800**
  16" **$2,000**
1303 Older woman; may be darker-complexion American Indian; good wig; glass eyes; CM.
  14" **$23,000**
  21" **$27,000**
1304 White-faced clown; oval, glass eyes; arched brows; CM; smiling.
  13" **$3,200**
  22" **$5,100**

10" Simon & Halbig #1428, **$3,200**, and an 11" Kestner #237, **$3,100**.
Courtesy of David Cobb Auction

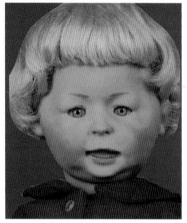

Impish 16" Simon & Halbig #1428 character baby, **$3,900**.
Courtesy of McMasters-Harris Auction

1305 Sharp-featured older woman; glass eyes; O/CM; smiling.
　16" **$18,000**
　20" **$32,000**
1307 Long-face lady; glass eyes; CM.
　20" **$25,000**
1308 Coke Maker; socket head painted to show smudges; mohair wig; glass eyes; smiling, CM*.
　14" **$22,000**
SH Gentleman; socket head; molded mustache; good wig; glass eyes; smiling, CM.
　16" **$26,000**
1339 Glass eyes; OM; "L.L. & S."
　18" **$1,500**
　24" **$2,600**
1358 Beautiful ebony child; glass eyes; OM.
　19" **$16,000**
1388 Socket head; good wig; glass eyes; O/CM, wide smile, molded teeth.
　24" **$38,000**
1398 Socket head; good wig; glass eyes; O/CM, wide smile, molded teeth.
　24" **$27,000**

Rare 22" Simon & Halbig #1358 black character child, **$20,000**.
Courtesy of James Julia Auctions, Inc.

15" closed mouth Simon & Halbig glass eye #1448 character doll, **$26,000.**
Courtesy of David Cobb Auction

1418 Socket head; good wig; glass eyes; CM, pouty; full cheeks.
   16" **$7,900**
1428 Crooked smile; good wig; glass eyes; O/CM, impish.
   16" **$3,900**
   21" **$4,800**
   25" **$5,200**
1448 Socket head; good wig; pierced ears; glass sleep eyes; CM.
   15" **$26,000**
   24" **$38,000**
1468 Socket head; sweet expression; glass eyes; CM.
   14" **$4,500**
1469 Lady's body; good wig; glass eyes; CM.
   16" **$5,000**
1478 Socket head; glass eyes; CM.
   16" **$14,000**
1488 Baby; glass eyes; O/CM.
   20" **$6,200**
1489 Baby; good wig; glass eyes; OM.
   22" **$4,900**
1498 Solid dome glass eyes; O/CM.
   16" **$3,700**
   22" **$5,700**

*Coke Maker's costume consists of a long black coat, black pants, red vest with two rows of brass buttons, and black felt hat.

OM = Open Mouth

CM = Closed Mouth

O/CM = Open/Closed Mouth

16" solid dome Simon & Halbig #1498, **$3,700,** with 20" Yes-No mohair bear.
Courtesy of David Cobb Auction

Société de Fabrication de Bébés & Jouets (S.F.B.J.)

The Société de Fabrication de Bébés & Jouets (Society for the Manufacturer of Bébés and Toys) is commonly referred to as S.F.B.J. In 1899, the society signed an agreement for locations in Paris and Montreuil-sous-Bois, France.

Most of the premier French firms joined the S.F.B.J. syndicate. Many continued to produce the same dolls under S.F.B.J. that they had previously made as individual independent companies. Dolls produced under the amalgamation rarely met the high standards set by the original firms.

S.F.B.J. 22" #60 bébé, **$1,300.**
Courtesy of David Cobb Auction

S.F.B.J. 24" #301 bébé, **$1,300.**
Courtesy of David Cobb Auction

S.F.B.J. 11" #60 with special
clown facial painting, **$1,400.**
Photo courtesy of James D. Julia Inc.

Prices listed are for appropriately costumed dolls in good condition.

Jumeau-Type Bébé: bisque socket head; jointed composition body; very pretty, obviously Jumeau modeling; good wig; paperweight eyes; open mouth; typically marked "S.F.B.J." and/or size number only.

16"-22" .... **$1,900-$2,600**
26"-28" .... **$3,000-$3,250**

S.F.B.J. Bébé: bisque socket head; jointed composition body; good wig; glass eyes; open mouth; typically marked "S.F.B.J.," "S.F.B.J./301/Paris," "S.F.B.J./60/Paris," and "Bluette #301."

60*:
    12"-18" .... $900-$1,100
    22"-28" .... **$1,300-$1,600**
301:
    14"-26" .... **$900-$1,500**
    28"-32" .... **$2,200-$2,400**
    38" **$3,200**
Bluette:
    10-1/2"-11" .... **$2,400-$2,700**
Black Dolly Face:
    12" **$1,300**
    16"-18" .... **$2,400-$2,600**

*Add $500 for special clown facial paint. Deduct $200 for painted eyes.

Character Dolls: bisque socket head; jointed body; molded and painted or flocked hair, or good wig; painted or glass eyes; open, closed, or open/closed mouth; typically marked "S.F.B.J./PARIS" and a mold number.

Boxed interchangeable heads, molds 233, 235, and 237:
    14" **$14,000**
52 CM, upward-glancing eyes, black:
    13" **$2,800**
225 O/CM, molded teeth:
    18" **$2,300**
226 O/CM, smiling:
    14" **$2,600**
227 OM, character:
    18" **$2,700**
229 OM, molded teeth:
    18" **$4,100**
230 OM, chin dimples (may be marked Jumeau):
    18" **$2,300**
233 OM, screamer:
    18" **$6,000**
234 OM, smiling, movable tongue:
    18" **$4,400**
235* O/CM, squinting eyes:
    20" **$3,800**

S.F.B.J. 18" #236 Laughing
Jumeau, **$2,300**; 15" #235
smiling character, **$3,000**; and
13-1/2" #251 flirty-eyed character toddler, **$2,500.**
Courtesy of David Cobb Auction

236* O/CM, laughing:
  20" **$2,600**
237 or 266 OM, wigged or flocked hair:
  16" **$3,000**
238 OM, smiling, expressive eyes:
  16" **$3,400**
239 CM, street urchin:
  18" **$9,250**
242 OM, nursing baby:
  16" **$7,500**
246 OM, round face child:
  16" **$3,900**
247 OM, overbite, deeply molded eyes socket:
  14" **$2,200**
248 CM, pouty, fly-away brows:
  16" **$14,000**
250 O/CM, smiling lady:
  18" **$4,200**
251 OM, overbite, cheek dimples:
  14" **$2,450**
252 CM, pouty:
  16" **$5,300**
262 OM, lower lashes only:
  18" **$2,300**
287 O/CM, intaglio eyes:
  12" **$2,700**

Add $500 for a jointed toddler body.
OM = Open Mouth
CM = Closed Mouth
O/CM = Open/Closed Mouth

S.F.B.J. 21" #247 Twirp character child, **$3,500.**
Courtesy of David Cobb Auction

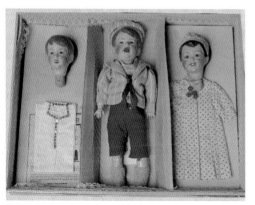

S.F.B.J. 14" boxed interchangeable character set with mold numbers 233, 235, and 237, **$14,000.**
Courtesy of James Julia Auctions, Inc.

S.F.B.J. 19" #252 Pouty child, **$5,500.**
Courtesy of James Julia Auctions, Inc.

Sonneberg Täufling

Sonneberg Täufling, often referred to as Motschmann Babies, were made by various manufacturers in the Sonneberg area of Germany as early as 1851. Täufling simply means a baby dressed in a shift.

Sonneberg Täufling dolls may be found stamped with the name Ch. Motschmann. Motschmann held the patent for the voice boxes often found within the doll bodies.

Sonneberg Täufling 10" papier-mâché baby, **$1,300.**
Courtesy of Susan Miller

Prices listed are for appropriately dressed dolls in good condition.

Sonneberg Täufling: wax over composition or papier-mâché shoulder head; cloth and composition body with floating joints; solid dome; painted wisps of hair above ears or fine mohair wig; very oval-shaped glass, black, pupilless eyes; no lashes; faint, single-stroke brows; closed or open mouth with bamboo teeth; unmarked.

    8"-12" .... **$1,100-$1,600**
    16"-20" .... **$2,200-$2,700**
    24" **$3,700**

Steiff

The German town of Gienger an der Brenz was the home of Margarete Steiff. Born in 1847, Margarete contracted polio at the age of two, weakening her legs and right hand. This did not, however, dampen her spirits, for she was determined to learn to sew in order to support herself. As a young woman, Steiff became an accomplished seamstress with her own workshop where she made clothing for women and children from wool felt. In 1880, a flash of inspiration changed her life forever. She designed and created a small felt elephant pincushion, which was popular among the neighborhood children, who wanted copies to use as playthings. Steiff then began to commercially produce small stuffed animals. In 1897, Steiff's nephew, Richard, joined the family business, assuming leadership when Margarete passed away in 1909. Although best known for its animals, Steiff also produced dolls advertised as "jovial lads and buxom maidens." Felt pressed heads with a seam down the middle of the face, mohair wigs, glass eyes, and large feet are classic Steiff doll characteristics. Beginning in 1988 and continuing into the 1990s, Steiff reintroduced several earlier popular characters.

Prices listed are for originally costumed dolls in very good condition.

Adult Doll: felt, velvet, or plush; seam down center of face; oversized nose; applied ears; large feet; glass button eyes; painted or embroidered features; original costume; typically marked with ear-button.

12"-14"	**$2,200-$2,600**
18"-22"	**$2,900-$3,700**

Child Doll: felt, velvet, or plush; seam down center of face; jointed body; applied ears; glass button eyes; painted features; original costume; typically marked with ear-button.

12"	**$1,600**
18"	**$2,100**

18" vintage Steiff child in excellent condition, **$2,200.**
Photo courtesy of Sotheby's Auction

Steiff 10-1/2" early center
seam Red Riding Hood
character, **$1,500.**
Courtesy of McMasters-Harris Auction

16" modern (1986/1987)
limited edition Steiff lady and
gentleman, **$500 pair.** (How
could you possibly separate
the pair, when he is so obviously captivated by her?)

Steiff 10" Gucki and Pucki
character elves, **$900.**
Courtesy of Susan Miller

Steiff 19" soldier from the
1910 military series, **$4,500**,
holding box of Irish Guard
Britains soldiers.
Courtesy of Bertoia Auctions

Wonderfully preserved Steiff
19" black character child,
$3000.
Courtesy of McMasters-Harris Auction

Black child:
 12"-18" .... **$2,300-$2,900**
Character Doll: felt, velvet, or plush; seam down center of face; applied ears; large feet; jointed body; glass
button eyes; painted and embroidered features; original costume; typically marked with ear-button.
 Military Officer or Soldier:
  18"-21" .... **$4,500-$4,750**
 Mickey or Minnie Mouse:
  10"-14" .... **$2,200-$3,200**
 Clown:
  14"-18" .... **$2,800-$3,400**
 Golliwog:
  14" **$4,600**
 Max and Moritz:
  16" **$7,800/pair**
 Comic Characters:
  12"-16" .... **$900-$3,000**
Modern Limited Edition: (tennis player, gentleman,
lady, clown).
 16" **$250**
Vinyl Steiff Doll: vinyl head and arms; cloth body;
marked with ear-button.
 20" **$350**

Jules Steiner

Jules Nicholas Steiner founded his famous doll company in 1855 in Paris. Steiner was succeeded by Amédée La Fosse from 1892-1893 and, following his death, by his widow, who ran the business until 1899. From 1899 to 1901, Jules Mettais headed the company. He, in turn, was succeeded by Edmond Daspres from 1904 until 1908.

A variety of markings will be found, including some that may seem strange:

Fl, Fire, or Figure = face or countenance
Bte = registered
Ste = Steiner
SUCCe = successor
S.G.D.G. = registered, but without government guarantee
Bourgoin = a Paris merchant dealing in porcelains and associated with Jules Steiner
Markings usually include a size number and a letter such as "A," "B," "C," "D," "E," "F," or "G."

Prices listed are for beautifully dressed dolls in good condition.

Early Round Face: very pale socket head; jointed wood-and-composition body; stubby fingers; mohair or skin wig; paperweight almond-shaped eyes; pink eye shadow; thin brows; with or without pierced ears; closed or open mouth; upper and lower teeth; thin lips; typically unmarked; body may be stamped "J. Steiner fabricante," "J. Steiner fabricate, rue de Saintonge, No. 25 Paris, Prissette, Imp. Pass du Carre 17."

    Closed mouth:
        18"-22" .... **$17,000-$21,000**
    Open mouth:
        11"-16" .... **$7,200-$8,200**
        18"-20" .... **$9,200-$9,700**
Täufling-Type Body*: round, very pale shoulder head with molded, full shoulder and upper body; bisque lower body/hip and tops of legs; cloth joints (same body-

Gorgeous 28" Steiner Series C bébé, **$16,000.**
Courtesy of David Cobb Auction

19" early round face, closed mouth Jules Steiner, **$8,000.**
Courtesy of David Cobb Auction

31" Steiner closed mouth Figure A bébé, **$12,000.**
Courtesy of David Cobb Auction

style as the Sonneberg Täufling); mohair or skin wig; paperweight, almond-shaped eyes; pink eye shadow; thin brows; most without pierced ears; closed mouth; typically unmarked.

15"-17" .... $7,500-$7,700
20" $8,200
Add $1,000 for swivel neck.

Gigoteur: Solid domed socket head; mechanism within carton moule torso; leather joints; skin or mohair wig; enamel or paperweight almond-shaped eyes; open mouth; upper and lower teeth; waves, kicks, moves head from side to side, and cries "mama."

17"-20" .... $2,900-$3,700

Series A, C, E, F or G Stamped in Red: socket head; jointed wood-and-composition body; short, stubby fingers; straight wrists; good wig; oval paperweight eyes with dark rim undercuts or beautiful glass porcelain-encased sleep eyes, may be operated by a lever; heavy feathered brows; pink eye shadow; pierced ears with light blush on rims; closed mouth typically marked incised "Sie (letter) and (size number)," also stamped in red script "J. Steiner Bte SGDG J. Bourgoin" or "J. STEINER B.S.G.D.G."

10"-16" .... $8,400-$8,700
22"-28" .... $13,000-$16,000
38" $27,500

Series E:
24" $25,000

Series F:
24" $52,000

Series G:
24" $36,000

Figure A, B, or C Bébé: socket head; jointed wood-and-composition body; short, stubby fingers; good wig; paperweight eyes; long, dark, thick lashes, beginning at the outer eye corners; black-outlined eyes; heavy feathered brows; detailed, pierced ears with deep molding; closed mouth; body may have a label with a picture of a girl holding a flag; typically marked incised "Figure (A B or C) No. (Size Number)/J. Steiner Bte. S.G.D.G./Paris" or "Figure (A B or C)

25" Steiner Figure A bébé, **$8,500.**
Courtesy of James Julia Auctions, Inc.

(Size Number)/J. Steiner Bte. S.G.D.G./ PARIS" or "J. Steiner/Bte. S.G.D.G./Paris/Fre (A B or C E) (Size Number)/(ABC or after 1892) (Size Number)/ PARIS"; may also be stamped "Le Petit Parisien/Bébé Steiner/Medaille d'Or/Paris 1889."

Closed mouth A/B:

12"-15" .... $4,700-$5,650
17"-20" .... $6,300-$6,950
28"-30" .... $9,950-$11,500
36" $13,500

Closed mouth C:

10"-13" .... $7,550-$8,200
16"-18" .... $8,600-$8,950
22"-24" .... $11,000-$12,000
28"-34" .... $14,000-$17,500

Open mouth figure:

13"-17" .... $5,000-$6,000
22"-24" .... $6,700-$7,400
28"-32" .... $8,000-$8,700

Le Parisien Bébé*: socket head; wood-and-composition body (later Le Parisien may have lesser quality composition straight-limb body); longer fingers; good wig; paperweight eyes; pronounced brows; sculptured, pierced ears with intricate folds and canals; open or closed mouth; typically marked incised "(Size Number)/Paris" or "A (Size Number)/ Paris," stamped in red "Le PARISIEN," body stamped in purple "Bébé Le Parisien/Medaille D'or/Paris" or "Marque Déposés/Article/FRANCAIS (within a triangle in black)."

Closed mouth:

13"-15" .... $6,500-$6,900
20"-24" .... $7,700-$9,200
28"-30" .... $12,000-$14,000
38" $16,000

Open mouth:

8-1/2" $2,000
11"-15" .... $2,400-$2,900
22" $3,800
30"-32" .... $5,000-$5,700

Deduct $1,000 for five-piece, straight-limb body.

23" closed mouth Figure A bébé, **$8,000**, and 33" open mouth Le Parisien bébé, **$5,800**.
Courtesy of David Cobb Auction

21" open mouth Le Parisien pull string talker, **$3,700**, and a 26" open mouth Figure A with two rows of teeth, **$7,800**.
Courtesy of David Cobb Auction

Swaine & Company

Robert Swaine owned and Swaine & Company porcelain factory in Hüttensteinach, near Sonneberg, Germany. The company produced beautifully sculptured bisque dolls for a short period of time beginning in 1910.

Many believe that Swaine produced only one doll, Lori, but with several expressions signified by the lettering system "DI," "DV," and so on.

Sweet 22" closed mouth Swaine & Company Lori baby, **$4,100.**

Courtesy of McMasters-Harris Auction

Prices listed are for appropriately costumed dolls in good condition.

Character Baby*: bisque socket head; composition bent-limb baby body; solid dome or good wig; fine detailing around painted or glass eyes; open or closed mouth; typically marked "232," "Lori," "DIP," "DI," "DV," "BP," "BO," "S&C," "FP," "AP," or "Made in Germany S&C," accompanied by a green stamp "Gestchutzt Germany S & Co." within a circle.

Closed mouth:
  14"-18" .... **$2,900-$3,550**
  22"-24" .... **$4,100-$4,550**
Open Mouth:
  8"-10" .... **$1,050-$1,250**
  16"-20" .... **$1,850-$2,400**
  24" **$3,250**
DIP closed mouth:
  14"-16" .... **$1,850-$2,100**
  18"-22" .... **$2,500-$3,100**
DV closed mouth:
  12"-16" .... **$1,800-$2,200**
DI closed mouth:
  12"-14" .... **$1,400-$1,600**
BP or BO closed smiling:
  14"-16" .... **$6,550-$7,400**
  20"-22" .... **$9,100-$9,850**
FP closed mouth:
  8"-10" .... **$1,100-$1,450**
AP closed mouth:
  16" **$8,500**

*Add $500 to any doll with jointed toddler body.

Child: bisque socket head; jointed composition body; glass eyes; nicely feathered brows; open mouth; typically marked "S&C" or "Made in Germany S&C"; may have green stamp.

10"-14"	$1,000-$1,100
20"	$1,400
24"-28"	$2,000-$2,900

Swaine & Company 20" closed mouth DIP character, **$3,100**, holding a McLaughlin book and a 4-4-0 locomotive and tender while playing with a lithograph tin touring car, American teddy bear, Hubley cast iron coupe, and Lehmann lithographed and painted dancing sailor.
Courtesy of Bertoia Auction

15" Swaine & Co. character BP girl with intaglio eyes and smiling closed mouth with molded teeth; wonderfully original rare doll, **$7,300.**
Photo courtesy of James D. Julia Inc.

Shirley Temple

The Christmas season of 2004 marked the 70th anniversary of Ideal's Shirley Temple doll. In the midst of the Great Depression, when people needed an escape from the worries of their everyday lives, a darling child danced and sang her way into the hearts of the nation.

Master doll artist Bernard Lipfert created the Shirley Temple doll to the specifications of Ideal's founder, Michtom, and Shirley's mother, Mrs. Gertrude Temple. Mrs. Temple's approval was obtained only after more than 28 molds were rejected.

Mollye Goldman designed Shirley Temple outfits from. Clothing had one of two types of labels. One type of label was blue and white rayon with "Shirley Temple" in red, and the second type of label was similar but also had a blue eagle and the initials "N.R.A." (National Recovery Administration).

Composition

Prices listed are for dolls in good condition with original costumes.

Ideal Shirley Temple*: jointed composition; blond mohair wig styled with curls; hazel sleep eyes; painted lashes; dimples; open, slightly smiling mouth; original, tagged "Shirley Temple" outfit; typically marked "Shirley Temple" and size number on back of head and/or body; "Cop./Ideal/N & T Co.," "Shirley Temple/Ideal" (within a diamond); "Shirley Temple Corp. Ideal"; and occasionally unmarked.

11"	$1,400
13"-17"	$1,250-$1,450
18"-25"	$1,500-$1,750
27"	$2,700

*Add $300-$800 for Texas Ranger or Curly Top costumed doll.

Baby Shirley Temple: composition head and limbs; cloth body; molded hair or wig; open mouth; original, tagged "Shirley Temple" outfit and pants; typically marked "Shirley Temple."

16"-21"	$1,750-$1,950
23"-25"	$2,100-$2,200

Brown Shirley Temple: (from the movie The Hurricane) jointed brown composition; black yarn hair; painted, side-glancing eyes; open/closed mouth with painted upper teeth; original grass skirt and leis; flowers in hair; typically marked "Shirley Temple."

18"	$1,400

Vinyl and Plastic

Prices listed are for dolls in near mint, original condition.

1957: vinyl head; plastic body; rooted hair; brown sleep eyes; open/closed, smiling mouth; molded and painted teeth; dimples; original costume; gold plastic script "Shirley Temple" pin; typically marked "ST-II."

12"-15"	$325-$425
17"-19"	$500-$575
36"	$1,800

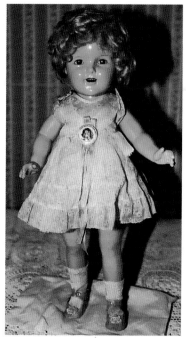

Original 18" Shirley Temple, **$1,500.**
Courtesy of Diane S. Hartman from "What-A-Doll," Adollisborn@hotmail.com

1972: vinyl head; plastic body; made for Montgomery Ward; original costume; typically marked "Hong Kong."

15"	$350

1973: vinyl head; plastic body; rooted hair; stationary brown eyes; open/closed mouth; molded and painted teeth; original costume; typically marked "1971/Ideal Toy Corp./ST-14-H-213."

16"	$225

1982: vinyl head; plastic body; original costume; typically marked "1982" on body and "1982 Ideal Toy Corp/S.T. 8-N-8371" on head.

8"-12"	$110-$135

1984: vinyl head; plastic body; original costume; typically marked "1984/Mrs. Shirley

Temple Black/Dolls, Dreams & Love."

36" **$550**

Porcelain

Prices listed are for original dolls in mint condition with boxes.

Display Doll: Marked "Danbury Mint."...**$250**

Foreign Shirley Temple Dolls

United States patent laws did not protect against infringements by other countries.

Prices listed are for originally costumed dolls in good to very good condition.

Canadian: Reliable Doll Company had the legal rights to manufacture Shirley Temple dolls. Marked "Celichle."

18" **$1,500**

French: felt swivel head; jointed cloth body; celluloid hands; face and neck painted; blond, curly, mohair wig; painted brown eyes, glancing slightly to side; single-stroke brows; open/closed, smiling mouth; finely molded teeth; dimples; various costumes from Shirley Temple films; typically unmarked (assumed to have been made by Raynal; not intended for export to the United States)

19" **$1,700**

German: Armand Marseille composition molds 452 and 452H; composition socket head; jointed composition body; 452 wears wig; 452H has molded, curly hair; glass sleep eyes; rosy cheeks with hint of dimples; smiling, open mouth with teeth; typically marked "Armand Marseille 452 Germany" or "AM/452H/Germany."

18" **$1,700**

20"-24" .... **$2,000-$2,400**

Rare brown 18" Marama Hawaiian closed mouth painted eye doll, **$1,400**, along with 27", 25", 17", and 15" Shirley Temple dolls. If in perfect condition, this group of dolls would have a value of **$2,700**, **$1,750**, **$1,450**, and **$1,250**, respectively. In their present conditions of being redressed, having messed hair, replaced wigs, and being obviously repainted, a more realistic value would be **$1,200**, **$500**, **$400**, and **$300**, respectively.

Japanese: jointed composition; molded and painted blond, curly hair; painted brown eyes; open/closed, smiling mouth; white between lips to simulate teeth; original, pink-pleated, dress; typically marked "S.T. Japan."

10" **$400**

Terri Lee Company

In 1946, Violet Gradwohl founded the Terri Lee Company in Lincoln, Nebraska, with 10 employees. The Terri Lee Doll Company, despite its success, was plagued with misfortune. The factory in Lincoln burned to the ground, prompting its relocation to Apple Valley, California. In 1958, the California factory closed its doors. There is a well-made copy, Mary Jane, often called an unmarked Terri Lee walker or sleep eye Terry Lee. She is not a Terri Lee even though she looks identical to the distinctive Terri Lee. Mary Jane was reportedly designed and manufactured by a former employee of Violet Gradwohl, advertised by Kathryn Kay-Toy Kreations.

Prices listed are for dolls in original tagged outfits in near mint condition.

Composition Terri Lee: 16"; jointed composition; wiry hair wig; painted eyes; closed mouth; typically marked "Terri Lee, Pat Pending." **$750**

Hard Plastic/Vinyl: 16"; jointed plastic; good wig; painted eyes; closed mouth; typically marked "Terri Lee Pat. Pending" on dolls made before 1949 and "Terri Lee" on dolls produced in 1949 and later years. **$900**

Talking Terry Lee...**$1,400**
Tiny Terry Lee:
10" **$500**
So Sleepy:
9-1/2".. **$325**

Companions:

Gene Autry: 16"; molded and painted brown hair; open/closed mouth with painted teeth; tagged cowboy outfit; "Gene Autry" pin and "Terri Lee" label; typically marked "Terri Lee/Pat. Pending" on back. **$3,750**

Jerry Lee: 16"; lamb's-wool wig **$950**
Tiny Jerri Lee: 10"..**$450**
Patti Jo, Bonnie Lu: 16"; black friends **$1,700**
Benji: 16" **$1,400**
Nanook: 16", Eskimo.......................................**$2,400**
Connie Lynn Baby: 19" **$850**
Baby Linda Lee: 10"..**$325**

Mary Jane: 17"; plastic walker body; similar facial molding to Terri Lee; sleep eyes; tagged "Mary Jane" costume; typically unmarked. **$500**

Mint condition 16" vinyl and hard plastic Terri Lee with original box, **$1,300.**
Courtesy of Diane S. Hartman from "What-A-Doll," Adollisborn@hotmail.com

Uneeda Doll Company

Uneeda Doll Company, founded in 1917 in New York, was also known as the Tony Toy Company of Hong Kong.

Uneeda supplied jobbers, mail-order houses, and department stores with a complete line of well-made, competitively priced play dolls.

By the 1930s, Uneeda was advertising over 400 different models of dolls. This 20th century doll manufacturer is still producing play dolls.

Uneeda Dollikin and her Lovable Baby in mint in box condition, **$600.**
Courtesy of David Cobb Auction

Composition

Prices listed are for appropriately costumed dolls in good condition.

Rita Hayworth as Carmen: 14"; jointed composition; red mohair wig; sleep eyes; exceptionally long lashes; gray eye shadow; closed mouth; original red dress with black lace overskirt and matching mantilla with silk flowers decorating both dress and scarf; gold shoes; typically unmarked; gold fan-shaped wrist tag "The Carmen Doll/W. I. Gould & Co., Inc. Mfrd. by Uneeda Doll Co.,/Inspired by/Rita Hayworth's/Portrayal of Carmen/in/The Loves of Carmen." **$750**

Baby Sweetheart: 17"; jointed composition; deeply molded hair; sleep eyes; open mouth metal tongue; two upper teeth; typically unmarked; hangtag "Everybody Loves Baby Sweetheart/Produced by Uneeda Doll Co." **$550**

Hard Plastic and Vinyl

Prices listed are for dolls in near mint, original condition.

Tiny Time Teens: (Fun Time, Beau Time, Bride Time, Winter Time, Date Time, Party Time, Vacation Time, and Prom Time) 5"; poseable vinyl head; plastic body; rooted hair; painted features with real lashes; typically marked "U.D. Co. Inc./1967/Hong Kong." **$100**

American Gem Collection: (Georgia, Carolina, Patience, Prudence, Priscilla, and Virginia) 8-1/2"; rooted hair; painted features; typically marked "U.D. Co. Inc./MCMLXXI/Made in Hong Kong" on head and body. **$85**

Little Sophisticates: (Kristina, Marika, Rosanna, Penelope, and Suzana) 8-1/2"; mod dolls; vinyl head; plastic body; rooted hair; closed eyes with eye shadow; typically marked "Uneeda Doll Co. Inc./1967/Made in Japan" on head and back. **$75**

Uneeda 19" collectible vinyl lady doll holding her original hat and purse, **$350**.
Courtesy of David Cobb Auction

Baby Sleep Amber: 11"; black vinyl head and limbs; cloth body; rooted black hair; sleep eyes; typically marked "Tony Toy/1970/Made in Hong Kong." **$65**

Pri-Thilla: 12"; vinyl; bent left arm; rooted hair; sleep eyes; open mouth; sucks thumb and inflates balloons; typically marked "4" on head. **$125**

Baby: 16"; vinyl; rooted hair; sleep eyes; open, nurser mouth; typically marked "3TD11/Uneeda." **$100**

Magic Fairy Princess: vinyl head; jointed plastic body; rooted, pink hair; sleep eyes; closed mouth; fairy costume with glitter wings; typically marked "Uneeda" on head, "210" on body.

    18"-22" .... **$225-$275**

Janie: 8"; vinyl; rooted hair; sleep eyes; typically marked "U." $150
Dressed in original Girl Scout or Brownie costume:... $250

Dollikins: vinyl head; unique fully jointed plastic body; rooted hair; sleep eyes; real lashes; pierced ears; closed mouth; polished fingernails and toenails; typically marked "Uneeda/25."

8" $150
12"-19" ....$250-$350
21" $250
Set of Baby and Me $400
Set of Wee Three.. $350

Glamour Lady: 20"; vinyl head; jointed plastic walker body; rooted hair; sleep eyes; real lashes; tiny, painted lower lashes; closed mouth; typically marked "3" (in circle), "Uneeda," "S2." $300

Country Girl: 22"; vinyl head; jointed plastic walker body; rooted hair; flirty, sleep eyes; real lashes; tiny, painted lower lashes; closed mouth; typically marked "Uneeda." $175

Toodles: 21"; vinyl head; jointed plastic walker body; rooted hair; sleep eyes; real lashes; tiny, painted lower lashes; wide open/closed mouth; molded tongue; typically marked "Uneeda."...$200

Needa Toodles: 22"; plastic head; composition upper arms and legs; vinyl lower arms and legs; weighted, screw-type walker body; saran wig; sleep eyes, real lashes; open/closed mouth; two upper teeth; hint of dimples; typically marked "20." ...$250

50th Anniversary Antebellum Southern Belle: 25"; vinyl; rooted hair; sleep eyes; long lashes; eye shadow; closed mouth; typically marked "8/Uneeda Doll Co./1967." ...$300

Pollyanna: vinyl head; jointed plastic body; blond, rooted hair; sleep eyes with lashes; eye liner; open mouth; painted teeth; typically marked "Walt Disney Prod./Mfd By Uneeda/N.F."

11"-17" ....$125-$175
31" $400

Freckles: 32"; vinyl head; jointed plastic body; rooted hair; flirty, sleep eyes with lashes; freckles; open/closed mouth; four molded and painted upper teeth. $250

Sarenade: 21"; vinyl and plastic; rooted hair; sleep eyes; closed mouth; typically marked "Uneeda Doll/1967"; phonograph and recorder with speaker in tummy. $275

Vogue Dolls, Inc.

Vogue Dolls was founded by Jennie H. Graves in Somerville, Massachusetts, shortly after World War I. Graves never dreamed that her modest doll costuming business would grow to be the largest doll-only manufacturer in the world.

Graves set out to design and make doll clothing. The company's sole enterprise remained the production of doll clothing until the mid-1930s. Graves then decided to buy undressed dolls and design clothing for them.

In 1948, the famous Ginny-type doll was introduced. Copies of this famous doll are numerous; see the Modern Collectible Dolls section for Ginny-type values.

Several Vogue dolls were original Arranbee dolls. Vogue purchased Arranbee in 1957, but the dolls continued to be marked and sold as Arranbee until as late as 1961.

Vogue Dolls 8" composition Toddles Hansel and Gretel in original tagged costumes, **$1,400** for the pair.
Courtesy of McMasters-Harris Auction

Vogue Dolls 8" composition painted-eye Toddles, **$500**, and #3 hard plastic, painted lash, straight leg walker Ginny, **$500**.
Courtesy of McMasters-Harris Auction

Bisque

Prices listed are for originally costumed dolls in good condition.

Just Me: bisque socket head; jointed composition body; mohair wig; glass eyes; closed mouth; typically marked "Just Me A. M.," "A. M. 310/11 Just Me," or round hangtag "Vogue."

    8"-9" .... **$2,000-$2,500**
    11"-13" .... **$3,000-$3,800**
Painted bisque: 8"-11" ...**$1,500-$2,000**

Composition

Prices listed are for originally costumed dolls in good condition.

Toddles: 8"; jointed composition; mohair wig; painted eyes; closed mouth; typically marked "Vogue" on head, "Doll Co," or "Vogue" on back................**$500**
Child: jointed composition; good wig; sleep eyes; real lashes, with or without eye shadow; open mouth; typically marked "13," "15," or "20," or unmarked; paper tag reads "Vogue Dolls, Inc/Medford, Mass."

    13"-15" ....**$650-$750**
    20" **$950**

Hard Plastic & Vinyl

Prices listed are for originally costumed dolls in near mint condition.

#1 Ginny: 1948-1950; 8"; jointed plastic; molded hair under mohair wig; painted, side-glancing eyes; closed mouth; typically marked "Vogue" on head and "Vogue Doll" on back; clothing tagged "Vogue Dolls." **$550**
#2 Ginny: 1950-1953; 8"; non-walker; jointed plastic; mohair wig with gauze strip forming cap; sleep eyes; painted lashes; closed mouth; typically marked "Vogue" on head and body; clothing tagged "Vogue.".................................**$800**
Ginny Poodle Cut: 1952 only; 8"; lamb's-wool, bubble "poodle" wig.............**$850**
Ginny Fluffy Bunny: 8"; lamb's-wool wig; tagged bunny costume.........**$1,750**

Crib Crowder Baby: 8"; bent-leg baby body...**$1,400**

#3 Ginny: 1954; 8"; straight-leg walker; jointed plastic; good wig; sleep eyes; painted lashes; closed mouth; typically marked "Ginny" on head and "Vogue Dolls Inc./Pat #2687594/Made in USA" on body; clothing tagged "Vogue Doll."**$500**

Black #3 Ginny:............................ **$2,800**

Queen Ginny:.................................**$1,450**

#4 Ginny: 1955-1957; 8"; straight-leg walker; jointed plastic; good wig; sleep eyes; molded plastic upper lashes; closed mouth; typically marked "Vogue" on head and "Ginny Vogue Dolls Inc./ Pat. #2687594/Made in USA" on body; clothing tagged "Vogue Dolls." **$450**

#5 Ginny: 1957-1962; 8"; jointed-knee walker; jointed plastic body; good wig; sleep eyes; molded plastic lashes; closed mouth; typically marked "Vogue" on head and "Ginny Vogue Dolls Inc./Pat. #2687594/Made in U.S.A." on body; clothing tagged "Vogue Dolls Inc."...........**$350**

#6 Ginny: 1963; 8"; vinyl head; jointed plastic body; rooted hair; sleep eyes; closed mouth; typically marked "Ginny" on head and "Ginny Vogue Dolls Inc./Pat. No. 2687594/Made in U.S.A." on back; clothing tagged "Vogue Dolls Inc."..**$200-$225**

Modern Ginny: 1972; 8"; jointed vinyl; rooted hair; sleep eyes; closed mouth; typically marked "GINNY" on head and "Vogue Dolls 1972/Made in Hong Kong/8" on body; clothing tagged "Made in Hong Kong." ....**$100-$125**

Sassoon Ginny: 1978-1979; thin body and limbs. ....**$75-$100**

Contemporary Ginny: made by Dankin. ....**$30-$50**

Jill: 10"; jointed, adult plastic body; high heel feet; saran hair; sleep eyes; molded lashes; pierced ears; closed mouth; typically marked "Vogue" on head and "Jill/ Vogue Made in U.S.A. 1957" on body; clothing tagged "Vogue." **$350**

Li'l Imp: 10-1/2"; vinyl head; jointed plastic, walker body; orange hair; freckles;

sleep eyes; open/closed mouth; typically marked "R & B" on head; clothing may be tagged "Vogue."................**$225**

Littlest Angel: vinyl head; jointed plastic walker body; rooted hair; sleep eyes; open/ closed mouth; typically marked "R & B" on head; clothing may be tagged "Vogue."

11"-13" ....**$225-$275**

Child: jointed plastic slender body; long legs; slightly bent arms; good wig; sleep eyes; real lashes; painted lower lashes; closed mouth; typically marked "14," "16," or other size number in inches on head and "Made in U.S.A." on back; clothing tagged "Vogue Dolls."

14".. **$500**

16"-18" ....$700-$850

Jan: 13"; jointed vinyl; high heel feet; rooted hair; sleep eyes; molded lashes; closed, smiling mouth; typically marked "Vogue" on head; clothing tagged "Vogue Dolls." **$250**

Jeff: 10"; vinyl head and limbs; plastic body; molded and painted hair; sleep eyes; molded lashes; typically marked "Vogue" on head; clothing tagged "Vogue Dolls." **$225**

Angel Baby: vinyl; bent-limb baby body; rooted hair; sleep eyes with lashes; smiling, closed mouth; typically marked "Vogue Doll/1965" or "1963."

14" **$150**

25" **$250**

Miss Ginny: 16"; jointed vinyl; teen body; rooted hair; sleep eyes; closed mouth; typically marked "Vogue Doll/1970"; clothing tagged "Vogue Dolls Inc."**$125**

Baby Dear: vinyl head and limbs; cloth body; rooted hair; painted eyes; closed mouth; typically marked with cloth tag "Vogue Dolls, Inc." Back of left leg marked "E. Wilkins/1960."

13"-18" ....$250-$375

27" **$700**

Baby Dear One:

25" **$375**

Baby Dear Two (toddler):

17" **$250**

23" **$375**

Posie Pixie: 17"; vinyl head and gauntlet hands; cloth body; rooted hair; black, side-glancing eyes; open/closed mouth; typically marked "1964/Vogue/71." **$175**
Ginny Baby: 22"; vinyl; rooted hair; sleep eyes with lashes; open nurser mouth; typically marked "Ginny Baby/10/Vogue Doll Inc." **$400**
Brickette: vinyl head and arms; plastic body; ball-jointed waist; rooted hair; sleep, flirty eyes with lashes; smiling, closed mouth; typically unmarked.

    16" **$250**
    22" **$350**
    18" (1980 re-issue)..**$125**

Original Vogue Dolls 22" 1961
Brickette, **$350.**
Courtesy of David Cobb Auction

W.P.A. Dolls

W. P.A. art dolls were made in the United States during the 1930s, under the Works Progress Administration (W.P.A.) The W.P.A. provided work for artists and seamstresses struggling during the Depression. Dolls represented characters from fairy tales; folklore; historical figures; and authentically costumed figures from the United States and various foreign countries. The quality, condition, artist's skill, and visual appeal make equally significant contributions to the value of a W.P.A. doll.

Prices are for originally costumed dolls in good condition.

Cloth
Painted features; yarn hair; typically marked "Michigan W.P.A. Toy Project," "W.P.A. Museum Project Wichita," "Museum Project 1865 W.P.A.," "W.P.A. Toy Project, sponsored by Michigan State College," "W.P.A.," or "WPA Handicraft Project Milwaukee, Wisconsin."

Child/Adult:
    12"-18" ....$500-$700
Fairy Tale Character Set: 15"-18"
    Mary and Her Lamb, Red Riding Hood and the Wolf, and other two- or three-character sets:...$1,000-$1,700/set
    Mother and Three Little Kittens, Goldilocks and the Three Bears, and other three or more character sets:.........................$2,500-$3,500/set
Nationality Doll: 14"-18" ....$700-$2,000
Famous Characters (George and Martha Washington, Paul Revere, etc.): 16"-18" ....$1,500-$2,500
Special Display Doll: 22"-24"..................$2,400-$3,500

18" W.P.A. Betsy Ross and a 16" child companion, **$1,500** and **$700**, respectively.
Photo courtesy of McMaster-Harris Autions.

Composition/Wood
International Wooden: 14"-17"; carved and painted facial features; authentically costumed dolls representing various classes from most countries; typically unmarked. ....**$700-$900**
Composition Character: 14"-18"; composition character faces; painted facial features; solidly stuffed bodies; appropriately dressed; typically unmarked. **$600-$700**
Puppets or Marionettes: 12" ....$250-$300

14" composition character dolls representing a couple from early 20th century Holland, **$600 each.**
Courtesy of Julia Burke, www.juliaburke.com

Izannah Walker

The 1865 Census of Rhode Island lists: "Walker, Izannah F., born of American parentage in Bristol, Rhode Island, living in the village of Central Falls in the town of Smithfield, occupation Doll Maker."

The quaint and charming beauty of an Izannah Walker doll is only surpassed by its historical significance. Izannah Walker's early American primitive sculpture dolls have heavily oil-painted features on slightly sculptured faces.

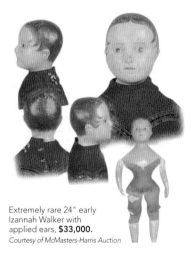

Extremely rare 24" early Izannah Walker with applied ears, **$33,000.**
Courtesy of McMasters-Harris Auction

Prices listed are for appropriately dressed dolls in fair to good condition. An Izannah Walker doll in very good condition is so rare that it could be valued at three or four times the amount listed.

Izannah Walker: cloth; oil painted covering; painted hair with soft wisps and tiny curls around the face; molded facial features; large, luminous eyes; applied or molded ears; closed, slightly smiling mouth; typically marked "Patented Nov. 4th 1873" or unmarked.

Early with applied ears:
> 15"-18" .... **$21,000-$25,000**
> 20"-21" .... **$28,000-$30,000**

After 1873 with molded ears:
> 15"-18" .... **$8,500-$9,500**
> 20"-21" .... **$11,000-$12,000**

Wax Dolls

There are three types of wax dolls: wax-over dolls; poured-wax dolls; and reinforced-wax dolls.

Prices listed are for appropriately dressed dolls in good condition.

Wax-Over Dolls

Wax-over dolls were made by various companies in England, France, and Germany during the 1800s and into the early 1900s. While dolls of many different materials were waxed over, papier-mâché/composition was by far the most frequently used.

By the end of the 19th century, the quality of wax-over dolls began to deteriorate.

Early "English Split-Head": German or English; round face; hair inserted in split in top of head; glass or wire operated sleep eyes; smiling, closed mouth; typically unmarked.

12"-18"	$1,000-$1,300
22"	$1,500
26"-30"	$1,700-$2,200

Molded Hair or Bonnet: wax-over shoulder head with molded hair and/or bonnet; glass eyes; closed mouth; typically unmarked.

14"-18"	$450-$600
22"-24"	$700-$800
30"-32"	$1,000-$1,100

Extraordinarily Elaborate: intricately styled hair with ornamentation or elaborately styled bonnet, often with human curls added; glass eyes; closed mouth; typically unmarked.

16"-20"	$3,500-$3,700
24"	$4,500

With Wig: wax-over shoulder head; good wig; glass eyes; open or closed mouth; typically unmarked.

Standard quality:

10"-14"	$200-$400
18"-24"	$500-$600

23" poured wax shoulder head with paperweight eyes, **$1,200**; 24" English split head, **$1,600**; 16" poured wax lady, **$1,000**; 18" reinforced shoulder head, **$600**; 17" open mouth reinforced shoulder head, **$550**; and 16" reinforced shoulder head lady, **$550**; and 17" English split head, **$400**, due to condition.
Courtesy of David Cobb Auction

28"-34"	$600-$850
36"-38"	$1,000-$1,200

Exceptional quality, heavily waxed, and nicely decorated:

10"-14"	$500-$550
18"-24"	$700-$900
30"-32"	$1,100-$1,200

Singing Doll: very pretty wax-over shoulder head; good wig; glass eyes; closed mouth; music box in torso with push bellows mechanism; typically marked "William Webber/Patented 1882/(name of tune)."

22"-24"	$2,200-$2,600
26"	$3,000

Two-Faced Doll*: wax-over shoulder head; molded bonnet hides one of the rotating head-faces; insert glass eyes; closed mouth; typically unmarked or body may be signed "Bartenstein." **$1,200**

*Add $500 for black version.

12" wax-over-composition shoulder head, **$400.**
Courtesy of McMasters-Harris Auction

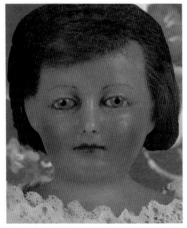

Nicely detailed 25" poured wax shoulder head, **$1,700.**
Courtesy of McMasters-Harris Auction

Poured-Wax Dolls

Poured wax dolls were produced as early as the Middle Ages in Italy and other parts of Europe. The wax dolls produced in England during the 19th century are a particular favorite. Poured-wax dolls are extremely lifelike. By the mid-1800s, wax dolls were being produced as toys.

Poured-Wax: lifelike shoulder head with well-molded plate; cloth body; hollow, poured-wax, molded arms and legs; human or fine mohair inserted wig and possibly lashes and brows; glass eyes; deeply molded eyelids; closed mouth; typically unmarked, name engraved on shoulder plate, or body stamped "Montarari," "Pierrotti," "Marsh," "Peck," "Meech," "Morrell," "Edwards," or "Cremer."

Standard quality:

14"	$900
20"-24"	$1,300-$1,500
26"	$1,900

Exceptional quality:

14"	$1,700-$2,500
20"-24"	$2,600-$4,200
30"	$4,400-$5,200

Reinforced-Wax Dolls

Reinforced-wax head dolls are generally accepted as having been made in Germany from about 1860 until 1890. Reinforced-wax dolls begin with a poured-wax head, which is reinforced from within.

Reinforced-Wax: shoulder head; cloth body; wax-over forearms; composition legs, molded and painted boots; good wig; glass eyes, molded lids; may have pierced ears; closed mouth; typically unmarked.

Fair quality:

14"-16"	$450-$550
20"	$700
26"	$850

Very good quality:

16"	$1,250
18"-20"	$1,600-$1,800
24"	$2,400

Norah Wellings

Norah Wellings was the chief designer at Chad Valley for several years, until she and her brother, Leonard, began manufacturing cloth dolls in 1926. The company, known as the Victoria Toy Works, was located in Arleston, England. Following the death of her brother in 1960, Wellings closed the business and retired.

Prices listed are for originally costumed dolls with good color.

Child*: mask type or molded face; jointed cloth body; mohair wig; painted or glass eyes; closed mouth; typically marked with cloth label; "Made in England/by/ Norah Wellings."

10"-12"	**$650-$750**
18"-22"	**$1,100-$1,250**
24"-28"	**$1,450-$1,850**
30"	**$2,300**

Add $100-$200 to any doll with glass eyes.

Island Doll or Black Ethnic*: velvet; stitched at shoulder and hip; mohair wig; painted, side-glancing or glass eyes; grinning mouth; typically marked with cloth label "Made in England/by/Norah Wellings."

12"-16"	**$400-$500**
20"-22"	**$600-$650**
24"-28"	**$750-$950**
36"	**$1,500**

Add $100-$200 to any doll with glass eyes.

Military*: sculptured face; velvet body; mohair wig; painted, side-glancing or glass eyes; authentic military uniform; typically marked with cloth label "Made in England/by/Norah Wellings"; wrist tag "Force Comforts Committee an agreed percentage of the manufacturer's sales of the R.A.F. mascot doll is contributed to the Royal Air Comforts Fund."

10"-14"	**$400-$550**
16"-18"	**$600-$650**

Add $100-$200 to any doll with glass eyes.

Novelty Souvenir*: stitched, long, thin, floppy limbs and oversized hands; typically marked with cloth label "Norah Wellings/Wellington England."

6"-10"	**$200-$275**

Add $100-$200 to any doll with glass eyes.

14" Norah Wellings character boy, **$850.**
Courtesy of McMasters-Harris Auction

26" swivel head character "doll, **$1,700**, holding 10" novelty golliwog, **$350.**
Courtesy of McMasters-Harris Auction

Wilson Novelty Company

In 1930, John Wilson founded the Wilson Novelty Company in Watsontown, Pennsylvania. The devastating effects of the Depression left this small central Pennsylvania town in desperate need. The little Wilson Walkies, also known as Watsontown Walkers, had a tremendous responsibility placed upon their sloping shoulders—to save the small town—and that is exactly what they did! In 1949, just one year after the death of its founder, the Wilson Novelty Company was sold to a Canadian business; and in 1951, production of the Walkies came to an end.

Prices listed below are for dolls with no damage.

Collectible Characters: 4" ....$250-$300
Disney and Cartoon Characters: 4" ....$350-$500
Military and Common Characters: 4" ....$200-$250
Four-Legged Animals: 3" ....$400-$500
Character Walkies: 10" ....$600-$800

Group of charming 4" Wilson Walkies, **$200-$250 each.**
Courtesy of Julia Burke, www.juliaburke.com

Wooden Dolls

Early English and German wooden dolls were handmade by unknown craftsmen. Generally, wooden dolls have had a retrograde development, having declined, rather than improved, in quality over the years. The crude peg wooden dolls made until quite recently give evidence to this statement.

Prices listed are for dolls in good condition.

English

William & Mary: 1680-1720; carved, one-piece head and torso with unique facial expression; human hair or flax nailed to head for wig; painted almond-shaped eyes with little detail; single-stroke brows extend from curve of nose and end at outer corner of eye; well-defined nose, mouth, ears, and rosy cheeks; limbs attached by various pinning and jointing methods; upper arms usually made of bound linen; carved wooden lower arms and hands; separate fingers and thumbs; often detailed fingernails; upper and lower legs, usually wooden with well-carved toes; entire body covered with gesso base layer, delicately painted with flesh color and varnished; dressed in fashionable period costume; unmarked.

    14"-17" .... **$55,000-$70,000**

Queen Anne: 1700-1750; more stylized, less individual appearance; great craftsmanship; one-piece head and body; linen upper arms nailed to shoulders; shaped bosom, very narrow waist; rounded fingers with fingernails; hips curved on each side to accommodate pegged tongue-and-groove joints; human hair or flax wig nailed to head; oval, almost egg-shaped head; bulbous glass or painted oval eyes; brows and lashes indicated by a series of dots; well-defined nose and ears; closed mouth; rosy cheeks; entire body covered with gesso base layer; painted very pale flesh color and varnished; dressed in fashionable period costume; unmarked.

    14"-18" .... **$22,000-$25,000**
    24" **$32,000**

Georgian: 1750-1800; one-piece carved head and body; somewhat rounded head; torso has rounded chest, narrow waist, squarish hips, and flat back; upper arms of linen stitched to torso through hole drilled in shoulders; lower arms and hands carved with separate

Wooden 17" English William & Mary doll, **$70,000.**
Courtesy of James Julia Auction, Inc.

Wooden 19" Queen Ann doll, **$27,000.**
Courtesy of James Julia Auctions, Inc.

flat fingers and thumbs, and covered in kid with fingers exposed; legs carved to fit into carved slots of hips with pegged tongue-and-groove joints; human hair or flax wig nailed to head; well-defined nose and mouth; inserted lozenge-shaped glass eyes; brows and lashes indicated by a series of dots; closed, small mouth; entire body covered with gesso base layer; painted very pale flesh color and varnished; dressed in fashionable period costume; unmarked.

14"	$3,800
18"-24"	$6,200-$7,200

Early 19th Century: 1800-1840; carved, one-piece head and torso; base of torso forms a point; arms attached to body with piece of linen; legs carved to fit against either side of pointed torso; then pegged with one single peg going first through one leg, then torso, and into other leg; stitched flax or human hair wig glued to head; nicely painted facial features; painted, oversized, oval-shaped eyes; single-stroke brows; no ears; closed mouth; dark, rosy cheeks; upper body and lower limbs covered with gesso layer; painted a flesh color and varnished; often dressed in gown much longer than legs, with matching bonnet; unmarked.

14"	$2,100
20"	$4,700

German

Early to Mid-19th Century: 1810-1840; carved, one-piece head and torso; often with high or empire waist; all wooden arms; tongue-and-groove joints applied to shoulders and elbows (despite the relatively unrefined workmanship, the joints are quite efficient), allowing easy mobility. Finishing techniques were less sophisticated than earlier English dolls, but faces reflect a more delicate look with carved and painted hair, at times in elaborate styles, with curls around the face and the important addition of a hair comb carved into the back of the head. (Collectors often speak of "yellow tuck comb" when they are referring to this particular characteristic.) The nose was most often a wedge inserted into the face and heavily painted, making it less obvious, but still somewhat sharp in appearance. Earrings were common, as were closed mouths. The costly gesso base layer was entirely omitted, with heavy paint applied directly to the wood and only on exposed areas. Fashionably dressed in period costume. Unmarked.

8"-12"	$1,300-$1,900
18"	$2,500
34"	$3,400

Later 19th Century: 1840-1900; carved, one-piece head and torso; very similar to the early to mid-19th century doll in body configuration and facial features; artist's application of facial decoration progressively deteriorated until, by the end of the century, the painting was quite crude; other noticeable changes include the elimination of the hair comb, and the hair styles tend to be less elaborate with perhaps only a bun or carved side curls; fashionably dressed in period costumes; unmarked.

8"	$500
12"-16"	$700-$850
20"	$1,200

Bohemian Wooden Doll: turned wooden head; kid joints arms and legs to carved, red-painted torso; small waist; spoon-like hands; carved nose; painted facial features; appropriately dressed; unmarked.

20"-24"	$950-$1,150

Late 19th Century: carved wooden shoulder head and limbs; cloth body; simple, carved hair style; painted eyes; closed mouth; appropriately dressed; unmarked.

    9"-12" ....$600-$650
    17" $800
    24" $1,200

Peg Wooden or Dutch Wooden: after 1900; simple construction; jointed and fastened with wooden pegs; sharp carved nose, protruding from simple, round face; painted, black hair; painted facial features; stick-type limbs; spoon-like hands; painted white lower legs; black shoes; appropriately dressed; unmarked.

    12" $150

12" peg wooden dolls, showing body construction and how to present a charming peddle rendition, **$100-$175, respectively.**

Photo courtesy of James D. Julia Inc.

Wooden 16" Bébé Tout en Bois, **$950**.
Courtesy of McMasters-Harris Auction

Wooden 12" Swiss doll, **$600**.
Courtesy of David Cobb Auction

Bébé Tout en Bois (Dolls All of Wood): 1900-1914; manufactured by F. M. Schilling, its subsidiary Rudolf Schneider, and possibly others. Nicely carved head, resembling dolly faced or character baby; fully jointed wooden or cloth body with wooden arms and legs; good wig; glass eyes; painted brows and lashes; closed or open mouth with teeth; appropriately dressed; typically marked with the trademark "Angle," a sticker in three languages "Tout Bois, Holz, All Wood," or unmarked.

14"-16" ....$700-$950
18"-20" .... $1,200-$1,300

Swiss

Early 1900s: socket head or shoulder head; nicely carved expressive face; all wood or cloth body with wooden limbs; carved and painted hair, often with intricate detailing; painted eyes; tiny lines through iris; closed mouth; often wearing regional costumes; typically stamped "Made in Switzerland," unmarked, or wrist tag only.

10"-12" ....$400-$600
14" $900
18"-20" .... $1,200-$1,500

Contemporary

The best known wooden dolls are Anri, Dolfi, Raikes, and Harold Naber's Kids. Prices listed are for original costumed dolls in near mint condition.

Anri: 14"; hand carved and painted; fully articulated; carved hair or good wigs; typically marked "Anri" and production number; wrist tag with artist name/"St. Christina South Tyrol Italy." $1,000
Dolfi: 16"; hand carved and painted; similar in construction and appearance to Anri. $600
Raikes: carved heads and limbs; cloth body; carved hair or good wig; insert or painted eyes; closed mouth; typically marked "Robert Raikes/production number"; body labeled "Applause."

12"-14" ....$225-$275
16" $375

Naber Kid*: originally handmade by Harold Naber while in Anchorage, Alaska; from 1988-1994 produced at his factory in Prescott, Arizona; happy, chubby-cheeked characters; fully articulated; large, painted eyes; typically marked "Harold Naber Original," "Naber Kid," or other variations; hangtag "Naber Kid" or "Wild Woods Baby."

1987 and before ....$3,000-$3,900
Early 1988-1989 ....$1,000-$1,500
1990 and beyond ....$400-$700

*Add $300 for Arizona Finish (heavy satin finish) and $500 for special Diver Suit.

Appendix of Additional Doll Companies

For detailed information regarding any of the following doll companies, consult *200 Years of Dolls 3rd Edition* (Krause 2005).

Acme Toy Company

Aetna Doll Company

Aich, Menzel & Co.
Don't confuse the A&M marking with the more commonly found AM of Armand Marseille.

Henri Alexandre

All Bisque Bathing Dolls

All Bisque Half Dolls or Pincushion Dolls

All Bisque Piano Babies

All Bisque Snow Babies

Allied Imported

Max Oscar Arnold

Arrow Novelty Company

Automata
Automata are French, German, or American-made mechanical dolls. Although references to automated dolls can be found dating as early as the mid-17th century, Automata's peak popularity spanned the years from 1860 to 1900.

Babyland Rag

E. Barrois

Beecher Baby

Bing Brothers

Boudoir Dolls

Albert Brückner

A. Bucherer

Century Doll Company

Columbian Dolls

Dollhouse Dolls

Edmund Edelmann

Eisenmann & Co.

J. K. Farnell & Company

Ralph A. Freundlich, Inc.

Godey Lady Dolls

Ludwig Greiner

H Mold Dolls

Hamburger & Company

Carl Hartmann

Karl Hartmann

Hertwig & Company

Hollywood Dolls

Adolf Hülss

Maison Huret

Illfelder Spielwaren

Japanese Dolls

Jullien

K & K Toy Company

Kamkins

C. F. Kling & Company

Gebrüder Knoch

Koenig & Wernicke

Richard G. Krueger Inc.

A. Lanternier et Cie

A. G. Limbach

Albert Marque

Mascotte

Metal-Head Dolls

Alexandre Mothereau

Motschmann Baby
See Sonneberg Täufling.

Multi-Faced Dolls

Munich Art Dolls

Gebrüder Ohlhaver

Oriental Dolls

Paper Dolls

Patent Washable Dolls

Peddler Dolls

Dr. Dora Petzold

Pintel & Godchaux

Rabery & Delphieu

Raleigh Dolls

Raynal

Reliable Toy Company Ltd.

Grace Corry Rockwell

Mme. Rohmer

Rollinson Dolls

Schützmeister & Quendt

Sheppard & Co. Philadelphia Baby

Ella Smith Doll Company

Soviet Union or Russian Dolls

Hermann Steiner

A. Thuillier

Unis

Van Rozen

Wagner & Zetzsche

Adolf Wislizenus

Index

Bibliography

Herlocher, Dawn. *200 Years of Dolls 3rd Edition*, Krause 2005.

—*Doll Makers & Marks*, Antique Trader, 1999.

—*Warman's Dolls Field Guide*, Krause 2006.

Define the Collection of Your Dreams

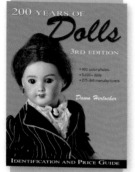

by Dawn Herlocher

This full-color doll guide is the most easy-to-use and comprehensive identification and doll value guide on the shelf! Designed for novice and experienced collectors, dealers and appraisers of vintage dolls, the production data and identifying details in this guide are unmatched.

Inside you'll find historical information on 180 different manufacturers, which helps you to gain a greater understanding of the doll making industry, as well as:

- Pricing grids with values for variations of the same dolls
- 5,000 listings for dolls, each featuring a description and current value
- Manufacturer marks data — the key to accurate identification
- Coverage of all types of dolls, cloth, china, vinyl, antique, molded, French, and German among others

Softcover • 8¼ x 10⅞ • 416 pages
400 color photos
Item# DOLY3 • $29.99

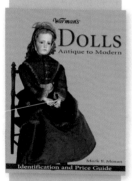

by Mark F. Moran

Dolls, dolls and more dolls – bisque to Barbie and everybody in between are in this glorious guide to dolls. Listings, descriptions and the 1,000 vibrant color photos featured in this book are the compilation of information gathered from a huge private collection, as well as major doll auctions. The depth of details and identifying data in this book will help you make smart doll collecting decisions every time!

Within the 1,500 listings for collectible dolls from the 1860s to the 1960s you'll also find:

- Information on manufacturers, body and head styles, costumes
- Keys to deciphering actual condition grade
- Current collector pricing for each doll
- More than 1,000 color photos useful for identification purposes

Softcover • 8¼ x 10⅞ • 256 pages
1,000+ color photos
Item# WCDL • $24.99

krause publications
An imprint of F+W Publications, Inc.
700 East State Street • Iola, WI 54990